Release 6.07

SAS® Technical Report P-216 SAS/AF® Software, SAS/FSP® Software, and SAS® Screen Control Language: Changes and Enhancements

SAS Institute Inc.
SAS Campus Drive
Cary, NC 27513

The correct bibliographic citation for this manual is as follows: SAS Institute Inc., SAS® Technical Report P-216, *SAS/AF® Software, SAS/FSP® Software, and SAS® Screen Control Language: Changes and Enhancements, Release 6.07,* Cary, NC: SAS Institute Inc., 1991. 313 pp.

SAS® Technical Report P-216, SAS/AF® Software, SAS/FSP® Software, and SAS® Screen Control Language: Changes and Enhancements, Release 6.07

ISBN 1-55544-468-7

1st printing, September 1991

Doc S18, Ver1.22, 082691

Contents

Illustrations

Tables

Using This Book

Introduction

SAS Technical Report P-216, *SAS/AF Software, SAS/FSP Software, SAS Screen Control Language: Changes and Enhancements, Release 6.07* provides reference information about changes from Release 6.06 to Release 6.07 of SAS/AF and SAS/FSP software and SAS Screen Control Language. This document is not intended as a primary source of product information. For complete information about these software products, users should refer to *SAS/AF Software: Usage and Reference, Version 6, First Edition, SAS/FSP Software: Usage and Reference, Version 6, First Edition, SAS Screen Control Language: Reference, Version 6, First Edition*, and SAS Screen Control Language: Usage, Version 6, First Edition.

Audience

This report is intended for users who are already familiar with Version 6 SAS/AF or SAS/FSP software and want a description of enhancements available in Release 6.07.

How to Use This Book

The following sections describe the organization of this report and its contents.

Organization

This report is divided into three parts, consisting of 19 chapters, and one appendix.

Part 1, "Changes to SAS/AF Software"
: Chapters 1 through 9 describe enhancements to the AF command, the new AFAPPLICATION command, PROGRAM entries, support for icons, and the new SLIST and SCL catalog entries.

Part 2, "Changes and Enhancements to SAS/FSP Software"
: Chapters 10 through 13 describe changes and enhancements to the FSEDIT procedure, the FSLIST procedure, and the FSVIEW procedure.

Part 3, "Updates to SAS Screen Control Language"
: Chapters 14 through 19 describe new features for controlling program execution at user interrupts and support for modular programming and for storing and manipulating data in SCL lists. It also provides examples using SCL lists and dictionaries of new and enhanced debugger commands and SCL elements.

Appendix "Icons"
: illustrates the icons available with the SAS System and provides the numbers with which you reference them in your SCL programs.

Reference Aids

This report includes the following sections to help you locate the information you need:

Contents	lists the chapters with their page numbers. Each chapter also includes a table of contents that lists the sections of that chapter and their page numbers.
Illustrations	lists all figures, displays, and tables in the report.
Index	provides the page numbers where specific topics and functions are discussed.

Examples

The examples in this book use code fragments (incomplete programs) and figures to illustrate the effect of new options or features in the software. Only those lines of the code directly related to the feature being described are included. Since these programs are not complete and do not include the data, they will not produce output if you submit them as shown.

Additional Documentation

This report updates information from the documentation on SAS/AF software and SAS/FSP software, which includes:

- *SAS/AF Software: Usage and Reference, Version 6, First Edition*
- *SAS/FSP Software: Usage and Reference, Version 6, First Edition*
- *SAS Screen Control Language: Reference, Version 6, First Edition*
- *SAS Screen Control Language: Usage, Version 6, First Edition.*

Summary of Changes and Enhancements to SAS/AF® and SAS/FSP® Software and SAS Screen Control Language

Release 6.07 of SAS/AF and SAS/FSP software and SAS Screen Control Language all include changes and enhancements. The following sections summarize these changes.

SAS/AF Software

SAS/AF software includes changes and enhancements to

- the AF command
- the AFAPPLICATION command
- the BUILD procedure
- support for icons
- SCL entry type

The AF Command

The AF command under Release 6.07 includes

- additional arguments that are passed to the application in a new type of data structure called an SCL list
- several new options that provide more flexibility in starting applications developed with SAS/AF software.

The AFAPPLICATION Command

The new AFAPPLICATION command starts an AF application in its own window. Unlike the AF command which always starts a command in the AF window, the application run by the AFAPPLICATION command gets its own window. This allows you to use the AFAPPLICATION command to execute several SAS/AF applications at the same time.

The BUILD Procedure

The BUILD procedure includes several general enhancements, which include

- several additional commands
- support for editing catalog entries created by other SAS procedures
- a new directory window
- support for running multiple concurrent BUILD sessions.

Support for Icons

SAS/AF software supports icons in this release, allowing you to

- □ create pushbuttons that display icons instead of text
- □ use the new ICON function in the SCL source code to assign icons to windows so that you can represent ideas with pictures instead of words, on menus, for example.
- □ display icons for block menu choices created with the SCL BLOCK function.

SCL Entry Type

The SCL entry is a new catalog entry type that contains an SCL program and its compiled code, but it does not include a DISPLAY window. You can use this entry for SCL programs that perform a task that does not require user interaction and therefore does not need to display a window.

SAS/FSP Software

Release 6.07 includes changes and enhancements to the FSEDIT, FSLIST, and FSVIEW procedures.

The FSEDIT Procedure

The FSEDIT procedure in SAS/FSP software includes the following changes and enhancements:

- □ Statement options and corresponding general parameters have been added to control whether users can add and delete observations from the displayed data set.
- □ A new field attribute controls how blanks in numeric field values are processed.
- □ The rules for when observations are updated have been modified.
- □ Scrolling between screens in multiscreen applications is allowed even when some screens contain invalid values.
- □ Search operations can be cancelled.

The following changes and enhancements to Screen Control Language (SCL) also provide new capabilities for FSEDIT applications:

- □ You can execute separate sections of SCL code when individual fields are modified.
- □ You can use the system variable _STATUS_ to monitor and control program flow.
- □ You can use data set variables marked as UNWANTED in your SCL programs.
- □ You can control which commands users can issue from the FSEDIT window.
- □ You can obtain additional information about the current observation and about the FSEDIT window.
- □ You can control the color and highlighting attributes of individual fields.
- □ You can determine which field the cursor is positioned on.

The FSLIST Procedure

The FSLIST procedure in SAS/FSP software has been enhanced to support attention handling during scrolling and search operations.

The FSVIEW Procedure

The FSVIEW procedure in SAS/FSP software includes the following changes and enhancements:

- Data set variables that have associated formulas can now be modified.
- Formats and informats for data set variables are no longer stored in FORMULA entries unless you explicitly specify them.
- Scrolling commands can now be interrupted if you decide that you don't want to wait for the commands to finish.
- Changes to Screen Control Language allow you to:
    - control the color and highlighting attributes of individual columns
    - determine which column the cursor is positioned on.

SAS Screen Control Software

Screen Control Language includes new and enhanced functionality in the following areas:

- control over program execution at user interrupts
- program modules
- SCL list functions
- debugger enhancements

Control Over Program Execution at User Interrupts

You can control program execution when users interrupt a program, for example, by a user pressing an interrupt key.

Program Modules

You can create program modules that can be called in the same program or from a different program. This allows you to write a module that performs one operation on an element of an SCL entry or FSEDIT window and use that module repeatedly instead of having to write the program segment into multiple programs. You can communicate values between program modules and the calling SCL program.

You can also create programs in which the MAIN section does not execute unless certain modules run without error. These modules contain statements that verify values in a window variable. You can include a module of this type for any number of window variables.

SCL List Functions

There is a whole family of new functions that allow you to store and manipulate data in a new data structure called an SCL list. SCL lists are ordered collections of data, similar to arrays. However, lists provide more flexibility in that they are created dynamically. You can reference list items by name or by index position. Lists can contain numbers, characters, or even other lists, and combinations of these item types. List functions enable you to insert items, replace or delete items, and move them around by reversing, rotating, or sorting them.

Debugger Enhancements

The SCL Debugger also includes several enhancements. You can specify a program label with the BREAK and GO commands. When you use the STEP command to debug a SELECT statement, the STEP command jumps to the appropriate WHEN or OTHERWISE clause without stepping through all the intervening WHEN statements.

Changes to SAS/AF® Software

PART 1

CHAPTER 1 Overview of Changes and Enhancements to SAS/AF® Software

Overview

Part 1 contains information on new and enhanced functionality for Release 6.07 of SAS/AF software. This information is divided into the following categories:

- □ the AF command
- □ the AFAPPLICATION command
- □ PROGRAM entries
- □ the BUILD procedure
- □ icons
- □ SCL catalog entries
- □ SLIST catalog entries
- □ the Procedure Management window.

Prerequisites
Several of the chapters in Part 1 discuss new features in SAS/AF software relating to changes and enhancements for Screen Control Language. SCL now supports new data structures and functions for manipulating lists of data. Lists, like arrays, are ordered collections of data. However, lists are more flexible than arrays in many ways.

Before you read Chapter 2, "The AF Command," and Chapter 8, "SLIST Catalog Entries," you should read Chapter 17, "Features for Storing and Manipulating Data in SCL Lists," in Part 3 of this book.

The AF command

Chapter 2, "The AF Command," describes the enhancements to the AF command in Release 6.07 of SAS/AF software. These enhancements include

- □ additional AF command options that provide more flexibility in starting applications
- □ the ability to use the AF command to pass information to your application for further processing.

The AFAPPLICATION Command

Chapter 3, "The AFAPPLICATION Command," describes the new AFAPPLICATION command. This command, which has the same form as the AF command, enables you to run multiple SAS/AF applications simultaneously. In this case, each SAS/AF application runs as a separate *task*.

PROGRAM Entries

Chapter 4, "Changes to PROGRAM Entries," describes the new capabilities you have when working with PROGRAM entries:

- you can specify that your application will handle SAS/AF commands over which you normally have no control
- you can execute individual labeled sections of code when users modify particular fields.

The BUILD Procedure

Chapter 5, "Changes to the BUILD Procedure," describes the changes and enhancements to the BUILD procedure in Release 6.07 of SAS/AF software, which include the following:

- new ways to invoke the BUILD procedure, including one method that supports multiple BUILD sessions at the same time.
- additional catalog entry types you can edit from the catalog directory.

Icons

Chapter 6, "Support for Icons," describes how you may be able to use *icons*, pictorial representations of objects or tasks, to represent the following:

- pushbutton fields on SAS/AF PROGRAM entries
- menu choices on block menus
- windows.

To use icons in Release 6.07 of SAS/AF software, your display device and operating system must support them.

SCL Catalog Entries

Often, your programs may perform tasks that do not require user interaction. Therefore, you do not need to display a window. In these cases, you can use the new SCL catalog entry type to take advantage of the full power of SCL. Chapter 7, "SCL Catalog Entries," describes how to

- □ edit an SCL program in an SCL entry
- □ compile and store the program
- □ execute the program directly from the SCL entry
- □ call the SCL entry from FSEDIT and SAS/AF entry types.

SLIST Catalog Entries

Chapter 8, "SLIST Catalog Entries," describes the new SLIST catalog entry. This entry type enables you to save SCL lists in a catalog so their contents may be recalled either later in the SAS session or during another SAS session.

The Procedure Management Window

The Procedure Management Window (PMW) is a new window you can use to access and manipulate catalogs in any SAS data library defined with a libref in the current SAS session, rather than just the single catalog available when you supply a catalog name with the PROC BUILD statement or BUILD command.

Chapter 9, "The Procedure Management Window," describes how you can use this window and its associated dialog windows to edit, copy, rename, and delete catalog entries.

CHAPTER 2 The AF Command

Overview

The AF command in SAS/AF software includes the following changes and enhancements for Release 6.07:

- □ additional AF command options which provide more flexibility in starting applications
- □ the ability to use the AF command to pass information to your application via an SCL list.

AF Command Syntax

The form of the enhanced AF command is

AF <AUTORECALL=YES> <AUTOSAVE=YES>
<AWS=NO>
<CATALOG=libref.catalog.name.type>
<CHECKLAST=NO>
<DEBUG=YES>
<FRAME=frame-number | frame-name>
<ICON=number>
<LABEL=label>
<MSG=YES>
<PMENU=YES>
<RESTART=YES>
<TITLE='title'>
<start-menu-number>
<...<option-name=>option-value>

The following section discusses the new AF command options.

Additional AF Command Options

You can use the following new options with the AF command:

AWS=NO

specifies that each of your application's windows appears in it's own native window rather than in an *Application Work Space*, AWS.

This option is useful when you run your SAS/AF application on systems that support a native window system such as the X Window System, DEC Windows, OS/2 Presentation Manager, or Microsoft Windows 3.0. These native window systems provide window management capabilities.

By default, SAS/AF software presents the application in an AWS. Therefore, all windows displayed by the AF application (including HELP windows and other windows displayed via the CALL DISPLAY routine) are confined to the single AWS window. The application user can minimize or maximize the entire SAS/AF application by minimizing or maximizing the AWS window.

This option has an effect only if the native windowing system supports Application Work Spaces.

ICON=*number*

specifies the number of the icon which is to represent an AWS window. By default, the SAS/AF icon is displayed. The Appendix, "Icons," lists the available icons.

This option has an effect only if the native windowing system supports Application Work Spaces and you specify AWS=YES.

LABEL=*label*

specifies the name of an SCL program label where execution begins when the AF command is used to execute a stand-alone SCL entry. Execution begins at the specified label and continues until a RETURN statement is reached. For more information about executing labeled sections of code in an SCL entry, refer to Chapter 7, "SCL Catalog Entries."

MSG=YES

enables the message window. The default is MSG=NO, which means SAS/AF software uses the LOG window instead of the message window for logging messages.

This option is similar to the MSG/NOMSG option used with the PROC BUILD statement.

PMENU=YES

specifies the PMENU facility for a window must remain on. If you have customized the action bars in your windows and wish to ensure users cannot turn the PMENU facility off for windows in your application, you may want to use this option.

If your SAS/AF application invokes other applications by specifying the AF or AFAPPLICATION command with the EXECCMD routine, include PMENU=YES in the command if you want the new applications to have the same behavior.

The default is PMENU=NO.

RESTART=YES
: specifies that when SAS/AF software is executing a CBT application, the CBT is restarted from the beginning.

  By default, RESTART= NO. In this case, when SAS/AF is executing a CBT application, the application starts at the CBT frame which was last accessed.

TITLE='*title*'
: specifies the title to display in the AWS window. If the title contains embedded blanks, enclose the title in single quotes. For example, you can specify an AWS window title with

```
af c=corp.fin.inv.program title='Inventory Analysis'
```

  This option has an effect only if the native windowing system supports Application Work Spaces and you specify AWS=YES.

Passing AF Command Options to an Application

In Release 6.07 of SAS/AF software, you can use the AF command to specify both options for the AF command and options to be used by your application. In either case, SAS/AF software passes the specified options to your SCL application for further processing. For example, you can design an application that requires a list of observations numbers as input, and invoke the application with the following AF command:

```
af c=a.b.obs.scl obs=17 23 19 47
```

SAS/AF software stores the specified options and their values in a special list called _CMDLIST_. This list is a sublist of the local environment SCL list that is created when either a SAS/AF or SAS/FSP application is invoked. (For more information about environment lists, refer to "Using Shared Data Environments" in Chapter 17, "Features for Storing and Manipulating Data in SCL Lists." If the option is specified in the form *name*=*value*, for example OBS=17, then both the name and the value are stored in the list; otherwise just the value, for example 23 or 19, is stored. In this case *value* is a number. However, it also can be one of the following:

- □ an unquoted text string such as YES or NO
- □ a quoted text string, such as 'Apply SAS Software' (If you want several words to be treated as one argument, you must enclose them in quotes.)
- □ a hex string such as '534153'x
- □ a date, time, or datetime literal such as '24Jul90'D.

Values Automatically Placed in the Command List

Regardless of whether you specify the CATALOG= option on the AF command, SAS/AF software automatically places the *library, catalog, name,* and *type* values for this option in the command list. If you reinvoke the AF command, omitting the CATALOG= option, SAS/AF software retrieves the last application name from the SASUSER.PROFILE.AF.AFGO catalog entry. Therefore, the command list is always at least four items long. For example, if you submit the following statement

```
af c=training.sas.intro.program
```

then _CMDLIST_ contains the following values:

```
_CMDLIST_=(LIBNAME='TRAINING'
           CATALOG='SAS'
           NAME='INTRO'
           TYPE='PROGRAM'
           ) 3
```

Note: This output was generated with a CALL PUTLIST statement:

```
call putlist(cmdlist,'_CMDLIST_=',0);
```

Differences in Storing AF Command and Application-Specific Options

Values you specify for application-specific options are stored a little differently than values you specify for the following AF command options:

AUTORECALL=

AUTOSAVE

AWS=

CATALOG=

CHECKLAST=

DEBUG=

FRAME=

ICON=

LABEL=

MSG=

NOBORDER=

PMENU=

RESTART=

TITLE=

Table 2.1 lists the differences in how SAS/AF software stores the specified options in the command list.

Table 2.1 *Comparison of how Values are Stored*

Comparing ...	**Values specified for AF command options**	**And values specified for application-specific options**
options users repeat on the same AF command	are ignored except for the last occurance, which is stored in the command list	are all stored in the command list
abbreviations users specify for "yes" and "no" values	are stored in the command list as YES and NO (the abbreviations are expanded and converted to uppercase)	are stored in the command list exactly as specified
values users specify in lowercase	are converted to uppercase unless quoted	are stored in the command list in lowercase

For example, if you use the following AF command,

```
af c=a.b.c.program  check=y check=n
```

then _CMDLIST_ contains the following values:

```
_CMDLIST_=(LIBNAME='A'
           CATALOG='B'
           NAME='C'
           TYPE='PROGRAM'
           CHECKLAST='NO'
           )[3]
```

Note: Notice CHECKLAST appears only once in the command list, reflecting the last occurrence of CHECKLAST on the AF command.

However, if you enter the following command

```
af c=a.b.c  name='David S.' Obs=17 23 19 term=y term=n
```

then _CMDLIST_ contains the following values:

```
_CMDLIST_=(LIBNAME='A'
              CATALOG='B'
              NAME='C'
              TYPE='PROGRAM'
              NAME='David S.'
              OBS=17
              23
              19
              TERM='y'
              TERM='n'
              )[3]
```

Note: The application-specific option NAME does not conflict with the *name* value which is recognized by the AF command and contains the name of the current SAS/AF program.

Using command macros

If your application accepts options when it is invoked, you can design a command macro which invokes the application. For example, if your application FINANCE.REPORTS.GENRPT.SCL accepts the following options on the AF or AFAPPLICATION command:

```
title="title"
date=sas-date
```

then you can design the following command macro to invoke the application:

```
%macro genrpt(title="Financial Report",date=0)/cmd;
   afapp c=finance.reports.genrpt.scl title=&title date=&date
%mend genrpt;
```

Then, users can invoke the application with the new GENRPT command, provided the macro is loaded in the current SAS session and the CMDMAC option is on. If users issue the command

```
genrpt
```

then the SCL entry is executed with the default title and date. However, users can specify a different title and date. For example, users can issue the following command:

```
genrpt date='24Jul90'D title="Personnel Report"
```

and the SAS macro facility will change this to the command

```
afapp c=finance.reports.genrpt.scl title="Personnel Report"
     date='24Jul90'D
```

CHAPTER 3 The AFAPPLICATION Command

Overview

There is a new command, the AFAPPLICATION command, in Release 6.07 of SAS/AF software that enables you to run multiple SAS/AF applications simultaneously. Each SAS/AF application is a separate *task.*

If you need to run only one application, you can continue to use the AF command.

AFAPPLICATION Command Syntax

The AFAPPLICATION command uses the same syntax as the AF command:

AFAPPLICATION <AUTORECALL=YES>
<AUTOSAVE=YES>
<AWS=NO>
<CATALOG=libref.catalog.name.type>
<CHECKLAST=NO>
<DEBUG=YES>
<FRAME=frame-number | frame-name>
<ICON=icon-number>
<LABEL=label>
<MSG=YES>
<PMENU=YES>
<RESTART=YES>
<TITLE=title>
<start-menu-number>
<...<option-name=>option-value>

Note: The AFAPPLICATION command may be abbreviated AFAPPL or AFA. For more information about the command options, see Chapter 2, "The AF Command" in this book, and Chapter 11, "The AF Command," in *SAS/AF Software: Usage and Reference, Version 6, First Edition.*

Comparison With the AF Command

Similarities
The AFAPPLICATION command is similar to the AF command in the following ways:

- □ command options have the same abbreviations, for example, CATALOG= may be abbreviated to CAT= or C=.
- □ both command options and application-specific options users specify on the command may be passed to the application for further processing
- □ the _CMDLIST_, which is a sublist of the local environment list, is supported
- □ if the CATALOG= option is omitted, the entry in SASUSER.PROFILE.AF.AFGO runs.

Differences
When you run a SAS/AF application with the AFAPPLICATION command, the AF checkpoint (which consists of the application name and CBT frame, if you are running a CBT) is not saved in SASUSER.PROFILE.AF.AFGO.

Sharing Data Between Multiple Applications

When you run a SAS/AF application with the AFAPPLICATION command, remember other applications may be running at the same time. Assumptions you make about the availability of data, such as SAS data sets or members of SAS catalogs, may be invalid when more than one application is running. For example, a typical application may read an SLIST catalog member using the FILLIST function. Before this application updates the list and writes the list back to the entry, another application having update access to the catalog may read from and write to the same SLIST entry. This situation may create problems with data integrity.

If your application may need to share data with another application, you should consider

- □ opening your data sets with member level locking. (For more information on opening data sets with member level locking, refer to Chapter 17, "Reading and Updating SAS Data Sets" in *SAS Screen Control Language: Usage, Version 6, First Edition" or Chapter 4, "Features of Screen Control Language," in SAS Screen Control Language: Reference, Version 6, First Edition.")*
- □ accessing your catalog through SAS/SHARE software, and locking your catalog entries and other SAS data files with the SCL LOCK function. (For more information about the SCL LOCK function, refer to Chapter 20, "Dictionary of New and Enhanced SCL Elements" later in this book.)

Example

The following SCL program shows you one way to account for data sharing using the new LOCK function.

```
entry='SASUSER.PROFILE.SAMPLE.SLIST';
rc=lock(entry,'LOCK');
if rc then _msg_=sysmsg(); /* can't lock the entry */
else
   do;
      /* We have locked the entry. Now, read it, */
      /* modify it, write it, then unlock it.    */
     list=makelist();
     rc=fillist('CATALOG',entry,list);
     if rc then _msg_=sysmsg();
     else
        do;
              /* ...place SCL code here to update the */
              /* list while holding the lock...       */
           rc=savelist('SLIST',entry,list);
           if rc then _msg_=sysmsg();
        end;
        /* Update done: clear the lock & delete the list */
     rc=lock(entry,'CLEAR');
     rc=dellist(list,'Y');
   end;
```

Note: This example only displays a message when the lock request fails. In your applications, handle the lock failure in a manner that is appropriate for the application.

CHAPTER 4 Changes to PROGRAM Entries

Introduction

When you work with PROGRAM entries in Release 6.07 of SAS/AF software, you now have the following additional capabilities:

- □ you can process SAS/AF commands over which you normally do not have control, in your application
- □ you can execute individual labeled sections of code when users modify particular fields.

Handling SAS/AF Window Commands

The new ALLCMDS option of the CONTROL statement enables you to process all SAS/AF commands within your application. You use this statement in the following form:

```
control allcmds;
```

When you specify this option with the CONTROL statement, the SAS/AF commands listed in table 4.1 return control to the MAIN section of your application. These commands can be issued on the command line, with function keys, or with an action bar.

Table 4.1 *Commands You Can Process with the CONTROL ALLCMDS Statement*

BACKWARD	FIND	KEYFIELD	QEND	TRACE
CANCEL	FONT	LEFT	QSTACK	TYPE
CLEAR	FORMNAME	LOCATE	RECALL	VSCROLL
DEBUG	FORWARD	MUSIC	RETURN	WREGION
DUP	HELP	PREVIEW	RIGHT	WSIZE
END	HSCROLL	PRTFILE	SAVE	=
EQUAL	ID	QCAN	SPRINT	

In your applications, you should process the commands listed in Table 4.1 the same way you currently process your other commands, including using the ALWAYS or ENTER option with the CONTROL statement to ensure that the MAIN section of your SCL program is executed whenever a user issues a command. For more information about these commands, refer to "Commands for Windows Displayed by the TESTAF and AF Commands" in Chapter 12, "SAS/AF Window Commands" in *SAS/AF Software: Usage and Reference, Version 6, First Edition*

For information about the ALLCMDS option, refer to "CONTROL" in Chapter 20, "Dictionary of New and Enhanced SCL Elements."

Executing SCL Code When Users Modify Individual Fields

SAS/AF software can now execute individual labeled sections of SCL code when users modify particular fields. To make use of this new feature, you must

□ use a CONTROL statement with the LABEL option in the following form:

```
control label;
```

□ put the statements to execute when a field is modified in a block of code labeled with the name of the field. For example, to display a message when a user modifies a field called NAME, you can use the following labeled section of code:

```
NAME:
   _msg_="The NAME field has been modified."
return;
```

When users modify a field while the CONTROL LABEL option is active, SAS/AF software

□ performs the usual field validation

□ executes any section of the SCL program labeled with the same name as the modified field

□ and then, executes the MAIN section.

This feature enables you to treat labeled statement blocks as subroutines associated with selected fields. You can write additional field validation code without using code in the MAIN section to determine which fields the user has modified. This technique is shown in the following example.

Example

The following example shows how you can perform cross-field validation using labeled sections of code.

The window
Display 4.1 shows the DISPLAY window for this example.

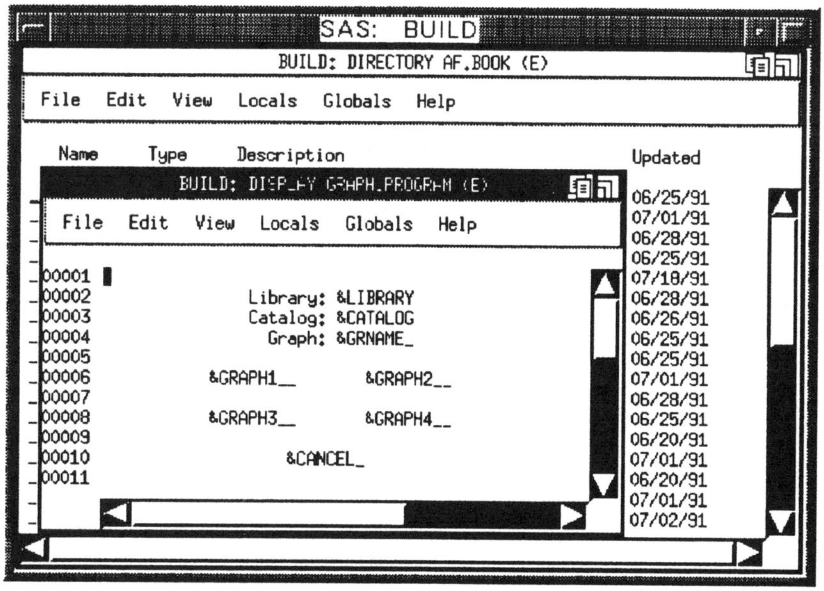

Display 4.1 DISPLAY Window for Graph Example

As you can see from the DISPLAY window, there are three entry fields in which users can enter the name of a SAS/GRAPH graph. (These fields have the type NAME.)

- LIBRARY
- CATALOG
- GRNAME

In addition to the three entry fields, the window has four pushbuttons which invoke a corresponding GRAPH window:

- GRAPH1
- GRAPH2
- GRAPH3
- GRAPH4

and a pushbutton called CANCEL. All of these fields have associated labeled sections of code in the SCL program.

SCL program

The complete SCL program for this example is shown here:

```
LIBRARY:
   erroroff library;
   if libref(library) then
      do;
         _msg_=sysmsg();
         erroron library;
         cursor library;
      end;
return;

CATALOG:
   erroroff catalog;
   if library='' then return;
   cat=library || '.' || catalog;
   if ¬cexist(cat) then link nocat;
return;

NOCAT:
   _msg_=sysmsg();
   erroron catalog;
   cursor catalog;
return;

GRNAME:
   erroroff grname;
   graph='';
return;

GRAPH1:
   gnum='1';
   link graph;
return;

GRAPH2:
   gnum='2';
   link graph;
return;

GRAPH3:
   gnum='3';
   link graph;
return;

GRAPH4:
   gnum='4';
   link graph;
return;
```

```
GRAPH:
   if cat='' then link nocat;
   else if graph='' then link nograph;
   else call execcmd('graph' || gnum || ' ' || graph);
return;

NOGRAPH:
   _msg_='Graph ' || graph || ' does not exist.';
   erroron grname;
   cursor grname;
return;

INIT:
   control label;
return;

MAIN:
   if (field('ERROR','LIBRARY CATALOG GRNAME')=0
      and cat¬=''
      and grname¬='' ) then
         do;
            graph=cat || '.' || grname || '.GRSEG';
            if (¬cexist(graph)) then link nograph;
            else _msg_='Select: Graph 1, 2, 3, or 4';
         end;
   else
      graph='';
return;

CANCEL:
   _status_='H';
return;

TERM:
   put 'TERM';
return;
```

You should note the following things about this SCL program:

- □ When users modify the entry fields, the SCL statements in the corresponding labeled sections are executed. If the fields are not in error, the MAIN section is executed.
- □ If the user selects one of the GRAPH push buttons, the SCL statements in the corresponding labeled section are executed. In this case, each of these labeled sections sets a graph number variable in GNUM and links to the labeled section GRAPH, which then displays the graph in the requested GRAPH window if the GRSEG exists.
- □ When users select the CANCEL button, the CANCEL label is executed. The code in this section halts the program by setting _STATUS_ to 'H'. (This prevents the MAIN section from executing).

Using the EXECCMD Routine in Labeled Sections of Code

When you use the EXECCMD routine to issue a command in a section of code labeled with a field name, the command is not executed until after the MAIN section executes. For example, if you use a PUSHBTNC field called CANCEL and include the following SCL code in your program:

```
CANCEL:
   call execcmd('CANCEL'); /* Caution!! */
return;
```

the CANCEL command does not execute until after the MAIN section executes.

Processing the CANCEL command
If you want to prevent MAIN from executing when the user selects the CANCEL button (assuming the CANCEL labeled section does not set _STATUS_ to 'H'), include the following statement at the top of your MAIN section:

```
MAIN:
   if field('MODIFIED','CANCEL') then return;
return;
```

Optionally, you could also name a choice group in the CANCEL button attribute window and MAIN could return if the choice group equals the cancel button. The following statement assumes the choice group is named CANCELG.

```
MAIN:
   if cancelg=cancel then return;
return;
```

In addition, you can bypass the MAIN section entirely and call the TERM section directly from your label exit. Then you can set the _STATUS_ variable to 'H' to halt the application. You should be careful to halt your program only after it has performed any cleanup activities, such as closing open data sets, directories, and external files or deleting allocated lists.

For example, you can put the following statements in the section of code with the CANCEL label:

```
CANCEL:
   _status_='C'; /* TERM runs as if the user had typed   */
   link term;      /* a cancel command and cleans up.      */
   _status_='H'; /* Halt the application after TERM runs */
return;
```

CHAPTER 5 Changes to the BUILD Procedure

Overview

In Release 6.07 of SAS/AF software, the BUILD procedure has been enhanced to enable you to

□ invoke the BUILD procedure using several alternative methods, including one method that supports multiple BUILD sessions at the same time

□ open catalog entries using the new OPEN command and edit several additional catalog entry types

Additional Ways to Invoke the BUILD Procedure

In Release 6.07 of SAS/AF software, you have several alternatives for invoking the BUILD procedure:

□ the enhanced PROC BUILD statement

□ the Procedure Management Window

□ the new BUILD command

□ the new SCL BUILD routine.

Enhancements to the PROC BUILD Statement

The following options for the PROC BUILD statement have been either changed or added in Release 6.07 of SAS/AF software:

CATALOG=
: specifies the catalog to invoke. If you omit the CATALOG= option on the PROC BUILD statement, SAS/AF software displays the Procedure Management Window, PMW, from which you can select a library, catalog, and catalog member for editing. The Procedure Management Window is described in Chapter 9, "The Procedure Management Window."

ENTRYTYPE=*type*
ETYPE=*type*
ET=*type*
: specifies the default catalog entry type for the EDIT and BROWSE commands. The default entry type is PROGRAM. You may change the entry type to CBT, HELP, MENU, or SCL with the ENTRYTYPE= option.

Procedure Management Window

The Procedure Management Window (PMW) is a new window you can use to access and manipulate catalogs in any SAS data library defined with a libref in the current SAS session, rather than just the single catalog available when you supply a catalog name with the PROC BUILD statement or BUILD command.

To invoke the Procedure Management Window, you can issue a PROC BUILD statement without specifying the CATALOG= option:

```
proc build;
run;
```

or you can use the BUILD command without specifying a catalog or catalog entry:

```
build
```

Display 5.1 shows a Procedure Management Window. In this window, the user has selected the **AF** library and the **BOOK** catalog.

Display 5.1 *The BUILD Procedure Management Window*

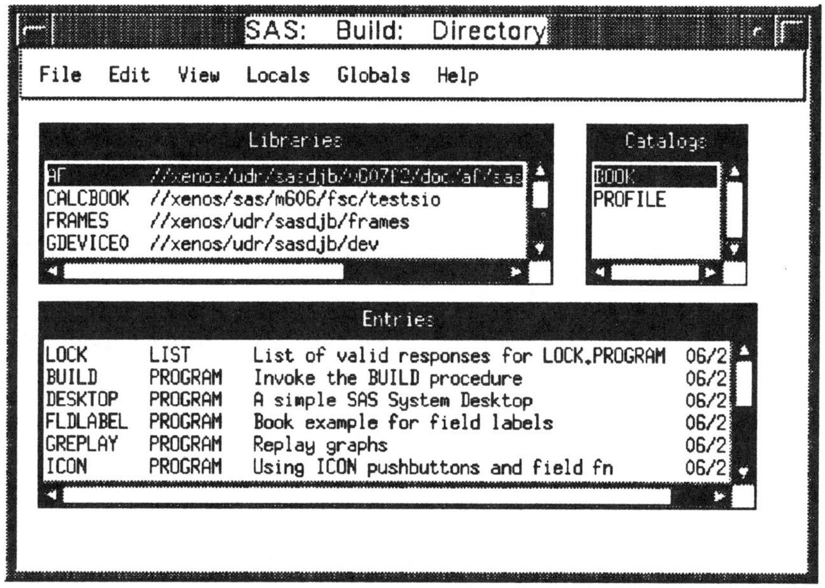

From the Procedure Management window you can invoke dialog windows to rename, copy, and delete catalog members. The Procedure Management window and its associated dialog windows are described in detail in Chapter 9, "The Procedure Management Window."

The BUILD Command

The BUILD command is a new Display Manager command you can use from any SAS window to invoke the BUILD procedure in its own window. Each BUILD command starts a separate BUILD procedure, so you can have several BUILD procedures running at the same time, each building different entries in the same or different catalogs.

▶ ***Caution:*** *Concurrent access to the same catalog entry is possible.*

It is possible to open the same catalog entry multiple times if multiple BUILD commands for the entry are issued. If this happens, and more than one copy of the entry is edited at the same time, the changes made to the entry that is closed last replace any changes that were saved previously. To avoid this problem, you may want to access the SAS data library through SAS/SHARE software. If you use SAS/SHARE software, you can lock the catalog entry (with the LOCK command) before you edit it, and then unlock the entry when you are finished with it.

BUILD Command Syntax

The form of the BUILD command is

BUILD <<libref.>catalog<.entry<.type>>>
<AWS=YES>
<TITLE='title'>
<ICON=number>
<MSG=NO>

If you omit the catalog or catalog entry, the BUILD procedure displays the Procedure Management Window from which you can select a library, catalog, and a catalog entry for editing. This window is described in "Procedure Management Window" earlier in this chapter.

If you specify a catalog, then the catalog directory is displayed just as if you had invoked the BUILD procedure via the PROC BUILD statement. The default library is WORK, so the command

```
build a
```

invokes the BUILD procedure on the catalog WORK.A.

If you specify a three- or a four- level name, the BUILD procedure opens the specified entry directly. (The default entry type is PROGRAM.)

The other options, AWS, TITLE, ICON, and MSG, are the same as the AF command options. See Chapter 2, "The AF Command" for more information about each of these options.

The BUILD Routine

A new SCL routine, the BUILD routine, enables you to open a BUILD window from within an application. You can use the BUILD window to construct any of the SAS/AF entry types, or to edit and browse FSP and GRAPH GRSEG entries. This is useful if you wish to design a SAS System desktop application that has pushbuttons for the most common tasks you perform. You can include a button for the BUILD procedure. You can then associate SCL code with the button's field label that prompts users to enter a catalog member and then invokes BUILD procedure for that entry.

For more information on the BUILD routine, refer to "BUILD" in Chapter 20, "Dictionary of New and Enhanced SCL Elements."

Example

Your desktop application can have the following field label definition for the pushbutton named BUILD.

```
BUILD:
   call display("build");
return;
```

You can then define a program entry BUILD.PROGRAM that prompts users for a catalog entry and invokes the BUILD procedure for that entry. The DISPLAY window for this program is shown in Display 5.2.

Display 5.2 *AF PROGRAM Display for Invoking PROC BUILD*

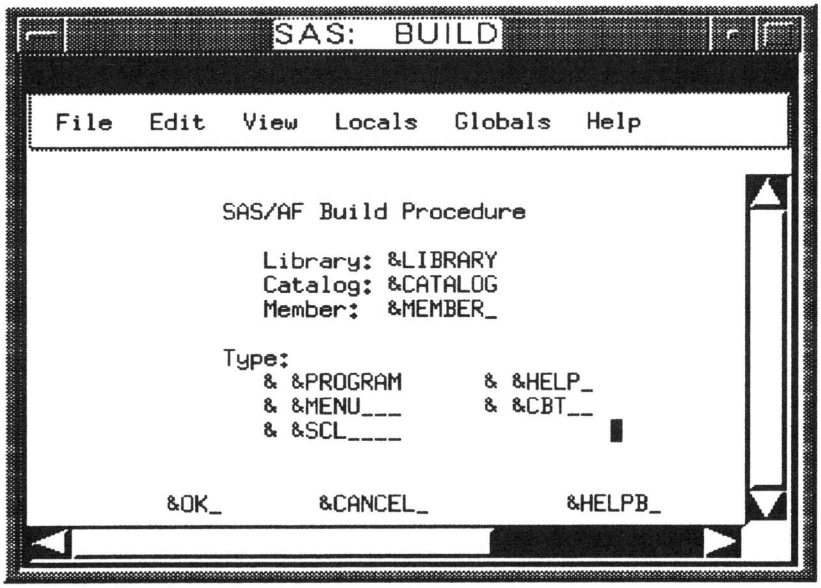

The fields PROGRAM, HELP, CBT, SCL, and MENU and the five action fields in front of them are all part of a single choice group named ETYPE.

The SCL program associated with the application is shown here.

```
   length afentry $ 26;

INIT:
   control label;
   etype='PROGRAM';
return;

OK:
   call build(afentry || '.' || etype);
return;

MAIN:
   if afentry='' then return;
   _msg_='Press the Ok button to edit ' || afentry || '.' || etype;
return;

HELP:
   /* Put statements to provide help in this section. */
return;

TERM:
return;

CANCEL:
   _status_='H';
return;
```

```
LIBRARY:
   /* Fall through to the CATALOG labeled section. */

CATALOG:
   afentry='';
   cat='';
   erroroff library catalog member;
   cat=library || '.' || catalog;
   if ¬cexist(cat) then
      do;
         erroron library catalog;
         cursor library;
         _msg_=sysmsg();
         return;
      end;

MEMBER:
   if member='' and cat ¬='' then
      do;
         choice=catlist(cat,etype,1,'N','Select an entry to build');
         if choice='' then return;
         member=substr(choice,1,index(choice,'.')-1);
      end;
   if member='' or cat='' then return;
   afentry=c at || '.' || member;
return;
```

Changes to the Catalog Directory

The catalog directory has been enhanced so that you can

- □ use a new command to open catalog entries for editing
- □ edit several catalog entry types, in addition to the valid SAS/AF catalog entry types.

Editing Catalog Entries

In addition to the valid SAS/AF entry types, you now can edit or browse the following from the catalog directory:

- □ SAS/FSP catalog entries
- □ SAS/CALC catalog entries
- □ SAS/GRAPH GRSEG catalog entries.

Note: To edit or browse SAS/FSP, SAS/CALC, or SAS/GRAPH catalog entries, your site must have licensed SAS/FSP, SAS/CALC, or SAS/GRAPH software, respectively.

Since you can edit spreadsheets or graphs directly from the SAS/AF catalog directory, you have much greater flexibility in designing integrated applications without having to exit the BUILD procedure.

Using selection field commands

To edit any catalog member, enter the E selection field command on the member name and press ENTER.

Using command line commands
If you use the command line, enter the command EDIT followed by the entry name:

```
edit primary.program
edit invtry.letter
edit division.calc
edit usamap.grseg
```

Using the PMENU facility
If you use the PMENU facility, select the **File** pull down menu and then choose one of the following:

□ **New..**, if you wish to create a new entry.

□ **Open..**, if you wish to edit an existing entry. When you select **Open..**, the **Edit..** dialog box is displayed.

Display 5.3 shows the **Edit..** dialog box for the BUILD procedure. This dialog box lists SAS/AF entry types such as PROGRAM, CBT, and MENU. Other products also display an **Edit..** dialog box that lists the catalog entry types appropriate for that product.

Display 5.3 *The Edit... Dialog Box*

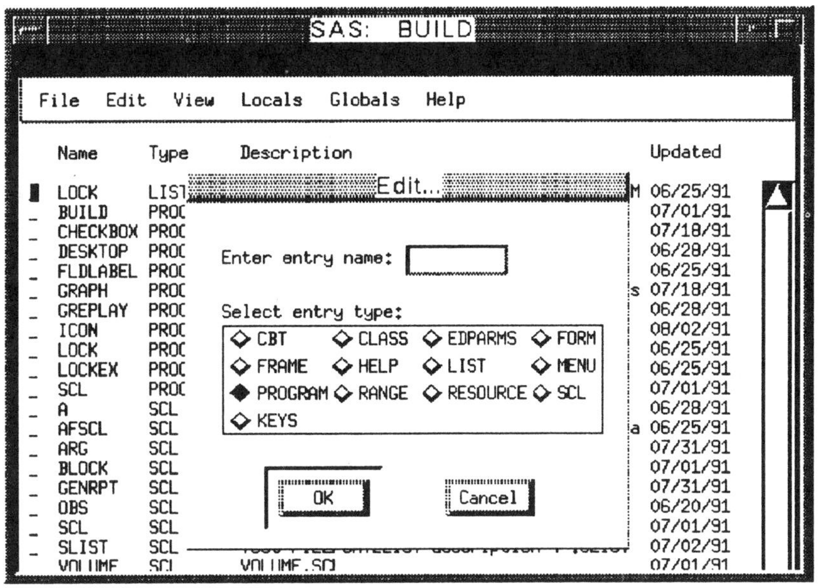

Note: If you select **New..** instead of **Open..**, the **New..** dialog box is displayed. The **New..** dialog box is similar to the **Edit..** dialog box shown here.

To complete the dialog boxes

□ select the desired entry type

□ enter the components of the name in the **Library**, **Catalog**, and **Member** fields

□ select the **OK** button

If you want to browse an entry, use the BROWSE command or place a B in the selection field.

Once you have issued the appropriate command, the BUILD procedure invokes the appropriate SAS Software product for editing or browsing.

New Command Available in the Catalog Directory

The following command is now available from the catalog directory window:

OPEN entry<.type>

opens a new or existing catalog entry for editing. The OPEN command is identical to the EDIT command for all SAS/AF entry types. However, if you have SAS/CALC software licensed at your site, the OPEN and EDIT commands operate differently. For more information, refer to *SAS/CALC Software: Usage and Reference, Version 6, First Edition*.

If you omit the entry type, it defaults to either PROGRAM or the entry type you specified with the ENTRYTYPE= option when you invoked the BUILD procedure.

To open a catalog entry using a selection field command, place an O next to the entry and press ENTER.

CHAPTER 6 Support for Icons

Overview

An *icon* is a pictorial representation of an object or task that you can use to either replace or supplement text in your windows. If your display device and host operating system support icons, you can use icons in Release 6.07 of SAS/AF software to represent

- □ pushbutton fields on SAS/AF PROGRAM entries
- □ menu choices on block menus
- □ windows.

Note: See your SAS Software Representative to find out if your system supports icons.

Using Icons For Pushbutton Fields

For fields that have the type PUSHBTNN or PUSHBTNC, you now can display icons instead of push buttons.

Identifying the initial icon to display
Every icon has an identification number. To display an icon for a push button field, you must identify the icon by entering its identification number between two backslash characters as the field's **List** attribute on the ATTR window. For example, to display the SAS/AF icon, icon number 17, enter

```
\17 \
```

for the field's **List** attribute.

Changing the icon that is displayed
You also can change the icon that is displayed for a push button while your SAS/AF application is running. To do this, you can use the SCL FIELD function with the new action, "ICON n." For example, to change the icon displayed for the field to icon number 32, use the following SCL statement:

```
n=field('icon 32','icon');
```

For information about the FIELD function, refer to "FIELD" in Chapter 20, "Dictionary of New and Enhanced SCL Elements."

Size of icons
The height of each icon is comparable to 6 lines of text, and the minimum width is equal to 10 columns of text. However, if the field which the icon represents is wider than 10 columns, the icon is displayed using the full width of the field.

Example

Suppose you want to design an application that enables users to browse a series of icons and determine their associate identification numbers. Display 6.1 shows several windows associated with an icon previewer application:

- the ICON.PROGRAM window, which contains four pushbutton icons: ICON, Up, Down, and Exit.
- the DISPLAY window for the application. Notice that each field is 10 characters wide to account for the width of the icons, and that there are five blank lines below each pushbutton field, ICON, UP, DOWN, and EXIT, to account for the height of the icons.
- the ATTR window for the Up pushbutton, icon number 166. Notice that the field type is PUSHBTNC. (The DOWN and EXIT fields are similarly PUSHBTNC fields, while the ICON pushbutton is a PUSHBTNN field which displays the current icon number).

Display 6.1 *Icon Previewer, DISPLAY and ATTR Windows*

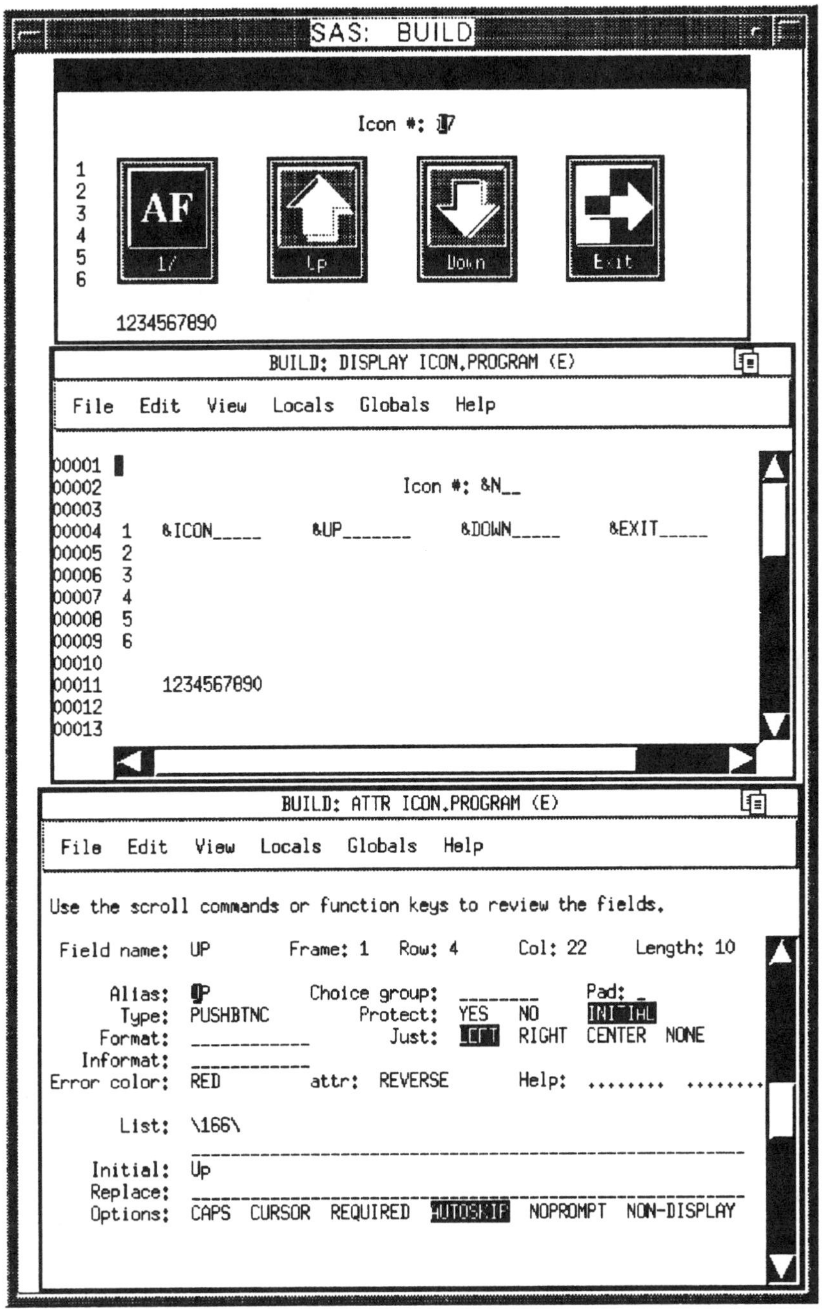

Note: Display 6.1 was captured on an X windows device running PROC BUILD in an Application Work Space.

The following SCL program controls the icon previewer application:

```
UP:                              /* UP Pushbutton */
   if n=1013 then return;
   n+1;
   link show;
return;

DOWN:                            /* DOWN Pushbutton */
   if n=1 then return;
   n=n-1;
   link show;
return;

N:    /* Change the icon displayed in field ICON to icon #N */

SHOW:
   rc=field("ICON" || putn(n,"BEST."),"ICON");
return;

EXIT:                              /* EXIT Pushbutton */
   call execcmd("Cancel");
return;

INIT:
   control label;
   n=17;                       /* fall through MAIN... */

MAIN:
   icon=n;                     /* fall through TERM... */

TERM:
return;
```

When the SCL program is executed, the first pushbutton (the AF icon) displays the icon whose number is shown in the field labeled **Icon #:**. The icon number is displayed in the icon itself, centered on the bottom line. When users change the icon number or select the **UP** or **DOWN** pushbuttons to increment or decrement the icon number, the program displays the corresponding icon. The **EXIT** pushbutton ends the preview application.

Using Icons on Block Menus

The BLOCK function has twelve new parameters allowing you to specify an icon to associate with each menu choice. For a detailed discussion of using icons with block menus, refer to "BLOCK" in Chapter 20, "Dictionary of New and Enhanced SCL Elements."

Note: If your device or system cannot display icons, the default BLOCK menu appears.

Assigning Icons to Windows

The new SCL ICON function identifies the icon that is to represent a window when the window is minimized using either the native window manager or the ICON Display Manager command. For more information about the ICON function, refer to "ICON" in Chapter 20, "Dictionary of New and Enhanced SCL Elements."

CHAPTER 7 SCL Catalog Entries

Overview

Your SAS/AF programs may perform tasks that do not require any user interaction. Therefore, you do not need to display a window. In these cases, you can use the new SCL catalog entry type, which enables you to do the following:

- □ edit an SCL program
- □ compile and store the program
- □ execute the program directly from the SCL entry
- □ call the SCL entry from other SAS/AF and FSEDIT entry types.

Editing SCL Entries

To edit an SCL entry, follow these steps:

1. Issue the EDIT command from a catalog directory window, specifying the name of the entry you want to edit:

   ```
   edit myprog.scl
   ```

   If you have set the default entry type to SCL (in your PROC BUILD statement or on the command line), the .SCL extension is unnecessary.

   Note: To issue the edit command, you may also use the **File** pull-down menu. From this menu, select **New...** to display the **New...** dialog box, select the SCL entry type, enter the entry's name, and then select the OK button.

2. When the SAS text editor is displayed, type the appropriate SCL statements in the window. (Use this window and text editor the same way you use the text editor for the SOURCE window in PROGRAM entries.)

3. Compile the SCL program as described in the next section, "Compiling SCL Entries."
4. Close the SCL editor window using the END command.

Compiling SCL Entries

Before you can execute your SCL program, you must compile it. To compile the program, issue the COMPILE command.

Note: The SCL window uses the BUILD procedure keys you may have defined in SASUSER.PROFILE.BUILD.KEYS. The default keys are defined in SASHELP.FSP.BUILD.KEYS if you do not have private definitions. You may issue the KEYS command or select **Keys...** from the **Help** menu bar to redefine your keys.

When you compile your program, the SCL compiler writes any error or warning messages to the MESSAGE window. However, if you edit the SCL entry from the BUILD procedure and you invoked the procedure with the NOMSG option, the SCL compiler writes the error and warning messages to the LOG window rather than the MESSAGE window.

When your program is compiled successfully, a message similar to the following is displayed at the top of the window.

```
Code generated for MYPROG. Code size=1276
```

However, if there are warning messages, you see a message similar to

```
Code generated (with messages) for MYPROG. Code size=1276
```

Finally, if there are errors in your program, you see the message

```
ERROR: Compile error(s) detected. No code generated.
```

When the SCL program is compiled successfully, SAS/AF software saves the compiled code along with the source code in the SCL entry. At this point, you may execute the SCL entry as described in "Executing SCL Entries."

▶ ***Caution:*** *Always compile an entry before you save it.*

If you save an SCL entry without compiling it, you cannot execute it. SAS/AF software provides a warning message indicating that the entry has been saved without intermediate code.

Executing SCL Entries

You can use several commands to execute a compiled SCL entry:

- □ TESTAF command (or you can use the T selection field command from the BUILD catalog directory window)
- □ AF or AFAPPLICATION command

Note: These commands do not tell you if the entry has not been compiled.

TESTAF Command

While you are still in the editor, you can issue the TESTAF command to execute a compiled SCL entry. This command executes the code in the INIT, MAIN, and TERM sections of the program, in that order.

Note: If you have not compiled your SCL program, or if you compiled it and then modified it without compiling again, the TESTAF command does not execute the entry. Instead, it issues the following message:

```
ERROR: You must compile first
```

AF and AFAPPLICATION Commands

If you have saved an SCL entry that has been compiled, you may execute the entry from the SAS Display Manager command line using either the AF command or the AFAPPLICATION command:

AF C=lib.cat.myprog.scl
AFAPPLICATION C=lib.cat.myprog.scl

If you execute the entry with the AF command, the name is saved in SASUSER.PROFILE.AF.AFGO. This enables you to execute the entry again without specifying the CATALOG= option on the AF command.

See Chapter 2, "The AF Command" and Chapter 3, "The AFAPPLICATION Command" for more information about these commands.

Example

Suppose you have an SCL entry called AF.SAMPLE.TEST.SCL that contains the following program statements:

```
A:
   put 'Executing label a.';
return;

INIT:
   put 'In init label.';
   link a;
   x=5;
return;

MAIN:
   put 'In main,' x=;
return;

TERM:
   x=x-1;
   put 'In term,' x=;
   if x>0 then _status_='R';
return;
```

You can execute the SCL from the command line with the AF command

```
af c=af.sample.test.scl
```

▶ ***Caution:*** *The special variable _STATUS_ is obeyed when executing an SCL entry.*

If the TERM section of the program sets _STATUS_='R', SAS/AF software returns control to the MAIN section. This can cause infinite loops, since an SCL entry does not interact with the user.

Putting the Commands in Macros

You may also define command-style macros that use the AF or AFAPPLICATION command to invoke your SCL entry. For example, the following macro defines a new command HELLO that executes the program SASUSER.PROFILE.HELLO.SCL:

```
%macro hello/cmd;
afa sasuser.profile\hello.scl
%mend;
```

If you load this macro in your SAS session and turn on the CMDMAC SAS option, you can execute the SCL program by issuing the HELLO command.

Executing a Specific Labeled Section

When you execute an SCL entry directly with the AF or AFAPPLICATION command, SAS/AF software normally executes the INIT, MAIN, and TERM sections of the SCL program, in that order. However, if you want to execute only one labeled section of your program, you can use the LABEL= option to specify the label name. If the label name, which may be INIT, MAIN, TERM or another label, exists in the SCL entry, SAS/AF software executes the code associated with that label and RETURN statement.

For more information about the LABEL= option, refer to Chapter 2, "The AF Command."

Calling SCL Entries from Other SAS/AF Programs

You can access SCL code that has been compiled and stored in SCL entries in two ways:

- □ Use the CALL DISPLAY routine in SCL to execute SCL entries
- □ Use the new CALL METHOD routine to execute individual routines in an SCL entry.

Using CALL DISPLAY to Execute SCL Entries

The CALL DISPLAY routine is most commonly used to execute PROGRAM, HELP, or CBT entries. Its purpose is to display the window associated with these entries and run the associated SCL code, if there is any. In the past, you could create a PROGRAM entry without a DISPLAY window and use CALL DISPLAY to execute the associated SCL program. For such cases, it is more efficient to isolate the SCL code into an SCL entry and invoke the SCL code directly. You may still pass parameters in the CALL DISPLAY statement and receive them via an ENTRY statement. When you invoke an SCL entry via CALL DISPLAY, SAS/AF software executes the statements in the following order before returning to the caller:

1. ENTRY statement
2. INIT section
3. MAIN section
4. TERM section

If you use CALL DISPLAY to execute an SCL entry, the entry must have at least one of the special labels INIT, MAIN, or TERM.

Using CALL METHOD to Execute SCL Routines

When you build large applications, or even several different applications, you usually generate common sequences of SCL code that you use repeatedly. Instead of duplicating the code in each application, or putting it in a PROGRAM entry with no display, you can now create modular SCL routines which you can invoke from any SCL application. Each module can have its own parameter list, analogous to an ENTRY statement. You can place several different modules in a single SCL entry. You identify each module with the METHOD statement, and invoke each module with CALL METHOD.

The default entry type for the METHOD routine is SCL. Thus, the call

```
call method("MYFUNC", "FUNC1", 10, 30, x);
```

looks for the entry MYFUNC.SCL in the current search path.

▶ *Caution: A program halts if you attempt to invoke a routine that does not exist in the SCL program.*

For example, if your application executes the following line:

```
call method("MYFUNC.SCL","FUNC1",10,30,x);
```

and the label FUNC1 does not exist in MYFUNC.SCL, your program will halt.

For a detailed description of the METHOD statement, refer to "METHOD" in Chapter 20, "Dictionary of New and Enhanced SCL Elements."

Example

Suppose you create an SCL entry named PARSE.SCL in which you place two modules: PARSE and NAMEDIV. The NAMEDIV module parses a text string containing the name of a SAS catalog object into its components: *library*, *catalog*, *member*, and *type*. PARSE is a more general module that parses any text string into its components, placing the components in an SCL list.

To call the NAMEDIV module, use the following statement:

```
call method("PARSE","NAMEDIV",sas_file_name,lib,cat,mem,type,rc);
```

where SAS_FILE_NAME, LIB, CAT, MEM, and TYPE are character variables and RC is a numeric variable. You should declare these variables with a length statement if this CALL METHOD statement contains the first occurrence of the variables in the program.

Table 7.1 shows how the NAMEDIV module parses several character strings.

Table 7.1 *Output of NAMEDIV Module*

Character String	LIB	CAT	MEM	TYPE
"A.B.C.D"	"A"	"B"	"C"	"D"
"A.B.C"	"A"	"B"	"C"	""
"A.B"	""	""	"A"	"B"
"A"	""	""	"A"	""

In the following SCL program, the NAMEDIV module calls the PARSE module in PARSE.SCL to parse the character string into its components, then validates the syntax of each component.

```
    /* Divide the SAS file name in PATH into its components: LIBRARY, */
    /* CATALOG, MEMBER and TYPE.  RC is 0 if OK.  RC is non-zero if   */
    /* PATH has invalid syntax at component #rc, or too many          */
    /* components if rc=-1.                                           */
  NAMEDIV:
    method path library catalog member type $ rc 8;
    components=makelist();
    call method("parse","parse",path,".",components);
    library ="";
    catalog ="";
    member  ="";
    type    ="";
    rc      = 0;
    length  =listlen(components);
          /* Convert the components to uppercase and trim the blanks.*/
       do i=1 to length;
          component =getitemc(components,i);
          component =upcase(trim(left(component)));
             /* Ensure each non-empty component is a valid SASNAME.  */
          if component ¬= '' then rc=rc + not(sasname(component));
          components=setitemc(components,component,i);
       end;
    select ( length );
       when(1) member=getitemc(components,1);
       when(2) member=getitemc(components,1);
               type=getitemc(components,2);
       when(3) library=getitemc(components,1);
               catalog=getitemc(components,2);
               member=getitemc(components,3);
       when(4) library=getitemc(components,1);
               catalog=getitemc(components,2);
               member=getitemc(components,3);
               type=getitemc(components,4);
      otherwise; rc=-1;
                 return;
    end;
    components=dellist(components);
 return;
 endmethod;
```

```
   /* Parse a string into the individual pieces that are separated  */
   /* by a character in DELIMITER and place each piece in the list   */
   /* of tokens, TOKENLIST (token list must already exist).          */
length substring $ 200;
PARSE:
   method istring delimiter $ tokenList 8;
   string=istring; /* make copy of input string */
   tokenList=clearlist(tokenList);
   tokenNum =1;
         /* Scan until no more components are found. */
      do until (substring=" ");
         substring=scan(string,tokenNum,delimiter);
         if substring ¬= " " then
            tokenList=insertc(tokenList,substring,-1);
         tokenNum+1;
      end;
return;
endmethod;
```

Functions That do not Work With SCL Entries

Because an SCL entry has no associated application window (and therefore no message line or command line), you cannot use the following elements with an SCL entry:

- functions that return information about the current window, such as FIELD, MODIFIED, WINFO, SETFKEY, GETFKEY, and NUMFKEYS
- the _MSG_ variable. If you have a PROGRAM entry that displays a message produced by an SCL routine in an SCL entry, pass the _MSG_ variable as one of the parameters to the SCL program.
- the EXECCMDI routine. Since there is no command line, any command issued via EXECCMDI is lost. However, the EXECCMD function works since the command is appended to the global command string that SAS/AF software collects and submits after MAIN has executed.

CHAPTER 8 SLIST Catalog Entries

Overview

In Release 6.07 of the SAS System, SCL supports new data structures and functions for storing and manipulating data in *SCL lists*. SCL lists are ordered collections of data, similar to arrays. However, SCL lists are more flexible than arrays. For example, using SCL, you can create lists and then insert numbers, character strings, and even other lists into them. You can replace or delete list items, and move them around by reversing, rotating, or sorting the list. You also can assign names to the items in a list and refer to items by their names rather than their index (position) in the list. Thus, you can use a list to implement data structures and access and assign values to list elements by their name. Using this feature, you can add new fields to the list data structure or change the order of the list's items without modifying your SCL program.

To store your SCL lists, Release 6.07 of SAS/AF software supports a new catalog entry type named SLIST. By using SLIST catalog entries with the new family of SCL list functions, you can create general data structures in SCL lists and save them between sessions.

For a detailed description of SCL lists, refer to Chapter 17, "Features for Storing and Manipulating Data in SCL Lists."

Creating SLIST Entries

To create an SLIST catalog entry, you use the new SAVELIST function in your SCL program. When you use this function, the entire contents of the list, including any nested lists, is saved to the SLIST entry. For more information about saving nested lists in an SCL entry refer to "Saving Nested Lists to SCL Entries" in Chapter 17, "Features for Storing and Manipulating Data in SCL Lists."

▶ ***Caution:*** *Lists are maintained in memory.*

SCL lists are maintained entirely in memory. Therefore, if you save an SCL list in an SCL entry, and then your application modifies the list, the SCL entry is not automatically updated. To update the list in the SCL entry, you have to resave the list after it is changed. In addition, the converse is also true. If you update an SCL entry, the list that is maintained in memory is not updated until you read the list from the SCL entry with the FILLIST function.

Using the Contents of SLIST Entries

Once you have saved a list in an SCL entry, you can use the contents of the SLIST entry to fill an SCL list you create. To do this, use the new SCL FILLIST function. For more information about the FILLIST function, refer to "FILLIST" in Chapter 20.

CHAPTER 9 The Procedure Management Window

Introduction

The Procedure Management Window (PMW) is a new window you can use to access and manipulate catalogs in any SAS data libraries defined with a libref in the current SAS session, rather than just the single catalog available when you supply a catalog name with the PROC BUILD statement or BUILD command.

In this chapter the PMWs are shown running on the Apollo operating system. When you open a PMW, its contents will display the names of your libraries, catalogs, and entries in the format required by your operating system.

Using the Procedure Management Window

When you use the PMW, you can use the global commands available for working with catalogs. (The global commands are discussed in Chapter 12 "SAS/AF Window Commands" in *SAS/AF Software: Usage and Reference, Version 6, First Edition*. The PMW also provides a set of special commands that display dialog windows for renaming, copying, and deleting catalog entries. This set of dialog windows and commands provides an interactive interface to selecting and manipulating catalogs and catalog entries.

Display 9.1 shows the default PMW with the PMENU facility active and scrollbars. The PMW contains three rectangular, scrollable windows called listboxes. For more information on listboxes, see SAS Technical Report P-222, *Changes and Enhancements to Base SAS Software, Release 6.07.*

Display 9.1 *Opening the Procedure Management Window*

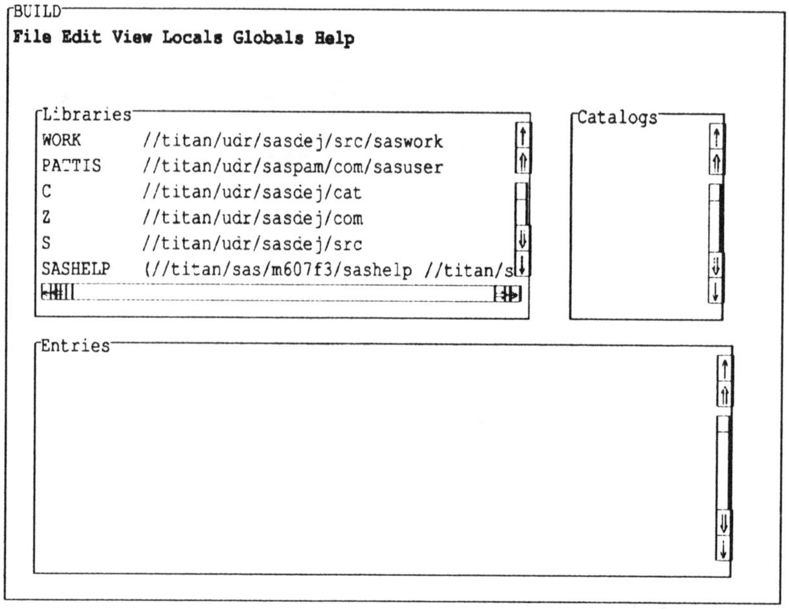

You can use scroll commands or a listbox's scroll bars to display additional information not currently visible. (For complete details on how to use scroll bars, see the SAS companion to your host operating system and the SCROLLBAR command in Chapter 18 of *SAS Language: Reference, Version 6, First Edition.*)

The Libraries listbox displays each libref and the name of the corresponding SAS data library. Initially, the Catalogs and Entries listboxes are empty because a library has not been selected.

Using the listboxes

To select an item in a listbox, position the cursor on the desired item and press the ENTER key or a mouse button. You can toggle the selected status off by selecting the item again.

When you select a library, the names of the catalogs stored in that library display in the Catalogs listbox. No catalogs are shown when you select a library that contains no catalogs.

When you select a catalog, the names of the entries stored in that catalog display in the Entries listbox. If no entries are shown, the catalog is empty. Display 9.2 shows the window displaying the entries in the catalog named FGXL.

Display 9.2 *Displaying Catalog Entries*

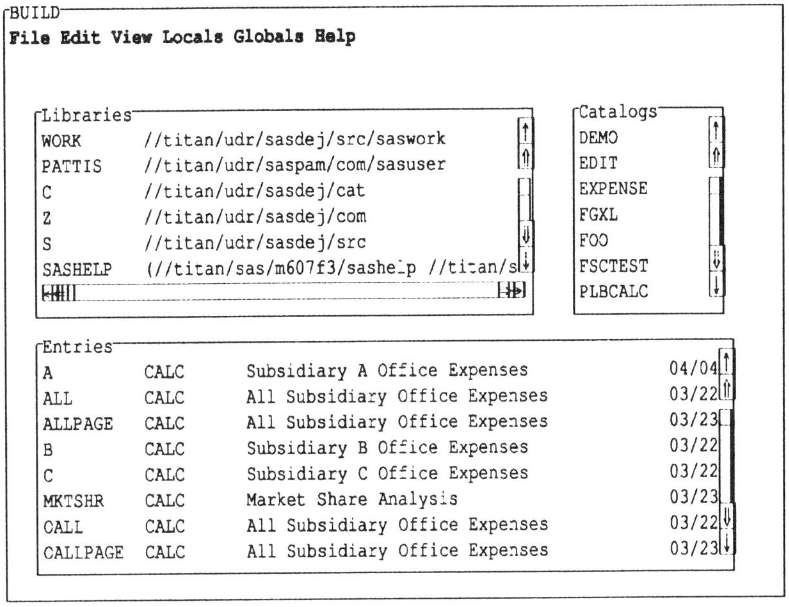

Manipulating catalogs
If you wish to perform an operation on a catalog or its entries, you

- □ select one or more entries
- □ issue the appropriate command
- □ take the actions required by the dialog window (Copy, Delete, or Rename) that opens displaying the selected entries
- □ select the OK or CANCEL pushbuttons.

For example, to copy one or more entries to another catalog, you select the entries to be copied and then issue the COPY command. The Copy dialog window displays the names of the selected entries in the order in which you selected them. You can name the catalog to which the entries are to be copied and specify new names for the copied entries before selecting the OK pushbutton.

You can issue the COPY, DELETE, and DELETE CATALOG commands without selecting any entries. When you do this, all the entries from the selected catalog display in the appropriate dialog window. This saves you from having to select every single catalog entry when you need to perform an operation on all, or most, of the entries.

Special PMW commands
In addition to global commands, the following commands are available from the Procedure Management window:

- □ COPY
- □ DELETE
- □ DELETE CATALOG
- □ RENAME
- □ RESET

The following sections describe each of these commands.

The COPY Command

When the PMENU facility is active, you access the COPY command from the FILE menu. The COPY command can copy one or more catalog entries to the current catalog or to a different one. The Copy window, shown in Display 9.3, opens when you issue the COPY command.

Display 9.3 *The Copy Window*

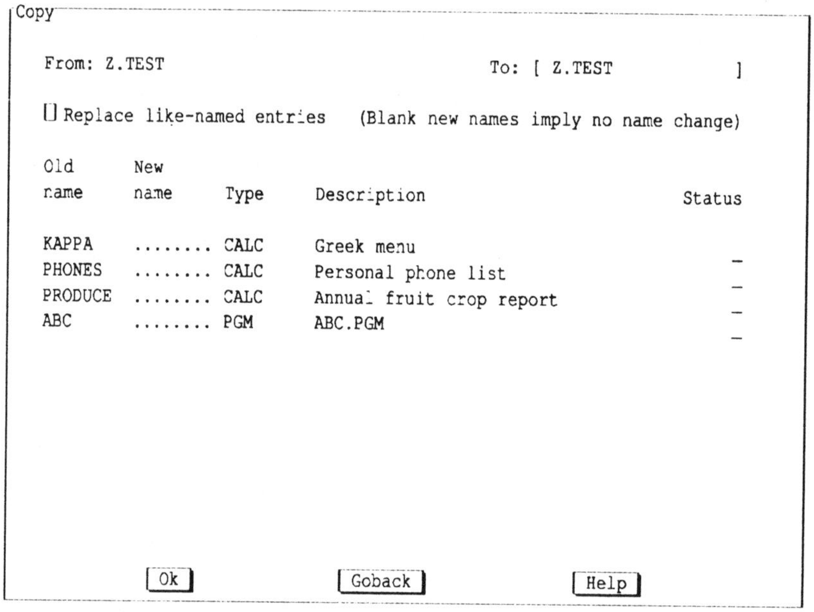

To copy the selected entries into another catalog, enter the name of that catalog in the **To** field, using the form *library.catalog*. You must supply a libref; WORK is not assumed to be the default. You cannot change the catalog named in the **From** field because this name is restricted to the current catalog.

Overwriting like-named entries
You can determine whether an entry being copied overwrites an entry with the same name in the catalog named in the **To** field. If you do not select the **Replace** checkbox, the copy operation does not replace like-named entries. If you do select the **Replace** checkbox, all entries are copied, regardless of their names.

▶ ***Caution:*** *If you wish to protect entries from being overwritten, do not select the replace option.*

Replacing entries overwrites any entries with duplicate names in the catalog to which you are copying. Be sure this is the behaviour you desire.

Assigning new names to copied entries
You can assign a different name to each copied entry by specifying the new name in the **New name** field. When you do not specify a name in the **New name** field for an entry being copied to a different catalog, the entry is copied with the same name. When you do not specify a name in the **New name** field for an entry being copied within the same catalog, the copy operation is not performed.

Copy operation reports
After you issue the OK command to exit from the Copy window, a message displays the number of entries that have been copied. If the copy operation generates any error conditions,

- □ an "E" displays in the **Status** field of each entry that generated an error
- □ a "C" displays in the **Status** field of each entry that was successfully copied
- □ the Copy window remains open.

Copy operation error conditions
The following list contains some of the error conditions that are reported.

- □ A circular reference is detected. For example, you are attempting to copy entry AAA to entry BBB and then BBB to AAA.
- □ An entry you are trying to copy or copy to is being used by another process or task.
- □ You are attempting to overwrite a like-named entry but you have not selected the **Replace** checkbox.
- □ One of the catalogs you named is damaged.
- □ The output device is full.
- □ The output device is faulty.

Viewing copied entries
When you copy entries to a different catalog, you must select that catalog to display the list of its entries after the new entries are copied in.

Copying within the same catalog
When the same catalog is named in the **From** and **To** fields, and the same entry is named in the **New name** and **Old name** fields, the entries are copied in an order that will not overwrite an entry before it has been copied. For example, if entry AAA is to be copied to entry BBB, and BBB is to be copied to entry CCC, entry BBB will be copied before AAA. If the copy operation cannot be performed without copying an entry before it is overwritten, an error message reports circular references and an "E" displays in the **Status** field of entries AAA, BBB, and CCC.

Using the COPY command without selecting entries
If you issue the COPY command but select no entries, all the entries in the selected catalog are listed in the Copy window. When all the entries from one catalog are copied to an empty catalog, the resulting catalog is identical to the first catalog except that all unused space is removed.

Creating new catalogs before copying
If the catalog named in the **To** field does not exist, but the libref in the **To** field has been assigned, the copy operation creates the new catalog and then copies the entries.

The DELETE Command

When the PMENU facility is active, you access the DELETE command from the EDIT menu. The DELETE command removes one or more entries from the selected catalog. The Delete window opens when you issue the DELETE command.

▶ ***Caution:*** *Be sure you do not need your catalog entries before you use the DELETE command.*

The DELETE command removes the catalog entries as well as the entry names from the catalog. It is good practice to have backup copies of your catalogs at all times so that you can recover from accidental deletions, overwrites and changes, and hardware failures.

The Delete window, shown in Display 9.4, displays a Catalog listbox containing the names of the entries you have selected before using the DELETE command.

Display 9.4 *The Delete Window*

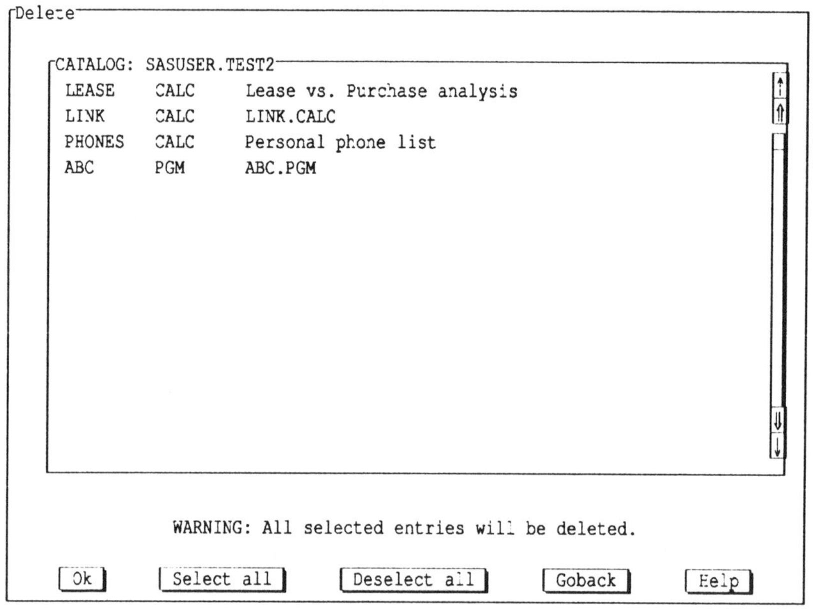

If you did not select any entries before using the DELETE command, the listbox displays the names of all the entries in the selected catalog.

Deleting entries
To delete one or more catalog entries,

□ select the entries you want to delete or issue the SELECT ALL command to select all of the catalog's entries at once

□ issue the OK command, to delete the selected entries.

Note: Issuing the GOBACK command closes the Delete window without deleting any of the remaining entries, even the selected ones.

Removing the selected status from entries
If you decide that you do not want to delete some of the entries that are currently selected, simply reselect those entries and the selected status is removed from those entries. To remove the selected status from all the entries in the list, select the DESELECT ALL pushbutton.

Delete operation reports
After the delete operation is performed, a message displays the number of entries that have been deleted. Entries no longer listed in the Delete window were either deleted or not selected for deletion. If any errors occur during the delete process, the Delete window remains open, and the entries that produced errors remain in the selection list. When the Delete window is still open, you can either try again to delete the remaining entries, or issue the GOBACK command.

Delete operation error conditions
The following list contains some of the error conditions that are reported by the delete operation.

- An entry you are trying to delete is being used by another process or task
- The entry you are trying to delete is in a damaged catalog.

The DELETE CATALOG Command

When the PMENU facility is active, you can access the DELETE CATALOG command from the EDIT menu. The DELETE CATALOG command deletes a catalog from a library.

Deleting catalogs
To delete a catalog,

- select the libref for the SAS data library containing the catalog you wish to delete
- select the catalog to be deleted
- issue the DELETE CATALOG command
- in the confirmation window that opens
  - select the confirmation checkbox and issue the OK command to delete the catalog.
  - issue the CANCEL command to cancel the deletion.

  Note: Issuing the OK command without selecting the checkbox has the same effect as issuing the CANCEL command.

▶ ***Caution:*** *Before you confirm the delete operation, be sure you do not need your catalog entries.*

This option removes all the entries in the selected catalog and removes the catalog from the library. It is good practice to have backup copies of your catalogs at all times so that you can recover from accidental deletions, entry overwrites and/or changes, and hardware failures.

The RENAME Command

When the PMENU facility is active, you access the RENAME command from the EDIT menu. The RENAME command enables you to change the name and description of one or more catalog entries. You can change an entry's description even if you are not changing the entry's name. The Rename window, shown in Display 9.5, opens when you issue the RENAME command.

Display 9.5 *The Rename Window*

```
Rename

     Catalog:  Z.TEST2

     Overwrite Name to rename, and/or you may overwrite Description.

     Name       Type       Description                              Status

     NUMBERS    CALC       Personal phone list                        _
     TEST1      CALC       Test Spreadsheet #1                        _
     ABC        PGM        ABC.PGM                                    _
     ALPHABET   PGM        ABC.PGM                                    _

            [Ok]              [Goback]              [Help]
```

Renaming catalogs
To rename a catalog entry,

- □ select the entries to be renamed
- □ issue the RENAME command
- □ enter the new name or description for the entries
- □ select the OK checkbox.

Order of renaming
The entries are renamed in the order they are specified in the Rename window. To swap the names of two entries, rename one entry to a temporary name, rename the second entry to the previous name of the first entry, then rename the first entry to the previous name of the second entry. For example, to swap the names of entry AAA and entry BBB when the catalog contains no entry named TEMP, rename entry AAA to TEMP, entry BBB to AAA, then entry TEMP to BBB.

Rename operation reports
An "R" displays in the **Status** field of each entry that is successfully renamed. If a renaming operation produces any error conditions, the entry is not renamed, an "E" displays in its **Status** field, and the Rename window remains open.

Rename operation error conditions
The following list contains some of the error conditions that are reported by the rename operation.

- □ You are attempting to assign a new name that is already assigned to an entry of the same type in the catalog.
- □ An entry you are trying to rename is being used by another process or task.
- □ The catalog containing the entry is damaged.

The RESET Command

When the PMENU facility is active, you access the RESET command from the VIEW menu. While you are running a SAS session, another person, process, or task may be updating or changing the information in your libraries or catalogs. The updated information may not be displayed in the Libraries, Catalogs, or Entries listboxes. Issuing the RESET command updates the listboxes with the most current information. In addition, the reset process attempts to maintain any selections you currently have in any of the library, catalog, and entry lists.

If the RESET command does not maintain your previous selections or if it leaves one of the listboxes blank, one or more of the libraries, catalogs, or entries has been changed or deleted.

Changes and Enhancements to SAS/FSP® Software

PART 2

CHAPTER 10 Overview of Changes and Enhancements to SAS/FSP® Software

Overview

Part 2 contains information on new and enhanced functionality for SAS/FSP software in Release 6.07. This information is divided into the following categories:

- □ new features for the procedures
- □ enhancements to the behavior of the procedure windows
- □ enhancements to Screen Control Language (SCL) that provide new capabilities in applications built with the procedure.

The FSEDIT Procedure

Chapter 11, "The FSEDIT Procedure," describes the enhancements to the FSEDIT procedure in Release 6.07 of SAS/FSP software. These changes include

- □ new PROC statement options and general parameters to control users' ability to add and delete observations
- □ a new field attribute to control the way numeric field values are processed
- □ enhancements in the FSEDIT window behavior, including allowing users to interrupt search operations
- □ enhancements in SCL, including support for executing individual labeled sections of SCL code when particular fields are modified.

Chapter 11 updates Chapter 13, "The FSEDIT Procedure," in *SAS/FSP Software: Usage and Reference, Version 6, First Edition.*

The FSLIST Procedure

Chapter 12, "The FSLIST Procedure," describes the enhancement to the FSLIST procedure in Release 6.07 of SAS/FSP software. The enhancement consists of allowing users to interrupt scroll and search operations.

Chapter 12 updates Chapter 15, "The FSLIST Procedure," in *SAS/FSP Software: Usage and Reference.*

The FSVIEW Procedure

Chapter 13, "The FSVIEW Procedure," describes the enhancements to the FSVIEW procedure in Release 6.07 of SAS/FSP software. These enhancements include

- □ enhancements in the FSVIEW window behavior, including allowing users to edit data set variables that have associated formulas
- □ enhancements in SCL, including support for the _STATUS_ system variable to control the execution of FSVIEW applications.

Chapter 13 updates Chapter 16, "The FSVIEW Procedure," in *SAS/FSP Software: Usage and Reference.*

CHAPTER 11 The FSEDIT Procedure

Overview

Introduction
Release 6.07 of the SAS System provides the following changes and enhancements to the FSEDIT procedure in SAS/FSP software:

- new features for the FSEDIT procedure
- changes in FSEDIT window behavior
- changes to Screen Control Language (SCL) that provide enhanced functionality in FSEDIT applications.

New features for the FSEDIT procedure
The following new features have been added to FSEDIT procedure for Release 6.07:

- PROC statement options and corresponding general parameters to control whether users can add and delete observations from the displayed data set
- A field attribute to control the way blanks in numeric field values are processed.

Changes in FSEDIT window behavior
The behavior of the FSEDIT window has changed in the following ways for Release 6.07:

- The rules for when observations are updated have been modified
- Scrolling between screens in multiscreen applications is allowed even when some screens contain invalid values
- Search operations can be canceled.

Changes to SCL for FSEDIT applications
Changes and enhancements to SCL for Release 6.07 provide new capabilities for FSEDIT applications. You can use new or enhanced SCL functions, routines, and statements to

- □ execute separate sections of SCL code when individual fields are modified
- □ monitor and control application execution
- □ use data set variables marked as UNWANTED in your SCL programs
- □ control which commands users can issue from the FSEDIT window
- □ obtain additional information about the current observation and about the FSEDIT window
- □ control the color and highlighting attributes of individual fields
- □ determine which field the cursor is positioned on
- □ submit statements to the SAS System for processing.

In this chapter
This chapter describes the changes and enhancements to the FSEDIT procedure for Release 6.07. This chapter updates Chapter 13, "The FSEDIT Procedure," in *SAS/FSP Software: Usage and Reference, Version 6, First Edition.*

Additional PROC FSEDIT Statement Options

You can use the following new options with the PROC FSEDIT statement:

NOADD
: prevents users from adding new observations to the data set. When you use the NOADD option, the ADD and DUP commands are disabled in the FSEDIT window. Users can still edit existing observations.

Note: The FSEDIT procedure also provides a new parameter that you can use to disable the ADD and DUP commands. Refer to "Additional General Parameters" later in this chapter for details. When you use the NOADD option in conjunction with the SCREEN= option, the NOADD option takes precedence over the parameter setting specified in the SCREEN entry.

NODEL
: prevents users from deleting observations from the data set. When you use the NODEL option, the DELETE command is disabled in the FSEDIT window. Users can still edit existing observations.

Note: The FSEDIT procedure also provides a new parameter that you can use to disable the DELETE command. Refer to "Additional General Parameters" later in this chapter for details. When you use the NODEL option in conjunction with the SCREEN= option, the NODEL option takes precedence over the parameter setting specified in the SCREEN entry.

Additional Field Attribute

The FSEDIT procedure now supports a new field attribute, NOAUTOBLANK, that controls the way values entered in numeric fields are processed.

You use the FSEDIT Attribute window (option 4 from the FSEDIT Menu window) to view and set the status of the NOAUTOBLANK attribute for each field in the FSEDIT window. If you specify a SCREEN entry for the FSEDIT session, the attribute settings are stored in the SCREEN entry.

The FSEDIT Attribute window has following new frame:

NOAUTOBLANK
: specifies which numeric fields are not automatically blanked.

  When the FSEDIT procedure processes the values that users enter in numeric fields, it by default automatically clears all character positions following the first blank encountered in the fields. This is a useful feature in most instances because it enables users to enter numeric values left-justified in the field without having to manually blank out the remainder of the field. (Values in numeric field values are by default displayed right-justified.) However, some numeric informats permit values with imbedded blanks. Examples include date informats such as DATE*w*. and MMDDYY*w*., as well as the BZ*w.d* informat. For fields that use these informats, you can specify the NOAUTOBLANK attribute to suppress the automatic blanking feature so that users can enter values containing blanks.

  Type an **N** in the first position of a field of the NOAUTOBLANK frame to prevent the automatic blanking of characters following the first blank in corresponding numeric fields in the FSEDIT window.

  Note: The NOAUTOBLANK attribute is ignored for character fields.

The NOAUTOBLANK frame appears after the NOAUTOSKIP frame in the FSEDIT Attribute window sequence. You can also use the NOAUTOBLANK command in the FSEDIT Attribute window to display this frame.

Additional General Parameters

The FSEDIT procedure now supports two additional general parameters that control whether users can add observations to or delete observations from the displayed data set.

You use the FSEDIT Parms window (option 5 from the FSEDIT Menu window) to view and set the status of the new parameters. If you specify a SCREEN entry for the FSEDIT session, the parameter settings are stored in the associated SCREEN entry.

The FSEDIT Parms window has the following new fields:

Allow ADD/DUP command
: controls whether users are allowed to issue the ADD or DUP commands to add new observations to the data set.

  Specify **Y** in this field (or leave it blank) if you want to allow users to add new observations to the displayed data set. (You can use the NOADD option with the PROC FSEDIT statement to override this parameter setting when the FSEDIT session is invoked.) Specify **N** in this field to disable the ADD and DUP commands in the FSEDIT window.

Allow DELETE command
controls whether users are allowed to issue the DELETE command to delete observations from the data set.

Specify Y in this field (or leave it blank) if you want to allow users to delete observations from the displayed data set. (You can use the NODEL option with the PROC FSEDIT statement to override this parameter setting when the FSEDIT session is invoked.) Specify N in this field to disable the DELETE command in the FSEDIT window.

Note: If you want to prevent users from changing the settings of these parameters, you can specify a password for the MODIFY command in the **Modify password** field in the FSEDIT Parms window.

Changes in FSEDIT Window Behavior

The following sections highlight some of the ways in which the functionality of the FSEDIT window has been enhanced for Release 6.07.

New Rules for Updating Data Sets

In previous releases of SAS/FSP software, modifying a computed field or assigning variables in the SCL program could sometimes cause the procedure to update the current observation when the update was not needed. In Release 6.07, an existing observation is not updated unless the values of one or more data set variables are changed.

New or duplicated observations are always written to the data set unless you issue a CANCEL command.

Note: By default, the TERM section of the SCL program in the FSEDIT session's SCREEN entry does not execute unless you change data set variables so that the current observation needs to be updated in the data set.

Scrolling Allowed When Fields Are in Error

In previous releases of SAS/FSP software, you were not allowed to scroll to a different screen within the current observation if any fields in the current screen contained invalid values. You can now scroll from screen to screen within the same observation when errors exist on one or more screens. However, you still must correct all invalid fields on all screens (or issue a CANCEL or OVERRIDE command) before you can display a different observation.

Interrupting Search Operations

You can now interrupt the commands that search for a particular string or numeric value (FIND, LOCATE, SEARCH, and so forth). This feature is useful when you want to halt a search request while editing or browsing a large data set.

To halt an active FIND, LOCATE, or SEARCH operation, press the interrupt key or key combination for your system. The FSEDIT procedure halts the search operation and displays the following message:

```
NOTE: Search was discontinued due to user break request.
```

To resume the search, issue an RFIND command.

■ **Host Information** .... The key or key combination you use to interrupt an active process varies according to YOUR host operating system and terminal device. For example, some systems have a key labeled BREAK or ATTENTION (or ATTN). Other systems use a combination of the CTRL key and another key. Refer to host documentation if you are unfamiliar with the interrupt key for your operating system and terminal device.
.... ■

Changes to SCL for FSEDIT Applications

The following changes and enhancements to Screen Control Language provide new capabilities for FSEDIT applications. Refer to Chapter 20, "Dictionary of New and Enhanced SCL Elements," for detailed information on the SCL features discussed in this section.

Executing SCL Statements When Individual Fields Are Modified

The FSEDIT procedure can now execute individual labeled sections of the SCL program when users modify particular fields. This feature allows you to treat labels as subroutines associated with selected fields.

Activating the feature
To activate this new feature, you must use a CONTROL statement with the LABELON option:

```
control labelon;
```

Note: You typically use the CONTROL LABELON statement in the FSEINIT section of your SCL program.

Determining which labeled sections to execute
When the LABELON option is active and users modify a field in the FSEDIT window and press the ENTER key, then the FSEDIT procedure checks whether the SCL program contains a labeled section that has the same name as the modified field. If so, the procedure executes the statements in that labeled section before executing the MAIN section. If more than one field is modified, the FSEDIT procedure executes the labeled sections in the order in which the fields appear in the FSEDIT window, from left to right and top to bottom.

For example, suppose you have an FSEDIT window with two fields, A and B, and the following SCL program:

```
FSEINIT:
   control labelon;
return;

MAIN:
   if (modified(b)) then
      do;
         More SCL statements
      end;
return;
```

```
A:
   if (a<b) then
      _msg_='ERROR: A must be greater than B';
return;
```

When users modify the value in the A field, the FSEDIT procedure executes the section of the SCL program with the label A before executing the MAIN section. Since there is no section of the program with the label B, modifying the B field causes only the MAIN section to execute.

For additional examples of this feature, see Chapter 16, "Support for Program Modules."

Monitoring and Controlling Application Execution

You can now use the SCL system variable _STATUS_ to monitor and control the flow of your FSEDIT applications.

Determining the current state of the FSEDIT session
To determine the current state of the FSEDIT session, you test the current value of the _STATUS_ variable. The _STATUS_ variable has one of the following values:

E — users issued an END command

C — users issued a CANCEL command

blank — neither END or CANCEL commands were issued.

Changing the current state of the FSEDIT session
To control the execution of your FSEDIT application, you can assign either of the following values to the _STATUS_ variable:

H — terminates the FSEDIT session when the next RETURN statement is encountered.

Note: In this case, the TERM and FSETERM sections of the SCL program are not executed. If users modified data set variable values in the current observation, the modified values are not written to the SAS data set.

R — resumes editing the current observation.

For example, if you do not want to allow users to move off of the current observation until some condition is met, use the following assignment statement in the TERM section of your application's program to resume editing the current observation:

```
_status_='R';
```

Note: Your SCL program should use the _MSG_ system variable to display a message explaining why users cannot leave the current observation.

Accessing UNWANTED Data Set Variables

In previous releases of SAS/FSP software, only those variables that were defined as WANTED in the SCREEN entry could be referenced in your SCL program. With Release 6.07, any variable in the data set can be referenced in SCL, even if you mark the variable as UNWANTED in the FSEDIT

Identify window when you build a custom FSEDIT window display for the application.

If you use a variable marked as UNWANTED in your SCL program, a warning message is written to the SAS log when you close the FSEDIT Program window. This helps reduce the possibility of inadvertently modifying a data set variable that you did not intend to change.

Overriding FSEDIT commands

When the CONTROL ALWAYS option is in effect, the FSEDIT procedure now executes the MAIN section of the SCL program before checking whether users issued any command. This means that your SCL program can now intercept global and procedure-specific commands before they are passed to the FSEDIT procedure for execution.

For example, you can examine the command using the WORD function and, if you do not want the command to be executed, you can discard it using the NEXTCMD routine. This enables you to control what commands users can issue within your application.

Obtaining Information About the Current Observation

The new OBSINFO function returns a variety of information about the observation currently displayed in the FSEDIT window. The following examples show some of the information that you can obtain using the OBSINFO function:

```
rc=obsinfo('deleted');     rc=1 if current obs has been deleted.
                           rc=0 otherwise.

rc=obsinfo('locked');      rc=1 if current obs is locked.
                           rc=0 otherwise.

rc=obsinfo('new');         rc=1 if current obs is a new obs.
                           rc=0 otherwise.

rc=obsinfo('modified');    rc=1 if current obs has been modified.
                           rc=0 otherwise.

rc=obsinfo('curobs');      rc=observation number of current obs.
                           rc=-1 if obs number not available.
```

Obtaining Information About the FSEDIT Window

The WINFO function now returns several additional items of information about the FSEDIT window. Two of these new options, CURSCREEN and NSCREEN, are useful in multiscreen FSEDIT applications. The following examples show how you can use these new options:

```
rc=winfo('nscreen');     returns the number of screens in the FSEDIT
                         window.

rc=winfo('curscreen');   returns the number of the screen currently
                         being displayed.
```

Setting Field Colors and Highlighting Attributes

The FIELD function now enables you to change the color and highlighting attribute of individual fields from within your SCL programs. For example, the following statement causes the fields for the variables X1 and X2 to appear in red and reverse video:

```
rc=field('color red reverse','x1 x2');
```

Any valid color and highlighting attributes can be used.

Determining the Cursor Position

The new CURFLD function enables you to determine the name of the field on which the cursor is currently positioned. The following statement shows how you can use the CURFLD function:

```
name=curfld();
```

The CURFLD function returns a blank if cursor is not on a variable field.

Submitting Statements to the SAS System

You can now use the SUBMIT statement in FSEDIT applications to submit DATA and PROC steps to the SAS System for processing, provided that SAS/AF software is also licensed at your site. (You must have SAS/AF software installed at the site where you compile the SCL program containing the SUBMIT statement. Users of your application do not need SAS/AF software at their site to execute the FSEDIT application containing the SUBMIT statement.)

Note: Of the *when* options for the SUBMIT statement described in Chapter 8 of *SAS Screen Control Language: Reference*, only the CONTINUE option is valid in the FSEDIT procedure. You will get an error message when you compile the SCL program if you use any of the other *when* option values.

Compatibility with Release 6.06

Because Release 6.07 of the SAS System uses the same catalog structure as Release 6.06, you can use SAS catalogs you created with Release 6.06 to store SCREEN entries you build using Release 6.07. You also can use any SCREEN entries you built using Release 6.06 under Release 6.07 without modification. However, due to changes in the structure of SCREEN entries and in SCL, any SCREEN entries you in build using Release 6.07 cannot be used under Release 6.06.

If you create a SCREEN entry using the FSEDIT or FSBROWSE procedure under Release 6.06 and then later use that SCREEN entry under Release 6.07, the entry will no longer be usable under Release 6.06 if you do any of the following while using Release 6.07:

- open the FSEDIT Program window for editing the SCL program in the SCREEN entry (option 3 from the FSEDIT Menu window).

  Note: The entry becomes unusable under Release 6.06 after the program is compiled in Release 6.07, even if you do not add any of the new Release 6.07 functions. The SCL program is always recompiled when you close the FSEDIT Program window after it was open for editing.

□ specify the new NOAUTOBLANK attribute for any numeric field in the FSEDIT Attributes window (option 4 from the FSEDIT Menu window).

□ specify a value for either of the new general attributes (**Disable ADD/DUP command** or **Disable DELETE command**) in the FSEDIT Parms window (option 5 from the FSEDIT Menu window).

CHAPTER 12 The FSLIST Procedure

Overview

The only change to the FSLIST procedure in SAS/FSP software for Release 6.07 is the addition of support for attention handling during scrolling and search operations.

This chapter describes the enhancement to the FSLIST procedure. This chapter updates Chapter 15, "The FSLIST Procedure," in *SAS/FSP Software: Usage and Reference, Version 6, First Edition.*

Interrupting Scrolling and Search Operations

You can now interrupt the commands that scroll the text of the external file (for example, TOP or BOTTOM) as well as the commands that search for a particular string in the file (for example, FIND or BFIND). This feature is particularly useful when you want to halt a scroll or search operation while viewing the contents of a large external file.

To halt an active search or scroll operation, press the interrupt key or key combination for your system. The FSLIST procedure displays a requestor window that gives you the options of aborting or resuming the current operation.

■ **Host Information** .... The key or key combination you use to interrupt an active process varies according to host operating system and terminal device. For example, some systems have a key labeled BREAK or ATTENTION (or ATTN). Other systems use a combination of the CTRL key and another key. Refer to host documentation to determine the interrupt key for your operating system and terminal device. ■

CHAPTER 13 The FSVIEW Procedure

Overview

Introduction
Release 6.07 of the SAS System provides the following changes and enhancements to the FSVIEW procedure in SAS/FSP software:

- changes in FSVIEW window behavior
- changes to Screen Control Language (SCL) that provide enhanced functionality in FSEDIT applications.

Changes in FSVIEW window behavior
The behavior of the FSVIEW window has changed in the following ways for Release 6.07:

- Data set variables that have associated formulas can now be modified
- Formats and informats for data set variables are no longer stored in FORMULA entries unless you explicitly define them
- Scrolling commands can now be interrupted if you decide that you do not want to wait for the commands to finish.

Changes to SCL for FSVIEW applications
Changes and enhancements to Screen Control Language (SCL) provide new capabilities for FSVIEW applications. You can now

- control the color and highlighting attributes of individual columns
- determine which column the cursor is positioned on
- determine whether the column for a given variable is currently displayed in the window
- monitor and control application execution.

In this chapter
This chapter describes the changes and enhancements to the FSVIEW procedure for Release 6.07. This chapter updates Chapter 16, "The FSVIEW Procedure," in *SAS/FSP Software: Usage and Reference, Version 6, First Edition*.

Changes in FSVIEW Window Behavior

The following sections highlight some of the ways in which the functionality of the FSVIEW window has been enhanced for Release 6.07.

Editing Data Set Variables with Formulas

The FSVIEW procedure now allows you to edit data set variables that have associated formulas. This allows you to create formulas that act on the values you enter in the variable columns.

As in Release 6.06, you cannot edited computed variables (variables that are defined by formulas and that do not appear in the displayed data set).

Using Formats and Informats

The format and informat for data set variables are no longer stored in the FORMULA entry unless you issue FORMAT or INFORMAT commands in the FSVIEW window to assign specific formats or informats to the variable columns. This allows you to use the formats and informats defined in the data set when you use a FORMULA entry, and to specify different formats and informats using FORMAT and INFORMAT statements in conjunction with the PROC FSVIEW statement at procedure invocation.

To remove a format or informat assignment from the FORMULA entry so that the format or informat defined the data set is used, issue FORMAT or INFORMAT commands that specify the variable name but no format or informat name. For example, to cancel the format for the variable X stored in the FORMULA entry, issue the following command in the FSVIEW window:

```
format x
```

The format and informat for computed variables (variables that do not exist in the data set) are always stored in the FORMULA entry. FORMAT or INFORMAT commands for computed variables are ignored if they do not specify a format or informat.

Interrupting Scrolling Commands

You can now interrupt the commands that scroll the observations displayed in the FSVIEW window (for example, TOP and BOTTOM). This feature is useful when you want to halt a scroll request while browsing or editing a large data set.

To halt an active scroll operation, press the interrupt key or key combination for your system. The FSVIEW procedure displays a requestor window that gives you the options of aborting or resuming the scrolling operation.

■ **Host Information** ....

The key or key combination used to interrupt an active process varies according to host operating system and terminal device. For example, some systems have a key labeled BREAK or ATTENTION (or ATTN). Other systems use a combination of the CTRL key and another key. Refer to host documentation to determine the interrupt key for your host operating system and terminal device. ■

Changes to SCL for FSVIEW Applications

The following changes and enhancements to Screen Control Language provide new capabilities for FSVIEW applications. Refer to Chapter 20, "Dictionary of New and Enhanced SCL Elements," for detailed information on the SCL features discussed in this section.

Setting Column Colors and Highlighting Attributes

The FIELD function can now change the color and highlighting attribute of individual columns from within your SCL programs. For example, the following statement causes the columns for the variables X1 and X2 to appear in red and reverse video:

```
rc=field('color red reverse','x1 x2')
```

Any valid color and highlighting attributes can be used.

Determining the Cursor Position

The new CURFLD function enables you to determine the name of the column on which the cursor is currently positioned. The following statement shows how you can use the CURFLD function:

```
name=curfld();
```

The CURFLD function returns a blank if cursor is not on a variable column.

Determining Whether a Variable Is Displayed

The DISPLAYED function enables you to determine whether a variable is currently displayed in the FSVIEW window.

```
if (displayed(salary)=0) then call execcmd('=salary');
```

Monitoring and Controlling Application Execution

You can now use the SCL system variable _STATUS_ to monitor and control the flow of your FSVIEW applications.

Determining the current state of the FSVIEW session
To determine the current state of the FSVIEW session, you test the current value of the _STATUS_ variable. The _STATUS_ variable has one of the following values:

E — users issued an END command

C — users issued a CANCEL command

blank — neither END or CANCEL commands were issued.

Note: By default, formulas are not executed when users issue END or CANCEL commands unless users have also modified a value in one of the displayed columns. When you want to test the value of the _STATUS_variable in a formula, you may need to use the CONTROL ENTER statement to ensure that the formula is executed even if no fields were modified when the user issued the END or CANCEL command.

Changing the current state of the FSVIEW session
To control the execution of your FSVIEW application, you can assign either of the following values to the _STATUS_ variable:

H
: terminates the FSVIEW session when the next RETURN statement is encountered.

  Note: In contrast to the FSEDIT procedure, formulas in the FSVIEW procedure are executed after data set variables are updated. If users modified data set variable values in the current observation, the modified values are written to the SAS data set before the FSVIEW session terminates.

R
: resumes editing the current observations.

For example, if you want to close the FSVIEW window when users enter the value 99 in the X column, use the following formula:

```
x=x;if (x=99) then _status_='H';
```

Compatibility with Release 6.06

Because Release 6.07 of the SAS System uses the same catalog structure as Release 6.06, you can use SAS catalogs you created with Release 6.06 to store FORMULA entries you build using Release 6.07. You also can use any FORMULA entries you built using Release 6.06 under Release 6.07 without modification. However, due to changes in the structure of FORMULA entries and in SCL, any FORMULA entries you in build using Release 6.07 cannot be used under Release 6.06.

If you create a FORMULA entry using the FSVIEW procedure under Release 6.06 and then later use that entry under Release 6.07, the entry will no longer be usable in Release 6.06 if you define any new formulas or edit any existing formulas.

Updates to SAS® Screen Control Language

PART 3

CHAPTER 14 Overview of Changes and Enhancements to Screen Control Language

Overview

Part 3 contains information on new and enhanced functionality for SAS Screen Control Language (SCL). Release 6.07 of the SAS System provides much new functionality for SCL in the areas of:

- controlling program execution at user interrupts
- creating program modules
- creating and manipulating lists of data
- new and enhanced SCL functions
- enhanced SCL debugger commands.

Controlling Program Execution at User Interrupts

Chapter 15 "Features for Controlling Program Execution at User Interrupts" describes the features that allow you to control the execution of the INIT, MAIN, and TERM sections when a user interrupts a program (for example, by pressing an interrupt key).

Writing SCL Programs in Modules

Chapter 16 "Support for Program Modules" describes new features that allow you to build SCL programs in modules. You can create modules called window variable blocks that contain statements verifying values entered in the field for a window variable. These blocks execute after window fields are modified and before the MAIN section so that MAIN only executes after all window variable blocks execute correctly.

You can also create program modules called method blocks that you can use repeatedly in the same program or in other programs instead of having to write the program segment into multiple programs. You can pass values between method blocks and the calling SCL program.

Storing Data in SCL Lists

Chapter 17 "Features for Storing and Manipulating Data in SCL Lists" describes a group of data structures and functions that enable you to store data using a new feature called SCL lists. These lists are ordered collections of data, similar to arrays. However, lists provide more flexibility because they are created dynamically at run time. SCL lists can contain numbers, characters, or even other lists, and combinations of these item types. You can insert items, replace or delete items, and move them around by reversing, rotating, or sorting them.

Chapter 18, "Examples Using SCL Lists," contains two examples using SCL lists.

New and Enhanced SCL Elements

Chapter 19, "New and Enhanced Elements by Category," is composed of a list of the new and enhanced SCL functions and routines by category. Chapter 20, "Dictionary of New and Enhanced SCL Elements," describes the enhancements to many SCL functions as well as the new SCL functions. These elements are listed in alphabetical order. The dictionary chapter contains updates for many SCL functions and call routines that provide enhanced functionality. It also contains descriptions of all the new SCL functions.

Enhanced Debugger Commands

Chapter 21, "Dictionary of Enhanced SCL Debugger Commands," describes the enhancements to debugger commands. You can specify a program label with the BREAK and GO commands. When you use the STEP command to debug a SELECT statement, this command jumps to the appropriate WHEN or OTHERWISE clause without stepping through all the intervening WHEN statements.

CHAPTER 15 Features for Controlling Program Execution at User Interrupts

Overview

Release 6.07 of SCL provides a new feature that enables you to control the execution of your SCL programs when a user interrupts them.

Controlling Program Execution at User Interrupts

You can control program execution at user interrupts through a new type of attention handler that you define. This *attention handler* is a labeled statement block that begins with a label you define and contains SCL statements that can alter the program flow or execution status. This statement block ends with a RETURN statement. For the attention-handler block to be honored, you specify the associated label name in a CONTROL BREAK *label* statement that executes before the interrupt occurs. You can have more than one attention-handler block in a single SCL program, but only one of them is in effect at one time. Execution of a CONTROL BREAK *label* statement replaces any attention handler block called with a CONTROL BREAK statement previously defined in the program.

When an interrupt occurs during program execution (for example, a user presses the ATTENTION key) and a CONTROL BREAK *label* statement has been executed (putting an attention-handler block is into effect), the associated statement block is executed. When an interrupt takes place and a CONTROL BREAK *label* statement has not been executed or a previously-defined attention handler block has been disabled through the execution of a CONTROL NOBREAK statement, a requester window opens and asks users to choose whether to resume application execution or halt it.

Using an Attention Handler Block

To use this technique for controlling program execution when an interrupt occurs, you

- create a labeled statement block containing the statements to run if program execution is interrupted, and end the block with a RETURN statement
- specify the name of the this block as the label in a CONTROL BREAK *label* statement that can be placed anywhere in the program.

You can cancel a CONTROL BREAK statement with a CONTROL NOBREAK statement. You can also replace a CONTROL BREAK statement with a succeeding CONTROL BREAK statement that specifies a different program label.

Syntax

You use the following syntax for a control break block:

CONTROL BREAK *label;*
more SCL statements

label:
  SCL program statements
RETURN;

Examples

The first example sets a control break handler labeled MYTERM when the first SCL statement in the INIT section has been executed. During the execution of this SCL program, if a user presses an ATTENTION key, the statement block labeled MYTERM is executed immediately, and control is returned to the calling SCL program or DM window.

```
INIT:
   control break MYTERM;
   id=open('myfile');
   more SCL statements
return;

MAIN:
   more SCL statements
return;

TERM:
   call close(dsid);
   id = 0;
   more SCL statements
return;

MYTERM:
   if id > 0 then all close(dsid);
return;
```

The second example sets a control break handler labeled STOPINIT when the first SCL statement of the INIT section is executed. When a user presses an attention key, the STOPINIT label is executed. If the loop index I is less than 1000, execution of the program resumes. After the loop is finished, the effect of the control break handler is nullified. If a user presses an attention key again, control returns to the calling SCL program or DM window. Then another control break hander block labeled STOPTERM label is set by the first statement of the TERM label. If a user presses an attention key after this statement is executed, the STOPTERM label will be executed. If the loop index J is less than 1500, execution of the program is resumed. After the loop is finished, the effect of this attention handler is nullified again.

```
INIT:
   control break STOPINIT;
   do i = 1 to 2000;
      more SCL statements
   end;
   control break;
   more SCL statements
return;

MAIN:
   more SCL statements
return;

TERM:
    control break STOPTERM;
    do i = 1 to 2000;
       more SCL statements
    end;
    control break;
    more SCL statements
return;

STOPINIT:
   if (i < 1000) then
      do;
         _STATUS_ = 'R';
         return;
      end;

STOPTERM:
   if (j < 1500) then
      do;
         _STATUS_ = 'R';
         return;
      end;
return;
```

CHAPTER 16 Support for Program Modules

Overview

Release 6.07 of SCL provides two language constructs for supporting modular programming. These constructs are labeled statement blocks called window variable blocks and method blocks.

Window Variable Blocks

You use window variable blocks as program modules that contain statements verifying values entered in the field for a window variable. This module is called a *window variable block* because its label is the name of the window variable whose value it is verifying. The window variable label marks the beginning of the labeled section, which ends with a RETURN statement.

Your program can include window variable blocks for any number of window variables. When users modify window variables, the window variable blocks execute for all window variables that have been modified. The MAIN section executes only after the window variable blocks for all modified variable have executed correctly. This feature reduces the overhead required each time the MAIN section is executed because the MAIN section executes only when all the program's window variable labeled sections execute without error.

Using a Window Variable Block

To use a window variable block, you

- □ specify the name of a window variable as the label statement for a labeled block of your program and end the block with a RETURN statement.
- □ use a CONTROL LABEL statement in the program's initiation section (INIT or FSEINIT).

Using window variable blocks in extended tables You can also use window variable blocks in programs for extended tables. In these programs, the window variable block for each modified field executes before the PUTROW section executes for the row.

Syntax
To create a window variable block, you use the following syntax:

window-variable-label:
SCL program statements;
RETURN;

Example

Suppose your application window displays the three numeric variables AMOUNT, RATE, and PAYMENT. The following program shows how to use window variable labels to validate these fields.

In this example, the CONTROL statement with the LABEL option is in the INIT section. If a user enters a numeric value for the window variable RATE, the label block RATE executes immediately. The MAIN sections executes only if the value of RATE is between 0 and 1. If a user changes both AMOUNT and RATE and accidently enters a character value for AMOUNT, this is an attribute error. In this case, only the RATE block executes and not the AMOUNT or the MAIN section.

```
INIT:
   control label;
   amount=100;
   rate=0.5;
return;

AMOUNT:
      /* The amount must be positive.  */
   if amount<0 or amount>500 then
      erroron amount;
   else
      erroroff amount;
return;

RATE:
      /* The rate must be between 0 and 1.  */
   if (rate<0) or (rate>1) then
      erroron rate;
   else
      erroroff rate;
return;

MAIN:
      /*  Calculate payment.  */
   payment=amount*rate;
   if payment>100 then
      do;
         _msg_='We can not afford this payment.';
         erroron amount rate;
      end;
   else
      erroroff amount rate;
return;

TERM:
return;
```

Method Blocks

You can use method blocks as program modules that can be called within the same program or from a different program. These modules are called *method blocks* because they begin with a METHOD statement and end with an ENDMETHOD statement. This feature allows you to write a module that performs one operation on an element of an SCL entry or FSEDIT window. Then, you can use that module repeatedly instead of having to write those statements into multiple programs. For example, if multiple programs in your application need to sort a numeric array, you can write a program module that performs the sort and then call the module from each program that needs to sort a numeric array. You can pass parameters to a program module, which allows you to execute it on any element that you name in the calling routine. After the module performs its operations, it can return modified values to the calling routine.

In the METHOD statement, you can list parameters for receiving values passed by the calling METHOD routine. When you want to pass parameters between a program and a METHOD block, you use the same principles as when you are passing parameters between a CALL DISPLAY statement an ENTRY statement. The parameter list and argument list must agree in the number of parameters passed and arguments received, their position in the lists, and their data type. They do not have to agree in name.

Using a Method Block

To use a method block, you

- □ write a labeled statement block that starts with a METHOD statement, then the SCL statements that perform the desired task, and ends with an ENDMETHOD statement.
- □ call the method block with a link statement in the same program or a CALL METHOD routine from the same program or another one.

Syntax

To create a METHOD block, you use the following syntax:

METHOD <*arg_list*< optional=*arg_list*>>;
  SCL program statements
ENDMETHOD;

Example

The following program contains two method blocks:

- □ NSORT, which sorts numeric arrays
- □ CSORT, which sorts character arrays.

```
array narr(100) _temporary_;
array carr(100) $ 200 _temporary_;
length msg $ 200;
length ntemp 8 ctemp $ 200;

   /* This method sorts a numeric array. */
NSORT:
   method size 8 msg $ optional=narr 8;
      msg=' ';   /* set return value */
      if (size<=0) then
```

```
            do;
               _msg_='Array size is too small';
               return;
            end;
         if (size>100) then
            do;
               _msg_='Array size is over 100';
               return;
            end;
            /*  Do a bubble sort.  */
         do i=1 to size-1;
            do j=i+1 to size;
               if narr(i)>narr(j) then
                  do;
                        /* Swap */
                     ntemp=narr(i);
                     narr(i)=narr(j);
                     narr(j)=ntemp;
                  end;
            end;
         end;
      endmethod;

      /* This method sorts a character string array. */
   CSORT:
      method size 8 msg $ optional=carr $;
         _msg_=' ';   /* set return value */
         if (size<0) then
            do;
               _msg_='Array size is too small';
               return;
            end;
         if (size>100) then
            do;
               _msg_='Array size is over 100';
               return;
            end;
            /*  Do a bubble sort. */
         do i=1 to size-1;
            do j=i+1 to size;
               if carr(i)>carr(j) then
                  do;
                        /* Perform a swap. */
                     ctemp=carr(i);
                     carr(i)=carr(j);
                     carr(j)=ctemp;
                  end;
            end;
         end;
      endmethod;
```

Learning More

See Chapter 20, "Dictionary of New and Enhanced SCL Elements" for the dictionary entries on the

- □ CONTROL LABEL statement
- □ METHOD statement
- □ ENDMETHOD statement
- □ CALL METHOD routine.

CHAPTER 17 Features for Storing and Manipulating Data in SCL Lists

Overview

In Release 6.07 of the SAS System, SCL supports new data structures and functions for manipulating data in SCL lists. SCL lists, like arrays, are ordered collections of data. However, lists are more flexible than arrays in many ways. This chapter highlights the features of SCL lists and compares lists to arrays. The example in the next section illustrates the kinds of things you can do with SCL lists.

Example

The following program creates a list containing the names of the variables in SAS data set SASUSER.MILEAGE. The program

- □ prints the names in the order in which they appear in the SAS data set
- □ sorts and prints the list by the variable names
- □ sorts and prints the list by the length of the variables.

```
mileage=open('SASUSER.MILEAGE','I');
if (mileage>0) then
   do;
      nv=attrn(mileage, 'NVARS');
         /* Make a list with NV items in it.  */
      vars=makelist(nv);
      do v=1 to nv;
         vname=varname(mileage, v);
         vlen=varlen(mileage, v);
            /* Set item #V in the VARS list to the numeric  */
            /* value VLEN, giving it the name VNAME.  The   */
            /* SETITEMN call is similar to the assignment:  */
```

```
         /*    array v  = vl;                                    */
         /* The NAMEITEM gives item #v the name VNAME.    */
      x=nameitem(setitemn(vars,vlen,v),v,vname);
   end;
      /* Close the data set.  */
   rc = close(mileage);
      /* Print the variable names in the data set order.  */
   call putlist(vars,'Data set order:',0);
      /* Sort the list of variables by name, then      */
      /* print the variable names in the name order.  */
   vars=sortlist(vars,'name ascending');
   call putlist(vars,'Name order:',0);
      /* Sort the list of variables by length.  The default     */
      /* sort is to sort by value (the var lengths) in          */
      /* ascending order.  Then, print the variable names in    */
      /* the variable length order.                             */
   vars=sortlist(vars);
   call putlist(vars,'Length order:',0);
      /* Delete the list of data set variables.  */
   rc=dellist(vars);
end;
else _msg_=sysmsg();
```

This program produces the output shown in Output 17.1.

Output 17.1 *Output of Example Program*

```
Data set order:(DATE=8
                E=15
                EXERCISE=15
                DISTANCE=8
                TMILES=8
                TIME=8
                RATE=8
                MILES=8
                CUM=8
                )[3]
Name order:(CUM=8
            DATE=8
            DISTANCE=8
            E=15
            EXERCISE=15
            MILES=8
            RATE=8
            TIME=8
            TMILES=8
            )[3]
Length order:(CUM=8
              DATE=8
              DISTANCE=8
              MILES=8
              RATE=8
              TIME=8
              TMILES=8
              E=15
              EXERCISE=15
              )[3]
```

Manipulating SCL Lists

You can create new lists and then insert numbers, character strings, and even other lists into them. You can replace or delete list items, and move them around by reversing, rotating, or sorting the list. You can also assign names to the items in a list and refer to items by their names rather than their index (position) in the list. Thus, you can use a list to implement data structures and access and assign values to list elements by their name.

Using this feature, you can add new fields to the list data structure or change the order of the list's items without modifying your SCL program.

SCL lists maintained in memory
SCL lists are maintained entirely in memory. Keep this in mind as you develop your applications. If your data is more appropriately maintained in a SAS data set, you will probably want to design your application in that manner instead of trying to read the entire SAS data set into a list. However, if you know your data set will not contain thousands of observations and many variables, and you do not need to maintain data sharing, you may find it convenient to read the data set into a list. That is, you can use SCL lists for data that you would have liked to put into an array but might not have been able to because of the restrictions imposed by arrays.

Creating Data Dynamically

SCL lists are dynamic rather than static. That is, your SCL program creates these lists at run time rather than statically declaring their size like you declare arrays with an ARRAY statement. This means list sizes are computed at run time rather than before the list is created. Further, a list's length can grow or shrink to accommodate the amount of data you want to maintain, unlike arrays, which have a fixed size.

SCL lists can store data of mixed types
SCL lists can contain items of mixed types, whereas SCL arrays are fixed in type. (Depending on its declaration, an array contains either numeric data or character data, but not both), One item in an SCL list can be a number and the next item can be a character string. Further, you have the freedom to replace a numeric value with a character value in a list, and vice-versa. Although you can make lists that are of fixed type, you have the freedom to allow multiple types in the same list.

Identifying SCL Lists

You access lists with a list identifier, which is a unique number assigned to each list you create. This is similar to the SCL data set identifier with which you reference an open SAS data set. As with SAS data set identifiers, you do not know what number will be assigned to a list before your program executes. Therefore, you must store the list identifier in an SCL variable and then reference that variable in each operation you perform on the list. All the SCL functions that manipulate lists use a list identifier as an argument.

Note that assigning a list identifier to another variable does not copy the list. The two variables simply refer to the same list.

Creating new lists
You create a new, empty list with the MAKELIST function. You can then insert numbers, characters, or other lists into the list with the functions INSERTN, INSERTC, or INSERTL, respectively. You can also specify the default number of items in the initial list by supplying an argument to the MAKELIST function. For example, the following statement makes a list containing N items.

```
mylist=makelist(n);
```

Note that N can be any non-negative SCL numeric expression that is computed at run time, or it can be a simple numeric constant such as 12, if you want to create a list with a known initial number of items. No matter how you create the list, you are free to expand or shrink it to contain as many items as you need, from 0 to as many items as your computer has memory to hold. You use the LISTLEN function to find out the length of a list.

Determining the type of a list item
In general, SCL list functions that process data values are suffixed with either N, C, or L to denote the item types of numeric, character, or sublist, respectively. You can use the ITEMTYPE function to determine the type of a list element and use a condition statement to determine which of the set of functions to use.

Inserting and replacing items in lists
You can insert and replace items in a list with the SETITEMN, SETITEMC, and SETITEML functions. These functions can assign values to existing items or optionally add new items. Use the SETITEM function to replace a list item. With arrays, you would use

```
A[i]=x
```

but with lists, you use

```
l=setitemn(L,x,i);
```

Use the INSERT function to add a new item to a list without replacing the existing items.

Retrieving values from lists
You can retrieve the value of an item in the list with the GETITEMN, GETITEMC, or GETITEML functions.

Deleting items from lists
You can delete items from SCL lists by specifying the position to delete, by clearing all the values from a list, or by deleting entire lists. You can also pop items from lists, which allows you to create queues or stacks (see "Using Lists as Stacks and Queues").

You can delete a list item with the DELITEM function and specify the number of the item to delete. You can clear all the values from a list with the CLEARLIST function, which leaves the list with a length of 0. You can also delete an entire list with the DELLIST function. This function returns to the system the memory required to maintain the list and its items.

Referencing List Items by Index Number

List indexing is similar to array indexing. An index *i* specifies the position of an item in the list. The first item is at index $i=1$, and the last item is at index $i=n$, where n is the length of the list. Thus, you can use DO loops to process all items in a list, as shown in the following example:

```
do i=1 to listlen(mylistid);
   t=itemtype(mylistid,i);
   put='Item ' i ' is type ' t;
end;
```

Accessing items relative to the end of a list
It is also useful for you to be able to access items at or relative to the end

of an SCL list. You can use negative indices to index an item from the end of the list. Counting from the end of a list, the last item is at index -1 and the first item is at position -*n*. Thus, you do not need to subtract indices from *n* to access items relative to the end of the list. All of the SCL list functions recognize negative indices. An invalid list index is any index that is outside the ranges -*n*..−1 and 1.. *n* , where *n* is the length of the list. List item indices should be integral numbers.

Indexing errors
Indexing errors occur when you supply an invalid index to a list function, just as it is an error to use an invalid array index.

Implementing Sublists and Nested Structures

SCL allows you to put one list of items inside another SCL list, thereby making a sublist of the outer list. For example, you can read the variables of a SAS data set observation into a list. You could then insert each observation into another list, and repeat this process for a range of observations in the data set. You then have a list of lists, where the "outer" list contains an element for each observation in the data set, and the "inner" sublists contain each observation. This is called nesting lists.

Limitless levels of nesting
Nesting lists is highly useful for creating collections of records or data structures. There is no limit to the amount of nesting or to the number of sublists that can be placed in a list, other than the amount of memory available to your SAS application. Further, you can create *recursive* list structures, where the list A can contain other lists that contain A either directly or indirectly. The list A can even contain itself as a list item.

Simulating multi-dimensional arrays with nested lists
You can declare multi-dimensional arrays in SCL, but all lists are one-dimensional. That is, to access an item in a list, you specify only one index. However, you can use nested lists to simulate multi-dimensional arrays. For example, to create a list structure that mimics a 2 by 3 array, you can use the following example:

```
listid=makelist(2);
lista=setiteml(listid,makelist(3),1);
listb=setiteml(listid,makelist(3),2);
```

You can then access or set the item corresponding to the array item A i,j using the following statements.

```
x=getitemn(getitemn(listid,i),j);          /* like: x = Arr i,j ; */
listid=setitemn(getitemn(listid,i),y,j);   /* like: Arr i,j  = y; */
```

Assigning Names to List Items

SCL supports a feature called *named lists*, which allow you to assign a name to each item in a list, or only to some list items. The name can be any SCL character string, not just character strings that are valid variable names. Using the GETNITEMC, GETNITEMN, and GETNITEML functions, you can access these items by their name rather than their position. This feature allows you to vary the contents of the list according to your application needs without having to keep track of where a particular item is in a list. You can also assign or replace values associated with a name with the SETNITEMC, SETNITEMN, or SETNITEML function. You can delete an item by its name with the DELNITEM function.

The names in a list do not have to be unique. Item names are converted to uppercase and trailing blanks are ignored when searching the list for a matching name. Thus, the names 'abc' and 'Abc ' are converted to 'ABC'. If there are duplicate names, the functions find the first occurrence of the name (although you can specify any occurrence of the item you want). By inserting a new item at the beginning of the list, you can "hide" a previous value since a named search will find your new item first. When you want to restore the previous value, simply delete the new item from the list.

You can freely mix named items with unnamed items in a list. You can also use both items of indexing (by name or by number) in any list, regardless of how the list was created or whether all, some, or no items have names.

Indexing a named item by its position

You can find the position of a named item in the list with the NAMEDITEM function. This allows you to access the item by its position in the list, which is a faster search if the position does not change. However, searching by position is not safe if the position of the item might change between the time you find the position and the time you use the position.

For example, the following statement replaces the value associated with the name "Acme" in the list NUMBERS with the value "(201) 555-2263". These statements do not modify the list if the name "Acme" is not found.

```
i=nameditem(numbers,'Acme');
if i>0 then setitemc(numbers,'(201) 555-2263',i);
```

Locating or replacing an item's name

You can replace the name of an item with the NAMEITEM function. You can also use NAMEITEM when you want to find out the name of an item but you do not want to change the item's name.

Finding an occurrence of a name

In general, the functions that allow you to access a list item by its name operate on the first occurrence of the name. However, you can combine the optional arguments *occurrence* and *index* to refer to items other than the first occurrence. *Occurrence* allows you to specify the number of the occurrence of a named item that you want to find. For example, a value of 3 references the third occurrence, and a value of 10 references the tenth occurrence. The following example demonstrates how to find the positions of the first and third item containing the name 'SCL'.

```
first=nameditem(listid,'SCL');    /* default occurrence is 1   */
third=nameditem(listid,'SCL',3);  /* Find the third occurrence */
```

Specifying where the search for an item starts

The *index* argument specifies the position in the list to begin the search for the named item. The default is 1, which means the search begins at the first item in the list. If the value for *index* is negative, then the search starts at position abs(*index*) from the end of the list. For example, an *index* of −1 references the list's last item while an *index* of −2 references the list's second to last item. Thus, to change the value of the last occurrence of a list item named 'X' to the value *y*, you can use a statement like the following:

```
listid=setnitemn(listid,y,'X',1,-1);
```

Using Shared Data Environments

A feature available with SCL lists is support for shared data environments. In earlier versions of SCL, if you wanted one PROGRAM entry to pass data to many other entries, you had to pass the data explicitly in each CALL DISPLAY statement or you had to put the values in macro variables. However, macro variables are limited to in the amount of data they can contain (only scalar values) and to names that are valid SAS names. By placing data in a shared data environment, other programs and even other SAS applications can retrieve the data via a name. These names can be any valid SCL string, and the value associated with a name can be a numeric or character value or an entire list.

Two data environments
The two kinds of shared data environments are implemented with local SCL lists and global SCL lists.

Local data environment
Each SAS System application (such as an FSEDIT application, or a SAS/AF application started with the AF command) maintains its own application environment in a local environment list. You can store data that is local to the application, but which you want shared among all of an application's PROGRAM entries, in this local environment list. The function ENVLIST('L') returns the list identifier of the environment list for the current application. Other applications' lists are maintained in the memory of each application, and even though two lists in different applications may have the same list identifier, the lists are actually different. This is analogous to the same data set identifier being used by different SAS applications but this identifier actually referring to different data sets opened at different times.

Global data environment
There is also a global environment list that stores data that can be shared across all SAS applications started in the same SAS session. For example, one SAS application may place some data in the global environment list and then close. Another application may then open and read the data created by the other application. The global environment list is accessible via the list identifier returned by ENVLIST('G'). For more details, see the ENVLIST function in Chapter 20 "Dictionary of New and Enhanced SCL Elements."

Using Lists as Stacks and Queues

You can create lists that function as stacks (first in, last out lists) or queues (first in, first out lists).

Using a list as a stack
When you want to use a list as a stack, you use the INSERTC, INSERTN, or INSERTL function to insert an item into a list. The default insertion position for these functions is the beginning of the list, so you need only specify the list and the data to insert. To pop an item from a stack, use either the POPN, POPC, or POPL function to pop a number, character, or sublist from the stack. You can use the ITEMTYPE function to determine the type of the item at the top of the stack if your application does not know the type. If your application always pushes the same data type onto your stack (for example, the stack is a stack of character strings and you only put items into the list with INSERTC), then you do not need to use ITEMTYPE to check the type of the top of the stack before popping. You

can delete the top item in the stack with the DELITEM function if you do not want to keep the popped value. You can replace the top item with the SETITEMN, SETITEMC, or SETITEML function. You should not attempt to pop or delete an item unless you are sure the list contains at least one item. You can use the LISTEN function to return the length of the list before you use a function to delete an item.

Using a list as a queue
When you use a list as a queue, you also put items in the list with the INSERTN, INSERTC, or INSERTL function. To remove an item, you use the POPN, POPC, or POPL function to pop items from the end of the list instead of the beginning. As with stacks, you should use the ITEMTYPE and LISTLEN functions to verify the queue's type and length before popping an item from the list. For example, ITEMTYPE(listid,-1) returns the type of the last item in a list.

Assigning List and Item Attributes

You can assign attributes to lists or to items in a list. Attributes are useful to control the use and modification of lists. For example, you can specify that a list is not available for update, which means that other programs that your program calls (for example, via CALL DISPLAY) cannot change the data in the list or cannot add or delete items from the list. You can also assign attributes such as NOUPDATE and/or NODELETE to individual items in a list.

Since it is easy to change the type of any item in a list by simply replacing the value with a new value, it would be quite easy for one application to accidentally change a list in a way you did not intend. You can also specify that a list or items in a list have fixed type, so that another program cannot change a numeric value to a character value, etc. By assigning the proper attributes to the lists and data you create, you need not worry about other parts of the application corrupting your data, and you can avoid adding additional data validation statements to your programs.

Assigning list and item attributes is not required, but it can ease the process of application development because an attempt to violate an attribute, which indicates a bug in the application, causes the application to stop with a fatal error. Use the SETLATTR function to set the attributes of a list or item. The GETLATTR function returns a string describing the current attributes, and the HASATTR function returns 1 if the list or item has the specified attribute and 0 if it does not.

Using File Interfaces

Two SCL list functions allow you to store lists in SAS catalog entries or external files and to read lists from these files. The SAVELIST function writes a list, and the FILLIST function reads data from a catalog entry or external file and fills a list with the text from the file. OUTPUT, LOG and SOURCE entries are recognized, as well as a new catalog entry SLIST, which is described in Chapter 8, "SLIST Catalog Entries."

Saving Nested Lists to SCL Entries

When you save a list that contains sublists, both the list and its sublists are saved in the same SLIST entry. Thus, if the list data structures you create are highly recursive and have many cycles, you should be careful about saving your lists.

Example
Suppose your application has a list A which contains lists B, and the list B contains an instance of the list A. Using a CALL PUTLIST of A and B,

```
call putlist(a,'A=', 0);
call putlist(b,'B=', 0);
```

you see the following results:

```
A=(PI=3.1415926536
   B=(SQTR(2)=1.4142135624
      A=(...) 5
      SQRT(3)=1.7320508076
      ) 7
   E=2.7182818285
   ) 5
B=(SQTR(2)=1.4142135624
   A=(PI=3.1415926536
      B=(...) 7
      E=2.7182818285
      ) 5
   SQRT(3)=1.7320508076
   ) 7
```

If you save list A, you also save list B at the same time. Therefore, you do not need to save list B separately; list B is already stored in list A. In fact, if you store the lists in two separate SLIST entries and tried to read them back, you do not get the same list structure you stored originally. For example, the following SCL statements do not work as you expect them to:

```
rc=savelist('SLIST','SASUSER.LISTS.A', A);
rc=savelist('SLIST','SASUSER.LISTS.B', B);
   /* later: */
a=makelist();
b=makelist();
rc=filllist('SLIST','SASUSER.LISTS.A', A);
rc=filllist('SLIST','SASUSER.LISTS.B', B);
```

When the application uses SAVELIST to save list A, it saves a copy of list A (call it prime A for this example) and a copy of list B (call it prime B). Then when it uses SAVELIST to save B, it saves another copy of list B (dblprime B) and another copy of list A (dblprime A). When the application reads the lists back in with the FILLIST function, it reads in the copies which yields the following results:

```
A=(PI=3.1415926536
   B=(SQTR(2)=1.4142135624
      A=(...) 9
      SQRT(3)=1.7320508076
      ) 13
   E=2.7182818285
   ) 9
B=(SQTR(2)=1.4142135624
```

```
A=(PI=3.1415926536
   B=(...) 11
   E=2.7182818285
   ) 15
SQRT(3)=1.7320508076
) 11
```

Note that the list B contained in list A, with a list id of 13, is not the same as list B, which has a list id of 11. Also, the list A contained in list B, with a list id 15, is not the same list as the list A, which has a list id of 9.

Advantages
There is an advantage to the recursive nature of the SAVELIST function. Instead of trying to write each individual list in separate SLIST entries, you can insert all the lists into a single application list of lists. You can then write the entire collection of application lists to one SLIST entry.

For example, instead of writing entries A.SLIST and B.SLIST, we create a list named APPLICATION and store A and B in it, then write the list to APPL.SLIST:

```
application=makelist();
application=setniteml(application, B,'B');
application=setniteml(application, A,'A');
rc=savelist('SLIST','AF.BOOK.APPL', application, 0,
'My         application lists');
rc=dellist(application,'N');
   /* ... */
application=makelist();
rc=fillist('CATALOG','AF.BOOK.APPL',application);
A=getniteml(application,'A');
B=getniteml(application,'B');
call putlist(application,'APPLICATION=',0);
rc=dellist(application,'N');
call putlist(a,'A=',0);
call putlist(a,'B=',0);
```

This method correctly restores the lists A and B from the SLIST entry, as shown here.

```
APPLICATION=(B=(SQTR(2)=1.4142135624
             A=(PI=3.1415926536
               B=(...) 11
               E=2.7182818285
               ) 13
             SQRT(3)=1.7320508076
             ) 11
           A=(...) 13
           ) 9
A=(PI=3.1415926536
   B=(SQTR(2)=1.4142135624
     A=(...) 13
     SQRT(3)=1.7320508076
     ) 11
   E=2.7182818285
   ) 13
B=(SQTR(2)=1.4142135624
   A=(PI=3.1415926536
     B=(...) 11
```

```
  E=2.7182818285
  ) 13
SQRT(3)=1.7320508076
) 11
```

If you look closely, you will see that the list named B inside the list A is the same as the list B (list id 11), and the list named A inside the list named B is the same as the list A (list id 13).

Listing of SCL List Functions

The following table lists the tasks you can perform with SCL functions.

When you want to ...	Use the function ...
clear the values from a list, and optionally clear its sublists	CLEARLIST
copy the contents of a list into another list or into a new list	COPYLIST
designate a list to contain selections returned by selection list functions	CURLIST
delete an item from a list	DELITEM
delete a list	DELLIST
delete a named item from a list	DELNITEM
return a description of a SAS data set, view, catalog or catalog entry	DESCRIBE
return the list identifier for an environment list	ENVLIST
read data from a SAS file or an external file into a list	FILLIST
fetch a character list item by its position	GETITEMC
fetch a sublist list item by its position	GETITEML
fetch a numeric list item by its position	GETITEMN
find the attributes of a list or list item	GETLATTR
fetch a character list item by its name	GETNITEMC
fetch a sublist list item by its name	GETNITEML
fetch a numeric list item by its name	GETNITEMN
find out whether a list or list item has an attribute	HASATTR
insert a new character item into a list	INSERTC
insert a new numeric item into a list	INSERTL
insert a new sublist item into a list	INSERTN
find the type of a list item	ITEMTYPE
find the length of a list	LISTLEN
designate a list to contain the unique formatted values of a SAS data set variable	LVARLEVEL

create a list	MAKELIST
create a named list	MAKENLIST
search a list for an item by its name	NAMEDITEM
find, and optionally change, the name of a list item	NAMEITEM
delete an item from a list, returning its character value	POPC
delete an item from a list, returning its sublist value	POPL
delete an item from a list, returning its numeric value	POPN
display a popup menu based on the contents of a list	POPMENU
print the contents of a list to the MESSAGE window	PUTLIST
reverse the order of a list's items	REVLIST
rotate a list's items	ROTLIST
save list contents to a SAS file or an external file	SAVELIST
return the position of a character item in a list	SEARCHC
return the position of a sublist item in a list	SEARCHL
return the position of a numeric item in a list	SEARCHN
change or replace a character item by its position	SETITEMC
change or replace a numeric item by its position	SETITEML
change or replace a sublist item by its position	SETITEMN
change or assign attributes to a list or list item	SETLATTR
replace or insert a character item by its name	SETNITEMC
replace or insert a sublist item by its name	SETNITEML
replace or insert a numeric item by its name	SETNITEMN
sort a list	SORTLIST

CHAPTER 18 Examples Using SCL Lists

Overview

Introduction
This chapter contains examples of using SCL lists. One example shows how to use the _CMDLIST_, which is a sublist of the local environment list. The second example saves a list and all its nested lists in the same SLIST entry.

Using the _CMDLIST_

After reading in Chapter 2 how SAS/AF software assembles the SCL list called
CMDLIST, you can write SCL programs that detect which options and values users specify on the AF command.

Accessing the Command List

To access the command list in an SCL program, use the new SCL function GETNITEML shown here:

```
cmdlist=getniteml(envlist('L'),'_CMDLIST_');
```

This statement, which you typically place in the INIT section of your SCL program, retrieves the list named _CMDLIST_ from the local environment list and stores its list identifier in the SCL variable CMDLIST. For more information about the GETNITEML function, refer to "GETNITEML" in Chapter 20, "Dictionary of New and Enhanced SCL Elements."

Accessing the Components of an Application Name

Since SAS/AF software automatically stores the components of your application name in the command list, you can always access these components. To do this, you can use the GETNITEMC function, as shown here:

```
libname=getnitemc(cmdlist,'LIBNAME');
catname=getnitemc(cmdlist,'CATALOG');
```

```
name=getnitemc(cmdlist,'NAME');
type=getnitemc(cmdlist,'TYPE');
```

For more information on the GETNITEMC function, refer to Chapter 20, "Dictionary of New and Enhanced SCL Elements."

Determining the Options and Values Users Specify

To determine whether the user specified a particular option, you can use the NAMEDITEM function to search the command list for the option name. For example, to determine whether the user specified the AUTOSAVE option, you can use the following statement:

```
autosave_specified=nameditem(cmdlist,'AUTOSAVE');
```

After executing the above statement, the SCL variable AUTOSAVE_SPECIFIED is either

- 0 if the user did not specify the AUTOSAVE option
- >0 if the user specified the option.

The actual value of AUTOSAVE_SPECIFIED indicates which item in the _CMDLIST_is the value specified for the AUTOSAVE option. Therefore, the SCL program can read the value of the option from the list. Since the default value for AUTOSAVE is NO, you can use one SCL function call to find the current option value:

```
autosave=getnitemc(cmdlist,'AUTOSAVE',1,1,'NO');
```

This function retrieves the value of the character value named AUTOSAVE from the list CMDLIST. If the value doesn't exist in the list, the function returns NO.

If you want to determine the *last* value associated with a named option, use a −1 as the fourth argument on the GETNITEMC or GETNITEMN functions. Chapter 20, "Dictionary of New and Enhanced SCL Elements," describes these functions in greater detail.

Example

The following example illustrates how you can manipulate option names and values from the command list. This SCL program, which expects an AF command that contains the OBS= keyword followed by a list of observation numbers, collects the specified observations in a separate list, and then sorts and prints the list.

```
INIT:
   cmdlist=getniteml(envlist('L'),'_CMDLIST_');
   obsarg=nameditem(cmdlist,'OBS');
   if (obsarg=0) then
      do;
         _msg_='No OBS= on command line.';
         _status_='H';
         return;
      end;
   if itemtype(cmdlist,obsarg)¬='N' then
      do;
           /* Value is character rather than numeric. */
```

```
         _msg_=
'Invalid OBS='|| getitemc(cmdlist,obsarg)|| 'on command line.';
         _status_='H';
         return;
      end;
      /* Start building the list of observations. */
   obslist=makelist();
   obslist=insertn(obslist,getitemn(cmdlist,obsarg));
   obsarg+1;
   cmdlistlen=listlen(cmdlist);
   done='N';
   do while (obsarg<=cmdlistlen and done='N');
      if (itemtype(cmdlist,obsarg)¬='N' or
         nameitem(cmdlist,obsarg)¬='') then
            /* done when arg is non-numeric          */
            /* or it has a name (it's another option) */
         done='Y';
      else
         do;
            obsnum=getitemn(cmdlist,obsarg);
               /* Insert OBS# at end of list  */
            obslist=insertn(obslist,obsnum,-1);
            obsarg+1;
         end;
      end;
   obslist=sortlist(obslist,'NODUPS');
   call putlist(obslist,'Observations:',0);
return;
```

For example, for the command line

```
af c=a.b.obs.scl Obs=17 23 19 47 23
```

the application prints the following results:

```
Observations:(17
              19
              23
              47
              )[5]
```

Note: As you can see in this program, you must use the GETNITEMC function to fetch a character value from the command list and the GETNITEMN function to get a numeric value from the command list. If you do not know the value's type, you can use the ITEMTYPE function to determine its type, and then use the appropriate function to fetch it from the command list.

Note: Generally, it is better to write such an application using an extended table to enter a list of observations numbers. This would allow SAS/AF software to do much of the validation. However, this example emphasizes the flexibility of command line arguments and shows some ways to handle variable command lines.

Saving Nested Lists in SCL Entries

When you save a list that contains sublists, both the list and its sublists are saved in the same SLIST entry. Thus, if the list data structures you create are highly recursive and have many cycles, you should be careful about saving your lists. A recursive list is an outer list that contains itself as a sublist or contains other lists that contain the outer list as a sublist.

Example

Suppose your application has a recursive list A, which contains list B, and the list B contains an instance of the list A. The following statements print the original lists.

```
call putlist(a,'A=',0);
call putlist(b,'B=',0);
```

The following output shows original contents of the lists.

```
A=(PI=3.1415926536
   B=(SQTR(2)=1.4142135624
      A=(...)[5]
      SQRT(3)=1.7320508076
      )[7]
   E=2.7182818285
   )[5]
B=(SQTR(2)=1.4142135624
   A=(PI=3.1415926536
      B=(...)[7]
      E=2.7182818285
      )[5]
   SQRT(3)=1.7320508076
   )[7]
```

If you save list A, you also save list B at the same time. Therefore, you do not need to save list B separately; list B is already stored in list A. In fact, if you store the lists in two separate SLIST entries and try to read them back, you do not get the same list structure you stored originally. This example assumes the catalog SASUSER.LISTS exists and provides an illustration of SCL statements that do not produce the results you expect them to:

```
rc=savelist('catalog','sasuser.lists.a.slist',A);
rc=savelist('catalog','sasuser.lists.b.slist',B);
   /* later: */
newa=makelist();
newb=makelist();
rc=fillist('CATALOG','sasuser.lists.a.slist',newa);
rc=fillist('CATALOG','sasuser.lists.b.slist',newb);
```

When the application uses SAVELIST to save list A, it saves a *copy* of list A (call it A2 for this example) and a copy of list B (call it B2). Then when it uses SAVELIST to save B, it saves another copy of list B (B3) and another copy of list A (A3). When the application reads the lists back in with the FILLIST function, it reads in the copies,

```
call putlist(newa,'NEWA= ',0);
call putlist(newb,'NEWB= ',0);
```

which yields the following results:

```
NEWA=(PI=3.1415926536
   B=(SQTR(2)=1.4142135624
      A=(...)[9]
      SQRT(3)=1.7320508076
      )[13]
   E=2.7182818285
   )[9]
NEWB=(SQTR(2)=1.4142135624
   A=(PI=3.1415926536
      B=(...)[11]
      E=2.7182818285
      )[15]
   SQRT(3)=1.7320508076
   )[11]
```

Note that the the sublist named B contained in list NEWA has a list identifier value of 13 and is not the same as list NEWB, which has a list identifier value of 11. Also, the sublist named A contained in list NEWB has a list identifier value of 15 and is not the same as list NEWA, which has a list identifier value of 9.

Advantages

There is an advantage to the recursive nature of the SAVELIST function. Instead of trying to write each individual list in separate SLIST entries, you can insert all the lists into a single application list of lists. You can then write the entire collection of application lists to one SLIST entry.

For example, instead of writing entries A.SLIST and B.SLIST, we create a list named APPLICATION and store A and B in it, then write the list to APPL.SLIST:

```
application=makelist();
application=setniteml(application, B,'B');
application=setniteml(application, A,'A');
rc=savelist('CATALOG','AF.BOOK.APPL.SLIST', application, 0,
            'My application lists');
rc=dellist(application,'N');
   /* ... */
application=makelist();
rc=fillist('catalog','AF.BOOK.APPL.SLIST',application);
newa=getniteml(application,'A');
newb=getniteml(application,'B');
call putlist(application,'APPLICATION=',0);
rc=dellist(application,'N');
call putlist(newa,'newa= ',0);
call putlist(newa,'newB= ',0);
```

This method correctly restores the lists A and B from the SLIST entry, as shown below.

```
APPLICATION=(B=(SQTR(2)=1.4142135624
               A=(PI=3.1415926536
                  B=(...)[11]
                  E=2.7182818285
                  )[13]
               SQRT(3)=1.7320508076
               )[11]
```

```
                    A=(...)[13]
                    )[9]
A=(PI=3.1415926536
   B=(SQTR(2)=1.4142135624
      A=(...)[13]
      SQRT(3)=1.7320508076
      )[11]
   E=2.7182818285
   )[13]
B=(SQTR(2)=1.4142135624
   A=(PI=3.1415926536
      B=(...)[11]
      E=2.7182818285
      )[13]
   SQRT(3)=1.7320508076
   )[11]
```

If you look closely, you will see that the sublist named B inside the list NEWA is the same as the list NEWB (list id 11), and the sublist named A inside the list named NEWB is the same as the list A (list id 13).

CHAPTER 19 New and Enhanced SCL Elements by Category

Overview

This chapter lists the new or enhanced statements, functions, and CALL routines that you can use in your Screen Control Language (SCL) programs when building applications using Release 6.07. This chapter updates Chapter 7, "Language Elements," in *SAS Screen Control Language: Reference, Version 6, First Edition.*

SCL Elements

Table 19.1 summarizes the SCL functions, routines, and statements that have been added or enhanced in SCL for Release 6.07. The elements are grouped by functional category. Refer to Chapter 20, "Dictionary of New and Enhanced SCL Elements," for complete descriptions of the SCL functions, routines, and statements listed in this table.

Table 19.1 *SCL Elements by Category*

	Choice Group
GRAY	grays a single station or an entire choice group
ISGRAY	indicates whether a choice group or station is grayed
UNGRAY	ungrays a single station or an entire choice group
	Command
LASTCMD	returns the text of the last command issued from the application window
	Control
CONTROL	controls the execution of statements in the SCL program

Data Set	
ATTRC	returns the value of a character attribute for a SAS data set
ATTRN	returns the value of a numeric attribute for a SAS data set
OBSINFO	returns information on the current observation in an FSEDIT application
OPEN	opens a SAS data set
SETKEY	defines an index key for retrieving observations from a SAS data set

Display	
BLOCK	displays a menu containing up to 12 choice blocks or icons and returns a number corresponding to a user's choice

Field	
CURFLD	returns the name of the field on which the cursor is currently positioned
FIELD	performs an action on or reports the state of window variables
FLDATTR	changes the color and highlighting attributes for a field based on an attribute string
FLDCOLOR	changes the color and highlighting attributes for a field
STRATTR	defines a color and highlighting attribute string

File	
FOPEN	opens an external file

Key	
EVENT	indicates whether users have pressed any key
LASTKEY	returns the number of the last function key issued from the window

List	
CLEARLIST	clears the items from a list without deleting the list and optionally clears all sublist items
COPYLIST	copies the contents of a list into an existing list or a new list
CURLIST	designates or reports the current list
DELITEM	deletes an item from a list
DELLIST	deletes a list and optionally deletes all of its sublists
DELNITEM	deletes a named item from a list
DESCRIBE	fills a list with items of descriptive information about a SAS data set, view, catalog or catalog entry
ENVLIST	returns the list identifier of an environment list
FILLIST	fills a list with text from a SAS file or an external file
GETITEMC	returns the value of a character item that is identified by its position in a list
GETITEML	returns the list identifier stored as a sublist item that is identified by its position in a list
GETITEMN	returns the value a numeric item that is identified by its position in a list
GETLATTR	reports the attributes of a list or an item in a list
GETNITEMC	returns the value of a character item identified by its name in a list
GETNITEML	returns the identifier for the sublist item identified by its name in a list
GETNITEMN	returns the numeric value of a list item identified by its name in a list
HASATTR	reports whether a list or list item has a specified attribute
INSERTC	inserts a character item into a list
INSERTL	inserts a sublist item into a list
INSERTN	inserts a numeric item into a list
ITEMTYPE	reports the type of an item in a list
LISTLEN	reports the length of a list
LVARLEVEL	fills a list with the unique formatted values of a variable from a SAS data set
MAKELIST	creates a list
MAKENLIST	creates a named list with named items
NAMEDITEM	searches a list for the item with the specified name
NAMEITEM	returns and optionally replaces the name of an item in a list
POPC	removes a character item from a list and returns the value stored there

POPL	removes a sublist item from a list and returns the identifier for the sublist stored there
POPMENU	displays a popup menu containing character elements of a list
POPN	removes a numeric item from a list and returns the value stored there
PUTLIST	displays the contents of a list in the MESSAGE window
REVLIST	reverses the order of the items in a list
ROTLIST	rotates the order of the items in a list
SAVELIST	stores list items in a SAS file or an external file
SEARCHC	searches for the value of a character item in a list and returns its position number
SEARCHL	searches for the list identifier of a sublist item in a list and returns its position number
SEARCHN	searches for the value of a numeric item in a list and returns its position number
SETITEMC	assigns a new value to a character item in a list or a value to a new character item
SETITEML	assigns a new identifier value to a sublist item or an identifier value to a new list item
SETITEMN	assigns a new value to a numeric item in a list or a value to a new numeric item
SETLATTR	changes the attributes of a list or a list item
SETNITEMC	assigns a character value to a named item in a list
SETNITEML	assigns a sublist identifier to a named item in a list
SETNITEMN	assigns a numeric value to a named item in a list
SORTLIST	sorts the items in a list

Method Block

ENDMETHOD	ends a statement block that can be called by the METHOD routine
METHOD (routine)	executes a method block defined in an SCL entry
METHOD (statement)	begins a statement block that can be called by the METHOD routine

SAS/AF Software Interface*

BUILD	invokes the BUILD procedure in SAS/AF software

* This SCL routine is valid only if SAS/AF software is licensed at the users' site.

SAS/CALC Software Interface*	
CALC	invokes the CALC procedure in SAS/CALC software

SAS/CONNECT Software Interface**	
RLINK	determines whether a link exists between the current SAS session and a remote SAS session
RSESSION	returns the name and description of a remote session
RSTITLE	defines a description for a remote session

Selection List	
CATLIST	displays a selection list window that lists entries in a SAS catalog and returns user selections
COLORLIST	displays a selection list containing the names of colors that are valid for a device and returns user selections
DATALISTC	displays a selection list window containing values of selected variables from observations in a SAS data set and returns user selections
DATALISTN	displays a selection list window containing values of selected variables from observations in a SAS data set and returns user selections
DEVLIST	displays a selection list window containing the names of graphic hardware devices and returns user selections
DIRLIST	displays a selection list window that lists members of a SAS data library and returns user selections
FILELIST	displays a selection list window containing the currently assigned filerefs and returns user selections
LIBLIST	displays a selection list window containing libref names and returns user selections
LISTC	displays a selection list window containing character values and returns user selections
LISTN	displays a selection list window containing numeric values and returns user selections
VARLIST	displays a selection list window that lists the variables in an open SAS data set and returns user selections

* This SCL routine is valid only if SAS/CALC software is licensed at the users' site.

** These SCL routines are valid only if SAS/CONNECT software is licensed at the users' site.

Submit Block	
PREVIEW	manipulates submitted statements in the PREVIEW buffer

Utility	
CEXIST	verifies the existence of a SAS catalog or SAS catalog entry
COPY	copies a SAS data set, view, catalog, or catalog entry
FILENAME	assigns or deassigns a fileref for an external file, directory, or output device
IMPORT	creates a SAS data set from an external file
LOCK	locks or unlocks a SAS file or SAS catalog entry
PATHNAME	returns the physical name of a SAS data library or an external file
RENAME	renames a SAS data set, view, catalog, or catalog entry
SEARCH	creates or manipulates the current catalog search path

Window	
DMWINDOW	sets the color and attributes of lines in the display manager OUTPUT and LOG windows
ICON	associates an icon number with the window
REFRESH	updates field values and redisplays the window
WINFO	returns information about the current window
WOUTPUT	manipulates the display manager OUTPUT window

CHAPTER 20 Dictionary of New and Enhanced SCL Elements

Overview

This chapter provides descriptions of all the functions, statements, and call routines that have been added or modified in Release 6.07 of Screen Control Language (SCL). This chapter updates Chapter 8, "Screen Control Language Dictionary," in *SAS Screen Control Language: Reference, Version 6, First Edition.*

Terminology

This section describes the terminology used in this chapter and throughout this book.

field
: an area of a window in which the value of a window variable is entered or displayed.

nonwindow variable
: an SCL variable that is defined in the SCL program but has no corresponding field in the window.

SCL data vector (SDV)
: a data buffer used to store the current value of all SCL variables for the current program.

SCL variable
: any variable that can be used in an SCL program.

window variable
: an SCL variable that is associated with a field in the window.

Common Arguments

The following terms are used to identify common arguments in this chapter's dictionary entries:

catalog-name
: the name of a SAS catalog. The catalog name must follow standard SAS naming conventions. The usual form is

  ⟨*libref.*⟩*member-name*

data-set-id
: the data set identifier value returned by the OPEN function. SCL can open multiple SAS data sets simultaneously. Each open SAS data set is identified to the SAS System and the SCL program by a unique numeric data set identifier. This *data-set-id* value is used to identify the desired data set in functions that manipulate SAS data sets. You can assign the *data-set-id* value to another variable or pass it as a parameter to another program.

data-set-name
: the name of a SAS data set. The value must follow standard SAS naming conventions. The syntax of *data-set-name* is

  ⟨*libref.*⟩*member-name*⟨(*data-set-options*)⟩

  where *data-set-options* are any valid SAS data set options. Refer to Chapter 15, "SAS Data Set Options," in *SAS Language: Reference, Version 6, First Edition* for details.

entry
: the name of an entry in a SAS catalog. The complete syntax of a catalog entry name is

  libref.catalog-name.entry-name.entry-type

file-id
: the file identifier value returned by the FOPEN function. SCL can open multiple external files simultaneously. Each open file is identified to the SAS System and the SCL program by a unique numeric file identifier value. This *file-id* value is used to manipulate the files. You can assign the *file-id* value to another variable or pass it as a parameter to another program.

list-id
: the list identifier value returned by the MAKELIST, MAKENLIST, or other list function. SCL can manage multiple lists simultaneously. Each list is identified to the SAS System and the SCL program by a unique numeric list identifier. This *list-id* value is used to identify the desired list in functions that manipulate SCL lists. You can assign the *list-id* value to another variable or pass it as a parameter to another program.

Organization

Each dictionary entry in this chapter contains the following information:

Name
: names the function, routine, or statement.

Synopsis
: provides a short description highlighting the element's main use.

Group
: indicates the type of element (function, routine, or statement) and whether it is new or modified, along with its functional grouping.

Syntax
: presents syntax in standard form. Arguments enclosed in angle brackets (⟨ ⟩) are optional and can be omitted.

Complete syntax descriptions are provided only for those elements that are new in Release 6.07. Refer to *SAS Screen Control Language: Reference* for details of the syntax of elements that were included in Release 6.06

If a new element is a function, then its return value is described first. The **Type** column contains either N for numeric or C for character. The **Value** column explains the return value.

If the element takes arguments, they are described in the same format as the return value, with a code for the argument type (either N for numeric or C for character). The **Value or Action** column describes the argument.

Description or
Updated Functionality
: provides a more detailed explanation of the element.

Note: This section is labeled Description for new elements and Updated Functionality for elements that have been modified for Release 6.07.

Examples
: presents one or more brief examples that demonstrate the syntax and usage of the element.

Notes
: provides additional information useful to developers.

See Also
: tells where to look for information on related functions, routines, and statements or other topics.

ATTRC

Returns the value of a character attribute for a SAS data set

Enhanced SCL Function

Data Set Function

Syntax

attr-value=ATTRC(*data-set-id,attr-name*);

The following argument has changed for Release 6.07. Refer to *SAS Screen Control Language: Reference* for details of the other syntax elements.

Argument	Type	Value or Action
attr-name	C	Name of the desired attribute. In addition to the attribute names listed for the ATTRC function in Chapter 8 in *SAS Screen Control Language: Reference*, the following new options are available: CHARSET — Returns an empty string if the data set is not sorted. Otherwise returns one of the following three values: ASCII — Data set sorted in ASCII order EBCDIC — Data set sorted in EBCDIC order HASCII — Data set sorted in extended ASCII order SORTEDBY — Returns an empty string if the data set is not sorted. Otherwise returns the names of the BY variables in the standard BY statement format. SORTLVL — Return an empty string if the data set is not sorted. Otherwise returns one of the following values: WEAK — User assertion of sort order is weak STRONG — User assertion of sort order is strong OFF — User assertion to cancel sort order SORTSEQ — Returns an empty string if the data set is not sorted. Otherwise returns the name of the sort sequence.

Updated Functionality

The ATTRC function includes several new arguments that cause the function to return information about how the data set is sorted.

Example

The following statements test whether the data set specified in the DSNAME variable is sorted in ASCII order. If so, statements report the variable by which the data set is sorted.

```
dsid=open(dsname);
if (dsid ne 0) then
   do;
      if (attrc(dsid,'charset')='ASCII') then
         do;
            svar=attrc(dsid,'sortedby');
            put dsname 'is sorted in ASCII order by' svar;
         end;
   end;
```

ATTRN

Returns the value of a numeric attribute for a SAS data set

Enhanced SCL Function

Data Set Function

Syntax

attr-value=ATTRN(*data-set-id*,*attr-name*);

The following argument has changed for Release 6.07. Refer to *SAS Screen Control Language: Reference* for details of the other syntax elements.

Arguments	Type	Value or Action
attr-name	C	Name of the desired attribute. In addition to the attribute names listed for the ATTRN function in Chapter 8 in *SAS Screen Control Language: Reference*, the following new attributes are available: ALTERPW — indicates whether a password is required to alter the data set 1 the data set is alter protected 0 the data set is not alter protected PW — indicates whether a password is required to access the data set 1 the data set is protected 0 the data set is not protected READPW — indicates whether a password is required to read the data set 1 the data set is read protected 0 the data set is not read protected WRITEPW — indicates whether a password is required to write to the data set 1 the data set is write protected 0 the data set is not write protected

Updated Functionality

The ATTRN function includes several new arguments that cause the function to return information about whether the data set uses password protection.

Example

The following statements use the ATTRN function to determine the level of password protection for an open SAS data set:

```
dsid=open(dsname);
if (dsid ne 0) then
   do;
      if (attrn(dsid,'ALTERPW')) then
         put 'This data set is alter protected';
      else
         put 'This data set is not alter protected';
      if (attrn(dsid,'PW')) then
         put 'This data set is protected';
```

```
   else
      put 'This data set is not protected';
   if (attrn(dsid,'READPW')) then
      put 'This data set is read protected';
   else
      put 'This data set is not read protected';
   if (attrn(dsid,'WRITEPW')) then
      put 'This data set is write protected';
   else
      put 'This data set is not write protected';
end;
```

BLOCK

Displays a menu containing up to 12 choice blocks or icons and returns a number corresponding to a user's choice

Enhanced SCL Function

Display Function

Syntax

choice=BLOCK(*window-name,title,color,text-1,. . .,text-12*
⟨*,icon-1,. . .,icon-12*⟩);

The following argument has been added for Release 6.07. Refer to *SAS Screen Control Language: Reference* for details of the other syntax elements.

Arguments	Type	Value or Action
icon-1,. . ., icon-12	N	Icon numbers for icons displayed on place of the corresponding choice blocks. If these values are omitted, or if the host system does not support icons, the standard rectangular blocks are used. See the Appendix , "Icons," for a list of the available Institute-supplied icons.

Updated Functionality

The BLOCK function can now display icons in place of the text blocks in block menus if your users' host operating system supports icons.

Example

The following statement displays a block menu with icons for the choice blocks (if your host system supports icons):

```
choice=block('SAS Procedure','Main Menu',6,
             'PGM','OUTPUT','LOG','GRAPH',
             'REGRESSION','FSEDIT','AF','DBMS',
             'LAB','INSIGHT','HELP','EXIT',
             5,4,3,16,
             133,23,17,120,
             50,54,2,111);
```

See Also

Chapter 6, "Support for Icons," for more information on using icons in SAS/AF applications

BUILD

Invokes the BUILD procedure

New SCL Routine

SAS/AF Software Interface Routine

SAS/AF software required

Syntax

CALL BUILD(*entry*⟨,*open-mode*⟩);

Arguments	Type	Value or Action	
entry	C	Name of a SAS/AF entry in a catalog.	
		A one-level name is assumed to be a catalog name in the WORK library. A two-level name is assumed to be a libref and catalog. Use a three- or four-level name to specify a particular catalog entry. If a three-level name is used, the type is assumed to be PROGRAM.	
open-mode	C	One of the following:	
		EDIT	Open the specified catalog entry for editing. (This is the default.)
		BROWSE	Open the specified catalog entry for browsing

Description

The BUILD routine opens a BUILD window from within an application. Users can construct any of the SAS/AF entry types in the BUILD window.

Note: SAS/AF software must be licensed at your users' site to use the BUILD routine.

Example

The following statement opens a PROGRAM entry named NAME in the catalog MYLIB.MYCAT:

```
call build('mylib.mycat.name.program');
```

CALC

Invokes the CALC procedure in SAS/CALC software

New SCL Routine

SAS/CALC Software Interface Routine

SAS/CALC software required

Syntax

CALL CALC(*entry*〈,*open-mode*〉);

Arguments	Type	Value or Action	
entry	C	Name of spreadsheet	
open-mode	C	One of the following:	
		EDIT	Open a spreadsheet for editing. A dialog window is first opened in which users enter various spreadsheet parameters.
		OPEN	Similar to EDIT mode, except the dialog window is not opened if the spreadsheet already exists.

Description

The CALC routine opens a SAS/CALC spreadsheet from within an SCL program.

Note: SAS/CALC software must be licensed at your users' site to use the CALC routine.

Example

The following statement opens a CALC window for editing a spreadsheet named EXPENSE.CALC in the catalog WORK.SHEETS:

```
call calc('work.sheets.expense.calc','edit');
```

CATLIST

Displays a selection list window that lists the entries in a SAS catalog and returns user selections

Enhanced SCL Function

Selection List Function

Syntax

cval=CATLIST(*catalog-name,type,num-sel,prefix*⟨,*message*⟨,*autoclose*⟩⟩);

Note: The syntax for the CATLIST function is unchanged from Release 6.06. See Chapter 8 in *SAS Screen Control Language: Reference* for details.

Updated Functionality

The CATLIST function now places values in the current environment list. When the CATLIST function is invoked, the current environment list is cleared. After invoking the CATLIST function, the environment list has the following named elements:

Element	Type	Description
TAG	C	Identifies the list as one created by the CATLIST function
COUNT	N	Number of elements selected. If users make no selections, or if they issue a CANCEL command in the list window, COUNT is 0.
NAME	C	Name of each catalog entry selected. If the *prefix* argument is `Y`, the prefix is appended to the beginning of each name. There is one NAME element for each selection made.
DESC	C	Description of each catalog entry selected. There is one DESC element for each selection made.
DATE	C	Date each selected catalog entry was last modified. There is one DATE element for each selection made.

Example

The following statements displays a selection list showing all the entries for the catalog MYLIB.TEST. Users can make up to five selections. The selected values are retrieved from the current environment list using the GETNITEMC function.

```
listid=makelist();
rc=curlist(listid);
list=catlist('mylib.test','all',5,'y');
n=getnitemn(listid,'COUNT');
do i=1 to n;
   name=getnitemc(listid,'NAME',i);
   desc=getnitemc(listid,'DESC',i);
   date=getnitemc(listid,'DATE',i);
   put name= desc= date=;
end;
```

CEXIST

Verifies the existence of a SAS catalog or SAS catalog entry

Enhanced SCL Function

Utility Function

Syntax

rc=CEXIST(*entry*⟨,'U'⟩);

The following argument has been added for Release 6.07. Refer to *SAS Screen Control Language: Reference* for details of the other syntax elements.

Argument	Type	Value or Action
U	C	Tests whether the specified catalog is opened for updating.

Updated Functionality

The CEXIST function now supports an extra parameter that allows you to test whether a SAS catalog or a particular entry in a SAS catalog can be opened for updates.

Example

The following statement uses the CEXIST function to determine whether the catalog LIB.CAT can be opened for updating:

```
if not(cexist('lib.cat','U')) then
   _msg_='The catalog LIB.CAT cannot be opened for updating';
```

CLEARLIST

Clears the items from an SCL list without deleting the list and optionally clears all sublist items

New SCL function

List function

Syntax

rc=CLEARLIST(*list-id*⟨,*recursively*⟩);

Returns	Type	Value	
rc	N	Indicator of the success of the clear operation.	
		>0	The list was cleared.
		≤0	An error occurred, and the list was not cleared.

Arguments	Type	Value or Action	
list-id	N	Identifies the list to be cleared.	
recursively	C	Specifies whether to recursively clear all the list's sublists and all sublists of all of its sublists.	
		Y	All sublists are also cleared.
		N	Sublists are not cleared. This is default.

Description

The CLEARLIST function clears all the items from the SCL list identified by *list-id*. The list is not deleted, but its length is reduced to 0. If the value of *recursively* is 'Y', all the list's sublists, including sublists of sublists, are also cleared unless they have the NODELETE attribute. That is, you can assign the NODELETE attribute to sublists if you do not want them deleted when you recursively delete a list that contains them.

(To check the attributes of a list or list item, use the HASATTR function. To change these attributes, use the SETLATTR function.)

▶ *Caution: Before you delete a list recursively, make sure it is not needed by other parts of the SCL program.*

Be careful when deleting lists recursively, since you have the potential to clear lists that are needed by other parts of the SCL program. The *recursively* option clears all of a list's sublists, even if they are referenced in other SCL lists or by other SCL variables. If you do not want a list to be cleared when it is a sublist item in a list, you should use the SETLATTR function to assign the NODELETE attribute to the sublist. See SETLATTR for a discussion of the NODELETE attribute.

Example

The following statements show how to clear all sublists from an existing list identified by MYLIST without deleting items that are not sublists.

```
   /* Copy the list.  */
cp=copylist(mylist);

   /* Clear the entire list, including sublists  */
   /* that also appear in CP.                    */
rc=clearlist(mylist,'Y');
```

CLEARLIST

continued

```
   /* Copy the old list data.  */
   /* Sublists have been cleared.  */
mylist=copyist(cp,'N',mylist);

   /* Delete the copied list. */
rc=dellist(cp);
```

Notes

An error condition results if

- the item has the NOUPDATE or FIXEDLENGTH attribute
- any item in the list (or its sublists, if *recursively* is 'Y') has the NODELETE attribute
- the value of *recursively* is 'Y', and any item in the list has the DELETE attribute and the NOUPDATE or FIXEDLENGTH attribute
- *list-id* is not a valid list identifier.

See Also

COPYLIST, DELITEM, DELNITEM, MAKELIST, MAKENLIST, POPC, POPL, and POPN in this chapter for information on related SCL functions

COLORLIST

Displays a selection list window containing the names of colors that are valid for a device and returns user selections

Enhanced SCL Function

Selection List Function

Syntax

selections=COLORLIST(*device*,*num-sel*⟨,*message*⟨,*autoclose*⟩⟩);

Note: The syntax for the COLORLIST function is unchanged from Release 6.06. See Chapter 8 in *SAS Screen Control Language: Reference* for details.

Updated Functionality

The COLORLIST function now places values in the current environment list. When the COLORLIST function is invoked, the current environment list is cleared. After invoking the COLORLIST function, the environment list contains one element for each color name selected. The selections can be retrieved using the GETITEMC function.

Example

The following statements list all the colors that can be used on the device selected in the device selection list. The selected colors are retrieved from the current environment list. The LISTLEN function is used to determine the number of selections because there is only one element in the list for each selection made.

```
listid=makelist();
rc=curlist(listid);
selection=devlist('sashelp.devices','monitor','Select a device.');
device=substr(selection,41,8);
devcolor=colorlist(device,4);
n=listlen(listid);
do i=1 to n;
   color=getitemc(listid,i);
   put color=;
end;
```

CONTROL

Controls the execution of statements in the SCL program

Enhanced SCL Statement

Control Statement

Syntax

CONTROL *options*;

The *options* argument accepts several new values for Release 6.07. The new option values are described in the "Updated Functionality" section. Refer to Chapter 8 in *SAS Screen Control Language: Reference* for details of the other valid values for the *options* argument.

Updated Functionality

The CONTROL statement now provides additional options that enable you to control the following aspects of SCL program behavior:

- which procedure commands users can issue on the command line.
- what happens if an interrupt condition occurs
- whether labeled blocks are executed when individual fields are modified.

The following additional options are valid in CONTROL statements:

ALLCMDS
NOALLCMDS

By default, any global or procedure-specific commands users issue on the command line (or using pull-down menus or function keys) are executed immediately. Your SCL program cannot intercept any global or procedure-specific commands issued in the application.

Use the ALLCMDS option to have SCL intercept any application command issued in the application. You can use the NEXTWORD function to ignore invalid commands.

Use the NOALLCMDS option to restore the default behavior.

BREAK *label*
NOBREAK

By default, no statement block is called if an interrupt occurs while the program is executing. A requestor window opens in which users are asked whether they want to resume executing the program (that is, ignore the interrupt) or halt the program. If users choose to halt execution, the _STATUS_ system variable is set to H.

Use the BREAK option to specify a labeled statement block to which control passes if an interrupt or break condition occurs while the program is executing. The *label* specified with the BREAK option names the label of the statement block to execute.

The requestor window is also displayed after execution of the statement block that is specified in the CONTROL BREAK statement. This statement block can only halt or resume the display of this window, but it cannot transfer control from the window.

A program can contain any number of CONTROL BREAK statements. For example, there can be one in each of the INIT, MAIN, and TERM sections. When a CONTROL BREAK statement is executed, any previous CONTROL BREAK statement is overwritten so that only one is in effect at a time.

Use the NOBREAK option to restore the default behavior. The NOBREAK option clears the current CONTROL BREAK specification.

Note: The BREAK and NOBREAK options are ignored in FSVIEW applications.

LABEL
NOLABEL

By default, the MAIN section of the SCL program executes after any field in the window is modified.

Use the LABEL option to execute blocks labeled with window variable names before executing the MAIN section. Statements in a block labeled with the name of a field are executed after the associated field is modified, but only if the value in the modified field does not introduce an error. That is, the field value must satisfy any attributes defined through the BUILD procedure or the FSEDIT procedure.

Statements in the MAIN section are not executed until the statements in all the blocks labeled for modified fields are successfully executed. The sequence for executing statement blocks labeled for fields is determined by the physical position of the field in the window.

If a field modification introduces an attribute error, the statement block labeled with that field name is not executed. However, statements in other blocks labeled with the names of fields that were modified do execute. To correct a predefined attribute error, you can allow users to correct the error in the window, or you can include statements that make a correction in the labeled block for other fields.

If the ERROR or ALWAYS option is also specified, the MAIN section executes after the window variable labeled blocks even if an error was introduced.

If the window displays an extended table, the labeled block for each modified window variable is executed for a row before the PUTROW block executes. The MAIN section executes after the PUTROW block executes.

Use the NOLABEL option to restore the default behavior.

Examples

The following examples illustrate the new features of the CONTROL statement.

Example: CONTROL ALLCMDS

The following program uses the ALLCMDS option to block the CANCEL command:

```
INIT:
   control allcmds;
return;

MAIN:
   cmd=lastcmd();
   if cmd='CANCEL' then
      call nextword();
return;

TERM:
   return;
```

CONTROL

continued

Example: CONTROL BREAK

The first example shows the CONTROL BREAK statement used in the INIT section, and the second examples shows the statement used on the MAIN section.

Illustrating CONTROL BREAK in the INIT section
If the following program is running and a user interrupt occurs while the loop in the INIT section is running, control transfers to the label STOPINIT. When the statements in that block have executed, control returns to the statement in the INIT section where the interrupt occurred. If the _STATUS_ variable is set to `'R'`, execution continues, otherwise execution of the program halts. In this example, execution continues if the value of the COUNT variable is less than 1000. Otherwise, execution of the INIT section halts when control returns from the STOPINIT block.

```
INIT:
   control break stopinit;
   do i=1 to 2000;
      put i;
      count=i;
   end;
return;

MAIN:
return;

TERM:
return;

STOPINIT:
   if (count<1000) then
      _status_='R';
   else
      _status_='H';
return;
```

Illustrating CONTROL BREAK in the MAIN section
The next example illustrates the use of the CONTROL BREAK statement in a program's MAIN section.

```
INIT:
return;

MAIN:
   control break stopmain;
   do j=1 to 1000;
      statements that perform various computations
   end;
return;

TERM:
return;
```

```
STOPMAIN:
   _status_='R';
return;
```

Example: CONTROL LABEL

Suppose your application window displays the three numeric variables AMOUNT, RATE, and PAYMENT. The following program shows how to use window variable labels to validate these fields.

In this example, the CONTROL statement with the LABEL option is in the INIT section. If users enter a numeric value for the window variable RATE, the label block RATE executes immediately. The MAIN sections executes only if the value of RATE is between 0 and 1. If users change both AMOUNT and RATE and accidently enter a character value for AMOUNT, this is an attribute error. In this case, only the RATE block executes and not the AMOUNT or the MAIN section.

```
INIT:
   control label;
   amount=0;
   rate=0.5;
return;

AMOUNT:
      /* The amount must be positive.  */
   if amount<0 or amount>500 then
      erroron amount;
   else
      erroroff amount;
return;

RATE:
      /* The rate must be between 0 and 1.  */
   if (rate<0) or (rate>1) then
      erroron rate;
   else
      erroroff rate;
return;

MAIN:
      /*  Calculate payment.  */
   payment=amount*rate;
   if payment>100 then
      do;
         _msg_='The payment must be less than $100.';
         erroron amount rate;
      end;
   else
      erroroff amount rate;
return;

TERM:
return;
```

COPY

Copies a SAS data set, view, catalog, or catalog entry

Enhanced SCL Function

Utility Function

Syntax

sysrc=COPY(*old-name*,*new-name*⟨,*type*⟩);

Note: The syntax for the COPY function is unchanged from Release 6.06. See Chapter 8 in *SAS Screen Control Language: Reference* for details.

Updated Functionality

The COPY function now supports data set options in data set name specification.

Example

The following statement creates a SAS data set named WORK.TWO containing the subset of the observations in SAS data set WORK.ONE for which the value of the variable X is greater than 10:

```
rc=copy('one(where=(x>10))','two');
```

Notes

The *new-name* argument is ignored when you use the COPY function to copy catalog entries of type GRSEG created using SAS/GRAPH software. A copied GRSEG entry will have either the same name as the original entry or, if an entry with that name already exists in the target catalog, a unique name generated by the SAS System.

COPYLIST

Copies the contents of an SCL list into an existing list or a new list

New SCL Function

List Function

Syntax

new-list-id= COPYLIST(*list-id*〈,*recursively*〈,*target-list*〉〉);

Returns	Type	Value
new-list-id	N	List identifier of the target list.

Arguments	Type	Value or Action
list-id	N	Identifies the list to be copied.
recursively	C	Specifies whether to recursively copy all the list's sublists. Y The values of all sublist items are copied. N Only sublist identifiers are copied as values for sublist items. This is default.
target-list	N	Identifies a list into which you want to copy the contents of the list identified by *list-id*.

Description

The COPYLIST function copies the contents of the SCL list identified by *list-id* into another list or into a new list. If the value for *target-list* is omitted, the COPYLIST function creates a new list in the same environment ('L' or 'G')* as the list being copied and makes the new list the *target-list*. When *target-list* is specified, the contents of the list identified by *list-id* are inserted at the end of the target list. Thus, the following statement makes the list MYLIST twice as long by appending the list to itself. The variables for both NEWLIST and MYLIST contain the list identifier for the copy of MYLIST.

```
newlist = copylist(mylist,'N',mylist);
```

If MYLIST contained the items 1, 2, and 3 before this COPYLIST call, it would contain the values 1, 2, 3, 1, 2, 3 after the copy operation.

When a list is copied recursively, the items in all sublists are also copied, rather than just the sublist identifiers. However, even this duplication is avoided if it would result in an infinite recursion. When copying a list recursively, SCL will not perform an infinite recursive copy. For example, if a list contains itself, there is a circular structure. The COPYLIST function detects this and recreates the structure in the copy.

All attributes of the list and its contents are preserved when a list is copied. The password** is not copied, so that you can modify the copy without knowing the password of the original list. The copy has no password.

* For a description of list environments, see the ENVLIST function.

** Passwords of lists are discussed under the SETLATTR function.

COPYLIST

continued

Examples

The following examples copy lists recursively and non-recursively. In the first example, the list is a simple one. In the second example, the list contains a copy of itself. Both examples use an SCL list named B, which is identified by BID, an SCL list named A, which is identified by AID, and an SCL list NREC, which is referenced by NRECID.

Copying a single instance of a list
The following example illustrates the difference between a simple copy and a recursive copy.

```
   /* make B a local named list with 2 items named x, y */
b=makenlist('L','x','y');
b=setnitemc(b,'ABC','x');
b=setnitemc(b,'XYZ','y');

   /* make A a local named list with 3 items named A, B, and C */
a=makenlist('L','A','B','C');
a=setnitemn(a,3.5,'A');
a=setniteml(a,b,'B');
a=setnitemn(a,9.75,'C');

call putlist(a,'A=',2);
NREC=copylist(a,'N');            /* non-recursive copy */
call putlist(NREC,'NREC=',2);
REC=copylist(a,'Y');             /* recursive copy */
call putlist(REC,'REC=',2);
```

This produces the following output:

```
A=(  A=3.5
     B=(  x='ABC'
          y='XYZ'
       )[3]
     C=9.75
   )[5]
NREC=(  A=3.5
        B=(  x='ABC'
             y='XYZ'
          )[3]
        C=9.75
      )[7]
REC=(  A=3.5
       B=(  x='ABC'
            y='XYZ'
         )[11]
       C=9.75
     )[9]
```

The sublist named B in the outer list NREC is the same list as the sublist named B in the outer list named A, from which NREC was copied non-recursively. Both lists named B have the same list identifier (3), which means they are in fact the same lists. However, the sublist named B in the outer list REC, which was copied recursively from list A, is a different list, although it has the same contents as the list named B from A. The sublist in the outer list REC has a list identifier of 11, not 3, which shows it is a different list.

Copying multiple instances of a list
This example shows how a list, which contains a copy of itself, is copied non-recursively and recursively. The outer list R1 contains two items, named SELF and R1, which are actually the same list as R1. When a non-recursive copy, R2, is made, the copy has items named SELF and R1 which are still the list R1. Only when R1 is copied recursively as R3 does the copy contain itself instead of R1.

```
    /* Create the list L, fill it, and print R1.  */
r1=makenlist('l','a','SELF','r1', 'x');
r1=setniteml(r1,r1,'SELF'));
r1=setniteml(r1,r1,'r1'));
r1=setnitemn(r1,1,'a'));
r1=setnitemn(r1,99,'x'));
call putlist(r1,'R1=',2));
    /* Copy R1 nonrecursively into R2 and print R2.  */
r2=copylist(r1,'n');
call putlist(r2,'R2=',2);
    /* Copy R1 recursively into R3 and print R3.  */
r3=copylist(r1,'y');
call putlist(r3,'R3=',2);
```

The list R2, which was created with a non-recursive copy operation, contains the list R1. Note that the structure of the list R3 is identical to that of R1: it contains two copies of itself, at items named SELF and R1, since these items are lists whose list identifier is the same as the list R3.

This program yields the following output.

```
R1=( a=1
     SELF=(...)[13]
     R1=(...)[13]
     x=99
   )[13]
R2=( a=1
     SELF=( a=1
            SELF=(...)[13]
            R1=(...)[13]
            x=99
          )[13]
     R1=(...)[13]
     x=99
   )[15]
R3=( a=1
     SELF=(...)[17]
     R1=(...)[17]
     x=99
   )[17]
```

COPYLIST

continued

Notes

An error condition results if

- □ the target list has attributes that prevent copying data into it, such as NOUPDATE and FIXEDLENGTH
- □ the target list was created in the global environment (with the MAKELIST function), then when lists are copied into it, their copies are also created in the global environment.

See Also

DELLIST, GETLATTR, HASATTR, MAKELIST, MAKENLIST, PUTLIST, and SETLATTR in this chapter for information on related SCL functions

CURFLD

Returns the name of the field on which the cursor is currently positioned

New SCL Function

Field Function

Syntax

wvar-name=CURFLD();

Returns	Type	Value
wvar-name	C	Name of the field on which the cursor is currently positioned

Description

The CURFLD function returns the name of the field on which the cursor is located when users press the ENTER key. If the cursor is not positioned on a window variable, a null string is returned.

The CURFLD function is usually used in conjunction with the ENTER option in a CONTROL statement.

Example

The following statements use the CURFLD function to control the behavior of the application:

```
field=curfld();
if (field='PHONE') then
   call display('phone.help');
else if (field='EMPLOYEE') then
   call display('employee.program');
```

Notes

In SAS/AF software, you can use choice groups to achieve the same result more efficiently. Choice groups are discussed in *SAS/AF Software: Usage and Reference, Version 6, First Edition.*

See Also

CURSOR and CURWORD in Chapter 8 in *SAS Screen Control Language: Reference* for information on related SCL functions

CURLIST

Designates or reports the current SCL list, which is filled automatically with the values returned when selection list functions are invoked

New SCL Function

List Function

Syntax

list-id=CURLIST(⟨*new-list-id*⟩);

Returns	Type	Value
list-id	N	Identifier for the list to be filled automatically with the values returned by the next SCL selection list function that is invoked. >0 The list identifier of the SCL list previously defined as current with the CURLIST function. 0 No list is defined as the current list.

Arguments	Type	Value or Action
new-list-id	N	Identifies the list to be designated as the current list.

Description

When a value is provided for *new-list*, the CURLIST function designates the SCL list identified by *new-list* as the current list. *New-list* must be the list identifier returned by the MAKELIST, MAKENLIST, or COPYLIST function that created this list. If you omit *new-list*, this function reports the identifier of the SCL list already designated as the current list by the CURLIST or LVARLEVEL function. If no argument is passed to the CURLIST function and no current list has been specified, the CURLIST function returns 0.

The current list is filled automatically with the values selected when the next SCL selection list function or LVARLEVEL function executes.

The functions that can fill the current list are the SCL selection list functions CATLIST, COLORLIST, COPYLIST, DATALISTC, DATALISTN, DEVLIST, DIRLIST, FILELIST, LIBLIST, LISTC, LISTN, LVARLEVEL, and VARLIST. For example, the CATLIST function is a SCL selection list function that a opens a selection list window displaying the names of catalog entries. The value returned by the CATLIST function is a character string containing each catalog name users select separated by blanks. Since SCL character variables are limited to 200 characters, the SCL selection list functions cannot return more entries than will fit in 200 characters. Selection list functions like CATLIST can also automatically fill the current list, as specified by CURLIST, with a character item for each selection users make. The length of that list is unbounded.

When one of the selection list functions is invoked, the values users select replace the entire contents of the current list. To preserve the contents of the current list, you should use the COPYLIST function to copy the list before calling another selection list function.

Example

The following statements show how to set up a selection list, invoke a selection list function, and access the selections.

```
clist=makelist();
oldcurlist=curlist(clist);
   /* Allow user to choose up to 16 graphs.  */
graphs=catlist('SASUSER.DEMO', 'GRSEG', 16, 'Y');
do g=1 to listlen(clist);
      graphName=getitemc(clist, g);
     put 'Selection #' g ' is ' graphName;
end;
   /* Delete temporary curlist and restore previous curlist. */
rc=dellist(clist);
oldcurlist=curlist(oldcurlist);
```

See Also

CATLIST, COLORLIST, COPYLIST, DATALISTC, DATALISTN, DELLIST, DEVLIST, DIRLIST, FILELIST, LIBLIST, LISTC, LISTN, LVARLEVEL, MAKELIST, MAKENLIST, PUTLIST, and VARLIST in this chapter for information on related SCL functions

DATALISTC

Displays a selection list window containing values of selected variables from observations in a SAS data set and returns user selections

Enhanced SCL Function

Selection List Function

Syntax

cval=DATALISTC(*data-set-id,var-list*〈*,message*〈*,autoclose*〈*,num-sel*〉〉〉);

The following argument has been added for Release 6.07. Refer to *SAS Screen Control Language: Reference* for details of the other syntax elements.

Arguments	Type	Value or Action
num-sel	N	Maximum number of items users can select from the list. Use 0 for no selections, that is, a list displayed for reference only.

Updated Functionality

The DATALISTC function now permits more than one selection. It also now places values in the current environment list.

When the DATALISTC function is invoked, the current environment list is cleared. After invoking the DATALISTC function, the environment list has the following named elements:

Element	Type	Description
TAG	C	Identifies the list as one created by the DATALISTC function.
COUNT	N	Number of elements selected. If no selections are made, or if users issue the CANCEL command in the list window, COUNT is 0.
var-name	N or C	Value of variable *var-name* in *var-list* for each selection.

Example

The following statements create a selection list containing observations with values of the variables NAME, STREET, STATE and ZIP from the open SAS data set identified by the variable CLASSID. Users can make up to three selections from this selection list. The values are then retrieved from the current environment list.

```
listid=makelist();
rc=curlist(listid);
name=datalistc(classid,'name street city state zip',' ','n',3);
n=getnitemn(listid,'COUNT');
do i=1 to n;
   name=getnitemc(listid,'NAME',i);
   street=getnitemc(listid,'STREET',i);
   city=getnitemc(listid,'CITY',i);
   state=getnitemc(listid,'STATE',i);
   zip=getnitemc(listid,'ZIP',i);
   put name= street= city= state= zip=;
end;
```

DATALISTN

Displays a selection list window containing values of selected variables from observations in a SAS data set and returns user selections

Enhanced SCL Function

Selection List Function

Syntax

nval=DATALISTN (*data-set-id*,*var-list*⟨,*message*⟨,*autoclose*⟨,*num-sel*⟩⟩⟩);

The following argument has been added for Release 6.07. Refer to *SAS Screen Control Language: Reference* for details of the other syntax elements.

Returns	Type	Value
num-sel	N	Maximum number of items users can select from the list. Use 0 for no selections, that is, a list displayed for reference only.

Updated Functionality

The DATALISTN function now permits more than one selection. It also now places values in the current environment list.

When the DATALISTN function is invoked, the current environment list is cleared. After invoking the DATALISTN function, the environment list has the following named elements:

Element	Type	Description
TAG	C	Identifies the list as one created by the DATALISTN function.
COUNT	N	Number of elements selected. If no selections are made, or if users issue a CANCEL command in the list window, COUNT is 0.
var-name	N or C	Value of variable *var-name* in *var-list* for each selection.

Example

The following statements create a selection list containing observations with values of the variables ITEMNUM, ITEMAMT, CUSTNAM, and CUSTADR from the open SAS data set identified by the variable SALESID. Users can make up to three selections from this selection list. The values are then retrieved from the current environment list.

```
listid=makelist();
rc=curlist(listid);
itemnum=datalistn(salesid,'itemnum itemamt custnam custadr');
n=getnitemn(listid,'COUNT');
do i=1 to n;
   itemnum=getnitemn(listid,'ITEMNUM',i);
   itemamt=getnitemn(listid,'ITEMAMT',i);
   custnam=getnitemc(listid,'CUSTNAM',i);
   custadr=getnitemc(listid,'CUSTADR',i);
   put itemnum= itemamt= custnam= custadr=;
end;
```

DELITEM

Deletes an item from an SCL list

New SCL Function

List Function

Syntax

new-list-id=DELITEM(*list-id*⟨,*index*⟩);

Returns	Type	Value
new-list-id	N	The list identifier of the modified list. The value returned is the same as *list-id*.

Arguments	Type	Value or Action
list-id	N	Identifies the list from which an item is to be deleted. This value was returned by the function that created the list.
index	N	Specifies the position of the item to delete from the list. *Index* defaults to 1, the first item in the list. If *index* is a positive number, the item at position *index* from the beginning of the list is deleted. If *index* is a negative number, the item at position abs(*index*) from the end of the list is deleted.

Description

The DELITEM function deletes the specified item from the list identified by *list-id*. The item is specified by its position in the list. The position can be specified as a positive or negative number. If the item at position *index* is a sublist, its list identifier is deleted from the outside list but the list is not deleted.

The DELITEM function does not make a copy of the list before deleting the specified item. The delete operation is performed in place on the list.

Notes

An error condition results if:

- the item has the NODELETE attribute
- the list has the NOUPDATE or FIXEDLENGTH attribute
- the absolute value of *index* is zero or greater than the number of items in the list
- *list-id* is not a valid list identifier.

To check the attributes of a list or list item, use the HASATTR function. To change these attributes, use the SETLATTR function.

See Also

COPYLIST, DELLIST, DELNITEM, GETLATTR, HASATTR, MAKELIST, MAKENLIST, POPC, POPL, POPN, and SETLATTR in this chapter for information on related SCL functions

DELLIST

Deletes a list and optionally deletes all of its sublists

New SCL Function

List Function

Syntax

rc=DELLIST(*list-id*⟨,*recursively*⟩);

Returns	Type	Value
rc	N	Indicator of the success of the delete operation. 0 The list was deleted. ≠0 An error occurred, and the list was not cleared.

Arguments	Type	Value or Action
list-id	N	Identifies the list to be deleted.
recursively	C	Specifies whether to delete sublists recursively. Y Delete each sublist recursively. N Do not delete sublists. This is the default behavior.

Description

The DELLIST function deletes a list by removing all items from the list and returning to the system the memory used to store the list and its items. A list's contents cannot be retrieved after the list is deleted.

If the value for *recursively* is `'Y'`, the DELLIST function recursively deletes all sublists that do not have the NODELETE attribute. That is, sublists and sublists of sublists that do not have the NODELETE attribute are all deleted. For sublists that have the NODELETE option, the sublist identifiers are removed from the deleted list but the contents are not deleted from the sublist. Thus, you should store list identifiers for sublists in an item in another list or in an SCL variable so that you can delete the lists when they are no longer needed.

You cannot delete either the local or the global environment lists (the lists returned by the ENVLIST function). All local lists not deleted are deleted when the application ends, at the same time when SCL closes open data sets and files.

▶ ***Caution:*** *Be careful when deleting lists recursively, since you have the potential to delete lists that are needed by other parts of the SCL program.*

Recursively deleting a list deletes all of its sublists, even if they are referenced in other SCL lists or by other SCL variables. If you do not want a list to be deleted when it is a sublist item in a deleted list, you should use the SETLATTR function to assign the NODELETE attribute to the sublist. See the SETLATTR function for a discussion of the NODELETE attribute.

You should delete lists when they are no longer needed because the SAS System has no way of knowing when you have completed your work with a list. Typically, a DELLIST statement is placed in the termination section (TERM or FSETERM) of the program. Although the program that creates a list is most often responsible for deleting the lists it creates, it does not have to delete them unless that is the appropriate action for the application.

DELLIST

continued

Notes

An error condition results if

- the list has the NODELETE attribute If a list might have the NODELETE attribute, you should use the SETLATTR function to assign the DELETE attribute before you use the DELLIST function.
- *list-id* is not a valid list identifier.

See Also

COPYLIST, DELITEM, DELNITEM, ENVLIST, GETLATTR, HASATTR, MAKELIST, MAKENLIST, POPC, POPL, POPN, and SETLATTR in this chapter for information on related SCL functions

DELNITEM

Deletes a named item from an SCL list

New SCL Function

List Function

Syntax

new-list-id= DELNITEM(*list-id*,*name*⟨,*occurrence*⟨,*index*⟨,*pos*⟩⟩⟩);

Returns	Type	Value
new-list-id	N	The list identifier of the modified list.

Arguments	Type	Value or Action
list-id	N	Identifies the list from which the item is to be removed. This value was returned by the function that created the list.
name	C	Specifies the name of the item to delete.
occurrence	N	Specifies the number of the occurrence of the named item to assign the specified value. The default is 1 for the first occurrence of the item.
index	N	Specifies the number of the position to start the searching the list for the item. *Index* defaults to 1, the first item in the list. If *index* is a positive number, the search starts at position *index* from the beginning of the list and continues toward the end of the list. If *index* is a negative number, the search starts at position abs(*index*) from the end of the list and continues toward the beginning of the list.
pos	N	Names the variable to contain the position number of the deleted item.

Description

The DELNITEM function deletes a named item from the SCL list identified by *list-id*. The name of the item must match exactly in spelling, although trailing blanks and case are ignored.

The DELNITEM function does not make a copy of the list. The delete operation is performed in place on the list. For example, the following statement deletes the first item named 'app' in the list identified by LISTID.

```
listid=delnitem(listid,'app');
```

When the item to be deleted is a sublist, the DELNITEM function deletes the item but not the sublist, since the list may be referenced by other SCL variables or lists.

This function cannot delete the item if it has the NODELETE attribute or the list has the NOUPDATE or FIXEDLENGTH attribute. (To check the attributes of a list or list item, use the HASATTR function. To change these attributes, use the SETLATTR function.)

DELNITEM

continued

Notes

An error condition results if

- the absolute value of *index* is zero or greater than the number of items in the list
- *list-id* is not a valid list identifier.

See Also

DELITEM, DELLIST, GETLATTR, GETNITEMC, GETNITEML, GETNITEMN, HASATTR, MAKELIST, MAKENLIST, NAMEDITEM, NAMEITEM, POPC, POPL, POPN, SETITEMC, SETITEML, SETITEMN, SETLATTR, SETNITEMC, SETNITEML, and SETNITEMN in this chapter for information on related SCL functions

DESCRIBE

Fills an SCL list with items of descriptive information about a SAS data set, view, catalog or catalog entry

New SCL Function

List Function

Syntax

sysrc=DESCRIBE(*object-name*,*list-id*⟨,*type*⟩);

Returns	Type	Value
sysrc	N	Indicator of the success of the fill operation. 0 The object was described. ≠0 An error occurred, and the object was not described.

Arguments	Type	Value or Action
object-name	C	Specifies the name of the object to be described.
list-id	N	Identifies the list to contain the object's description.
type	C	Specifies the type of object to be described. Valid values are: ACCESS access descriptor created using SAS/ACCESS software CATALOG SAS catalog or catalog entry DATA SAS data file (This is the default.) VIEW SAS data view

Description

The DESCRIBE function fills an SCL list with items of information describing a SAS data set, view, catalog or catalog entry. The list referenced by *list-id* must be an existing SCL list that was created with one of the SCL list functions. The DESCRIBE function replaces the previous values in the list, so the same list can be used repeatedly.

The items of descriptive information are placed into the list as named items, and the names are the attributes described. Only the named attributes that appear in the list are filled in. The following table shows the attributes that the DESCRIBE function can place in an SCL list.

If the *type* argument is ...	The attribute items named in the list are ...
DATA or VIEW	any attribute returned by the ATTRN and ATTRC functions.
CATALOG or ACCESS	DESC, for the description of the object, and DATE, for the SAS data value. If DATE is specified, and the current value of DATE is numeric or list, DESCRIBE places a SAS date value in that entry. If the current value of DATE is a string, DESCRIBE places the formatted date in that entry (using the MMDDYY8. format).

DESCRIBE

continued

Example

The following statements create a named SCL list containing the items named DESC and DATE. The DESCRIBE statement fills in that list with information about the catalog entry SASUSER.MYCAT.A.PROGRAM.

```
desc_list=makenlist('L','DESC','DATE');
rc=describe('SASUSER.MYCAT.PROGRAM',desc_list,'CATALOG');
```

See Also

ATTRC, ATTRN, and MAKENLIST in this chapter for information on related SCL functions

DEVLIST

Displays a selection list window containing the names of graphic hardware devices and returns user selections

Enhanced SCL Function

Selection List Function

Syntax

selections=DEVLIST(*catalog-name,device*〈*,message*〈*,autoclose*〈*,num-sel*〉〉〉);

The following arguments have been changed or added for Release 6.07. Refer to *SAS Screen Control Language: Reference* for details of the other syntax elements.

Arguments	Type	Value or Action
device	C	Type of device to list. In addition to the devices listed for the DEVLIST function in Chapter 8 in *SAS Screen Control Language: Reference*, the following new values are available: EXPORT — List device catalog entries for device drivers that produce a graphics stream file. DEFAULT — Return the current device name.
num-sel	N	Maximum number of items users can select from the list. Use 0 for no selections (that is, a window displayed for reference only).

Updated Functionality

The DEVLIST function now permits more than one selection. It also now places values in the current environment list.

When the DEVLIST function is invoked, the current environment list is cleared. After invoking the DEVLIST function, the environment list has the following named elements:

Element	Type	Description
TAG	C	Identifies the list as one created by the DEVLIST function.
COUNT	N	Number of elements selected. If no selections are made, or if users issue a CANCEL command in the selection list window, COUNT is 0.
DESC	C	Device description. There is one DESC element for each selection.
DEVICE	C	Device name. There is one DEVICE element for each selection.
TYPE	C	Device type. There is one TYPE element for each selection.

DEVLIST

continued

Example

The following statements display a list of the devices of type PRINTER that are available in the catalog SASHELP.DEVICES. Users can make up to three selections. The selection values are retrieved from the current environment list.

```
listid=makelist();
rc=curlist(listid);
selection=devlist('sashelp.devices','printer',
                  'Select a device','n',3);
n=getnitemn(listid,'COUNT');
do i=1 to n;
   descript=getnitemc(listid,'DESC',i);
   device=getnitemc(listid,'DEVICE',i);
   devtype=getnitemc(listid,'TYPE',i);
   put descript= device= devtype=;
end;
```

DIRLIST

Displays a selection list window that lists the members of a SAS data library and returns user selections

Enhanced SCL Function

Selection List Function

Syntax

selections=DIRLIST(*lib-spec,member-type, num-sel,prefix*⟨,*data-set-type* ⟨,*sel-excl*⟨,*message*⟨,*autoclose*⟩⟩⟩⟩);

Note: The syntax for the DIRLIST function is unchanged from Release 6.06. See Chapter 8 in *SAS Screen Control Language: Reference* for details.

Updated Functionality

The DIRLIST function now places values in the current environment list. When the DIRLIST function is invoked, the current environment list is cleared. After invoking the DIRLIST function, the current environment list has the following named elements:

Element	Type	Description
TAG	C	Identifies the list as one created by the DIRLIST function.
COUNT	N	Number of elements selected. If no selections are made, or if users issue a CANCEL command in the list window, COUNT is 0.
NAME	C	Name of each library member selected. If the *prefix* argument is Y the prefix is appended to the beginning of each name. There is one NAME element for each selection made.
DESC	C	Description of each library member selected. There is one DESC element for each selection made.
TYPE	C	Type of each library member selected. There is one TYPE element for each selection made.

Example

The following statements display the SAS data sets in SAS data libraries MYLIB1 and MYLIB2 and enable users to select three of them. The selections are retrieved from the current environment list.

```
listid=makelist();
rc=curlist(listid);
select=dirlist('mylib1 mylib2','data',3,'Y',' ','^mylib1.answers');
n=getnitemn(listid,'COUNT');
do i=1 to n;
   member=getnitemc(listid,'NAME',i);
   descript=getnitemc(listid,'DESC',i);
   memtype=getnitemc(listid,'TYPE',i);
   put member= descript= memtype=;
end;
```

DMWINDOW

Sets the color and highlighting attribute of lines in the display manager OUTPUT and LOG windows

New SCL Function

Window Function

Syntax

rc=DMWINDOW(*window-name,line-type,color,attribute*);

Returns	Type	Value	
rc	N	0	The operation was successful
		1	The operation failed for some reason

Arguments	Type	Value or Action
window-name	C	Name of the window in which colors and highlighting attributes are to be set. Valid names are: OUTPUT — The OUTPUT window LOG — The LOG window
line-type	C	Type of line for which the colors and highlighting attributes are to be set. Valid values are: DATA — Data line ERROR — Error line NOTES — Notes line (LOG window only) SOURCE — Source line (LOG window only) WARNING — Warning line (LOG window only) BYLINE — Byline line (OUTPUT window only) HEADER — Header line (OUTPUT window only) TITLE — Title line (OUTPUT window only)
color	C	Name of the desired color, or ' ' for no color. The following values are valid for *color* argument: BLACK CYAN MAGENTA RED BLUE GRAY ORANGE WHITE BROWN GREEN PINK YELLOW
attribute	C	Name of the desired highlighting attribute. The following values are valid for the *attribute* argument: ALLOFF HIREV BLINKING REVERSE HIGHLIGHT UNDERLINE

Description

The DMWINDOW function enables you to set the color and highlighting attribute of various lines in the OUTPUT and LOG windows

Example

The following statement sets the highlighting attribute of the title line in the OUTPUT window to blinking and its color to yellow.

```
rc=dmwindow('output','title','yellow','blinking');
```

ENDMETHOD

Ends a statement block that can be called by the METHOD routine

New SCL Statement

Method Block Statement

Syntax

ENDMETHOD;

Description

The ENDMETHOD statement marks the end of a method block in an SCL program. Use the ENDMETHOD statement with a METHOD statement to indicate a block of statements that can be called using the METHOD routine. When the method block is executed, control returns to the calling program when the ENDMETHOD statement is encountered.

See Also

Chapter 16, "Support for Program Modules"
for examples of using method blocks

METHOD (routine) and METHOD (statement) in this chapter
for information on related SCL elements

ENVLIST

Returns the list identifier of an SCL environment list

New SCL Function

List Function

Syntax

list-id=ENVLIST(⟨*class*⟩);

Returns	Type	Value
list-id	N	List identifier of the specified environment list.

Arguments	Type	Value or Action
class	C	Specifies the environment list to be identified. G Return the identifier for the global environment. L Return the identifier for local environment list. This is the default.

Description

The ENVLIST function returns the list identifier of the specified environment list. When the SAS session begins, a global environment list is created that persists for the entire session. When a SAS/AF or SAS/FSP application begins (for example, with the AF command or FSEDIT command, respectively) a local environment list is created for that application. This local environment list persists for the duration of that application and is available to each program that runs in that application (for example, invoked by the DISPLAY routine).

Environment lists are special lists that can contain numeric, character, and sublist items. These items can be fetched by their names. Environment lists provide a means of creating "global variables" that can be shared among different SCL programs, much like macro variables. Unlike macro variables, the names in an environment list do not have to be valid SAS names, and the values in an environment list can be other lists, if you want to associate a lot of data with a single name. For example, you can read the contents of a small SAS data set into a list and place the contents in the global environment list so that other SCL programs do not have to read the data set to fetch data.

The local environment list

The local environment list, which is returned by ENVLIST('L'), contains data that is available only to the current SAS/AF application invoked with the DISPLAY procedure or the AF command. Each such application has its own unique local environment list. Both the contents of a application's environment list and the list itself are deleted when the application ends.

The global environment list

The global environment list, which is returned by ENVLIST('G'), contains data that all SAS applications can share during the same SAS session. The data remains in the global environment list until an SCL program explicitly removes it. Thus, one application can put data into the global environment list, the application can exit, and another application can fetch the data.

ENVLIST

continued

You can only insert global lists into the global environment list. Global lists are those created with the 'G' option to the MAKELIST or MAKENLIST function or new lists copied from other global lists. A fatal error results if you try to insert a local list into the global list.

Recommendations for modifying environment lists
Although it is not required, it is strongly suggested that you only insert named items into the environment lists and that you choose names that are unambiguous. If you add items with simple names, there is a greater likelihood that another application may unknowingly use the same name and accidentally overwrite your data.

See Also

COPYLIST, DELITEM, DELLIST, DELNITEM, GETLATTR, GETNITEMC, GETNITEML, GETNITEMN, HASATTR, LISTLEN, MAKELIST, MAKENLIST, NAMEDITEM, NAMEITEM, SETLATTR, SETNITEMC, SETNITEML, and SETNITEMN in this chapter for information on related SCL functions

EVENT

Indicates whether users have pressed any key

New SCL Routine

Key Routine

Syntax

rc=EVENT();

Returns	Type	Value	
rc	N	1	Users pressed a key in the window since the last event call

Description

The EVENT function is useful when you want your program to continue some task while waiting for user interrupt. For example your application can read data from an external source and display the results. When users press any key, you can interrupt processing and handle the request.

■ **Host Information** .... The EVENT function does not work on MVS and CMS. On these systems you should use the attention handler exit provided in SCL. Refer to the discussion of the BREAK option for the CONTROL statement elsewhere in this chapter.

Example

The following program updates a counter and stops when users press any key.

```
INIT:
   control always;
return;

MAIN:
   if (word(1,'U')='RUN') then
      do while(event()=0);
         x+1;
         refresh;
      end;
return;

TERM:
return;
```

The variable X is a window variable. This loop increments X and redisplays the value while waiting on users. If users press any key, the program exits the loop and returns control to the procedure. The procedure then handles keystrokes. When users issue a RUN command, the loop resumes.

See Also

CONTROL BREAK statement in this chapter for information on a related SCL function

FIELD

Performs an action on or reports the state of window variables

Enhanced SCL Function

Field Function

Syntax

rc=FIELD(*action*⟨,*var-1*⟨,. . .,*var-3*⟩⟩);

The following argument has changed for Release 6.07. Refer to *SAS Screen Control Language: Reference* for details of the other syntax elements.

Arguments	Type	Value or Action

action	C	Action to perform on the specified field or fields. In addition to the actions listed for the FIELD function in Chapter 8 in *SAS Screen Control Language: Reference*, the following new options are available:
		COLOR *color* ⟨*attribute*⟩
		Changes the color and highlighting attribute of a field in the window.
		The following values are valid for the *color* argument:
		`BLACK` `CYAN` `MAGENTA` `RED`
		`BLUE` `GRAY` `ORANGE` `WHITE`
		`BROWN` `GREEN` `PINK` `YELLOW`
		The following values are valid for the optional *attribute* argument:
		`ALLOFF` `HIREV`
		`BLINKING` `REVERSE`
		`HIGHLIGHT` `UNDERLINE`
		ICON *icon-number*
		Assigns an icon number for the icon used to represent the field if it is a pushbutton. See the Appendix for a list of the available Institute-supplied icons.
		Note: The ICON option is available only in SAS/AF software.

Updated Functionality

The FIELD function now provides the capability to change the color and highlighting attribute of individual fields or groups of fields.

In SAS/AF PROGRAM entries, pushbutton fields can now be represented with icons, providing your users' host operating system and terminal devices support icons. The FIELD function enables you to define which icon will be used to represent a particular pushbutton field.

Examples

The following statement changes the color of the DATASET field to yellow and the field's highlighting attribute to underlined:

```
rc=field('color yellow underline','dataset');
```

The following statement assigns icon 17 to the pushbutton field VAR1:

```
rc=field('icon 17','var1');
```

See Also

Chapter 6, "Support for Icons," for more information on using icons in SAS/AF applications

FILELIST

Displays a selection list window containing the currently assigned filerefs and returns user selections

Enhanced SCL Function

Selection List Function

Syntax

selections=FILELIST(⟨*sel-excl*⟨,*message*⟨,*autoclose*⟨,*num-sel*⟩⟩⟩⟩);

The following argument has been added for Release 6.07. Refer to *SAS Screen Control Language: Reference* for details of the other syntax elements.

Arguments	Type	Value or Action
num-sel	N	Maximum number of items users can select from the list. Use 0 for no selections, that is, a list displayed for reference only.

Updated Functionality

The FILELIST function now permits more than one selection. It also now places values in the current environment list. When the FILELIST function is invoked, the current environment list is cleared. After invoking the FILELIST function, the current environment list has the following named elements:

Element	Type	Description
TAG	C	Identifies the list as one created by the FILELIST function.
COUNT	N	Number of elements selected. If no selections are made, or if users issue a CANCEL command in the list window, COUNT is 0.
FILEREF	C	Name of each fileref selected. There is one FILEREF element for each selection made.
FILENAME	C	Physical name of the external file for each fileref selected. There is one FILENAME element for each selection made.

Example

The following statements open a window that displays a list of all defined filerefs except for LISTNUM. Users can make to make up to five selections. The selections are retrieved from the current environment list.

```
listid=makelist();
rc=curlist(listid);
select=filelist('^listnum',' ','n',5);
n=getnitemn(listid,'COUNT');
do i=1 to n;
   fileref=getnitemc(listid,'FILEREF',i);
   physname=getnitemc(listid,'FILENAME',i);
   put fileref= physname=;
end;
```

FILENAME

Assigns or deassigns a fileref for an external file, directory, or output device

Enhanced SCL Function

Utility Function

Syntax

sysrc=FILENAME(*fileref,filename*⟨,*device*⟨,*options*⟨,*dir-ref*⟩⟩⟩);

The following argument has been added for Release 6.07. Refer to *SAS Screen Control Language: Reference* for details of the other syntax elements.

Arguments	Type	Value or Action
device	C	Type of device (if the fileref points to a hardware device rather than to a physical file). In addition to the values for this argument in Chapter 8 in *SAS Screen Control Language: Reference,* the following new option is available: PIPE — a named pipe **Note:** Some host operating systems do not support pipes.
dir-ref	C	Fileref associated with the directory or partitioned data set in which the external file resides

Updated Functionality

The FILENAME function now provides an additional parameter to specify the name of a directory or partitioned data set in which the external file resides.

Example

The following statements use the FILENAME function to assign the fileref MYFILE to the partitioned data set member V606(SCLMAN).

```
rc=filename('myfile','sclman',' ',' ','v606');
if (rc ne 0) then
   _msg_=sysmsg();
```

FILLIST

Fills the items from a saved SCL list or an SCL list with text from a SAS file or an external file

New SCL Function

List Function

Syntax

rc=FILLIST(*type,source,list-id*⟨*,attr-list-id*⟨*,description*⟩⟩);

Returns	Type	Value
rc	N	Indicator of success of the fill operation. 0 The list was successfully filled. ≠0 The list could not be filled.

Arguments	Type	Value or Action
type	C	Specifies the object containing the source for the SCL list CATALOG The text is contained in a catalog entry. FILE The text is contained in an external file named by SOURCE. FILEREF The text is contained in an external file identified by a fileref named in SOURCE.
source	C	Specifies the name of catalog entry, external file, or fileref. For catalog entries, this must be a four-level name: libref.catalog.name.etype.
list-id	N	Identifies the list to be filled.
attr-list-id	N	Identifies the list to fill with text attribute information when the value for *type* is CATALOG.
description	C	Names the variable to contain the description of the catalog entry when the *type* is CATALOG. This argument is ignored when the *type* is FILE or FILEREF.

Description

The FILLIST function fills an SCL list with text from a SAS file, an external file, or from a catalog entry. Each line of text is placed into a separate character element of the list identified by *list-id*. An item from this list can be retrieved with the GETITEMC or POPC function. The number of items contained in the filled list is determined by the number of lines of text. The lists identified by *list-id* (and *attr-list-id*, if specified and the file is a text file) must have been created with the MAKELIST function before calling the FILLIST function.

When the list is being filled with text from a catalog entry, the first character in each item in the list contains a Fortran carriage control: 1 means a new page starts with this line. All other control codes can be safely ignored for now.

When the *type* is CATALOG and the entry type specified in *source* argument is SLIST, the types of the items in the filled list are determined by the saved list, and may be character strings, numbers, and other lists. All item attributes and names are duplicated, as are the list attributes. However, the list identifier numbers are different.

If the value for *type* is CATALOG, and the text contains text attributes (such as color and highlight attributes), this information is read into the list identified by *attr-list-id*, if it is specified, one element per line of text. These attributes consist of a character item for each line of text, containing one character for each character in the line. The first character is T for a title line, H for a header line, and D for a data line. The other characters represent the text highlight attributes and color.

Attribute specifications

The attribute list returned by the FILLIST function contains one string for each line of text from the SAS catalog entry. The attribute string for each line has one character for each character of text. Each attribute character describes the SAS Display Manager (DM) color and highlight attribute.

```
Color      Value
BLUE         '10'x
RED          '20'x
PINK         '30'x
GREEN        '40'x
CYAN         '50'x
YELLOW       '60'x
WHITE        '70'x
ORANGE       '80'x
BLACK        '90'x
MAGENTA      'A0'x
GRAY         'B0'x
BROWN        'C0'x
```

Not all display devices support all DM colors.

The highlight character is coded as follows:

```
Attribute     Value
NONE          '00'x
HIGHLIGHT     '01'x
UNDERLINE     '02'x
BLINK         '04'x
REVERSE       '08'x
```

The attributes may be added to specify combined attributes. For example, the attribute value '0C'x, which is 8+4=12, represents BLINK and REVERSE. By combining the color and highlight values, you get one character. For example, the color/attribute pair GREEN UNDERLINE is represented by adding '40'x to '02'x to yield '42'x.

FILLIST

continued

Examples

Suppose you have a PROGRAM entry named FINANCE.REPORTS.MONTHLY.PROGRAM that produces the text "Net: ($45,034)" on line 45, where the text " Net: " is white with no highlight attributes while the text "($45,034)" is red reverse. The following statements read the text and attributes and print line 45:

```
text_list=makelist();
attr_list=makelist();
rc=fillist('CATALOG','FINANCE.REPORTS.MONTHLY.PROGRAM',
           text_list,attr_list);
text=substr(getitemc(text_list,45),1);
attr=substr(getitemc(attr_list,45),1);
attrhex=putc(attr,'$HEX15.');
put attrhex;
```

Note: The SUBSTR function removes the carriage control characters.

The previous statements produce the following output:

```
Net: ($45,034)
7070707070282828282828282828
```

The line of text consists of five white characters with no attributes, represented by the attribute '70'x, followed by nine red reverse characters, represented by '28'x.

The following statements perform an operation similar to a recursive list copy:

```
   /* Assume the catalog WORK.TEMP has already been created. */
rc=savelist('CATALOG','WORK.TEMP.MYLIST.SLIST',mylist);
new_list=makelist();
rc=fillist('CATALOG','WORK.TEMP.MYLIST.SLIST',new_list);
rc=delete('WORK.TEMP.TEMP.SLIST','CATALOG');
```

Lists saved in a permanent catalog with the SAVELIST function can persist across SAS sessions.

The FILLIST function automatically clears the list identified by *list-id* (and *attr-list-id*, when reading in a SAS text file) before it fills the lists.

Notes

Do not confuse text attributes (color, highlight, etc.) with list attributes as specified with the SETLATTR function.

An error condition is produced if

- either list has the NOUPDATE, NUMONLY, or FIXEDLENGTH attribute
- any item in either list cannot be removed because it has the NODELETE attribute
- *attr-list-id* is not a valid list identifier.
- *list-id* is not a valid list identifier

To check the attributes of a list or list item, use the HASATTR function. To change these attributes, use the SETLATTR function.

See Also

GETITEMC, LISTLEN, MAKELIST, POPC, SAVELIST, and SETITEMC in this chapter for information on related SCL functions

FLDATTR

Changes the color and highlighting attributes for a field based on an attribute string

New SCL Function

Field Function

Syntax

nval=FLDATTR(*field,string*);

Returns	Type	Value	
nval	N	0	The color and highlighting attribute were successfully set
		≠0	An error occurred during the setting color or highlighting attribute

Arguments	Type	Value or Action
field	C	Name of the field to be changed
string	C	String containing the color and highlighting attribute to apply and the starting and ending character positions within the field.

Description

The FLDATTR function changes color and highlighting attributes for a field based on an attribute string. You can use the STRATTR function or the FILLIST function to generate the attribute string.

Example

The following statements use the FLDATTR function to sets the color and highlighting attribute of the ABC field based on the attribute string in the variable STR.

```
   /* Define an attribute string for red and reverse video */
str=strattr('red','reverse',1,mlength(abc));
   /* Change field ABC to the attributes defined in STR */
rc=fldattr('abc',str);
```

Notes

The combination of STRATTR function and FLDATTR function is equivalent to the FLDCOLOR function.

The FLDATTR function changes the internal buffers of SAS/AF windows, so, for extended tables, you must call this function in the GETROW section of your SCL program.

See Also

FLDCOLOR and STRATTR in this chapter for information on related SCL functions

FLDCOLOR

Changes the color and highlighting attribute for a field

New SCL Function

Field Function

Syntax

nval=FLDCOLOR(*field,color,attribute,start,length*);

Returns	Type	Value	
nval	N	0	The color and highlighting attribute were successfully set
		≠0	An error occurred during the setting the color or highlighting attributes

Arguments	Type	Value or Action
field	C	String containing the name of window variable
color	C	Name of the desired color. The following values are valid for the *color* argument: BLACK CYAN MAGENTA RED BLUE GRAY ORANGE WHITE BROWN GREEN PINK YELLOW
attribute	C	Name of the desired highlighting attribute. The following values are valid for the *attribute* argument: ALLOFF HIREV BLINKING REVERSE HIGHLIGHT UNDERLINE
start	N	Character position within the specified field at which to begin applying the specified color and highlighting attribute
length	N	Number of character positions within the specified field to which the specified color and highlighting attribute are to be applied.

Description

The FLDCOLOR function sets the color and highlighting attribute of selected character positions within a field.

Note: In SAS/AF PROGRAM entries, the FLDCOLOR function works only for fields in which at least one character position has a different color or highlighting attribute than the rest of the field.

Example

The following statement uses the FLDCOLOR function to change the color of the third through seventh character positions in ABC field to red and the highlighting attribute of those positions to high intensity.

```
rc=fldcolor('abc','red','highlight',3,5);
```

FLDCOLOR

continued

See Also

FLDATTR and STRATTR in this chapter for information on related SCL functions

FOPEN

Opens an external file

Enhanced SCL Function

File Function

Syntax

file-id=FOPEN(*fileref*⟨*,open-mode*⟨*,record-length*⟨*,record-format*⟩⟩⟩);

The following argument has changed for Release 6.07. Refer to *SAS Screen Control Language: Reference* for details of the other syntax elements.

Arguments	Type	Value or Action
open-mode	C	Open mode. In addition to the mode identifiers listed for the FOPEN function in Chapter 8 in *SAS Screen Control Language: Reference*, the following new options are available: S — Sequential input mode for pipes and other sequential devices such as hardware ports. The file is opened for reading only. W — Sequential output mode for pipes and other sequential devices such as ports. The file is opened for output at the beginning of the file.

Updated Functionality

The FOPEN function now supports two additional open modes:

- Sequential input mode for pipes and other sequential devices such as hardware ports.
- Sequential output mode for pipes and other sequential devices such as ports.

Examples

The following statement opens the file with the fileref MYFILE for sequential input:

```
rc=fopen('myfile','S',0,'D');
```

The following statement opens the file with the fileref MYFILE for sequential output:

```
rc=fopen('myfile','W',0,'D');
```

GETITEMC

Returns the value of a character item that is identified by its position in an SCL list

New SCL Function

List Function

Syntax

cval=GETITEMC(*list-id*⟨,*index*⟩);

Returns	Type	Value
cval	C	The character value stored at the specified position.

Arguments	Type	Value or Action
list-id	N	Identifies the list to which the character item belongs.
index	N	Specifies the item's position in the list. *Index* defaults to 1, the first item in the list. If *index* is a positive number, the item is at position *index* from the beginning of the list. If *index* is a negative number, the item is at position abs(*index*) from the end of the list.

Description

The GETITEMC function returns the value of a character item from the SCL list identified by *list-id*. The item is specified by the number of its position in the list. To determine whether a list item is character before using the GETITEMC function, you can use the ITEMTYPE function.

Example

The following statements return the third and first character items from the list identified in the LISTID variable:

```
citem=getitemc(listid,3);
citem=getitemc(listid);
```

Notes

An error condition is produced if

- the indexed item is not a character value
- the absolute value of *index* is zero or greater than the number of items in the list
- *list-id* is not a valid list identifier.

See Also

DELITEM, GETLATTR, GETITEML, GETITEMN, GETNITEMC, GETNITEML, GETNITEMN, HASATTR, INSERTC, INSERTL, INSERTN, ITEMTYPE, LISTLEN, MAKELIST, MAKENLIST, POPC, POPL, POPN, SEARCHC, SEARCHL, SEARCHN, SETITEMC, SETITEML, SETITEMN, SETLATTR, SETNITEMC, SETNITEML, and SETNITEMN in this chapter for information on related SCL functions

GETITEML

Returns the list identifier stored as a sublist item that is identified by its position in an SCL list

New SCL Function

List Function

Syntax

sublist-id=GETITEML(*list-id*⟨,*index*⟩);

Returns	Type	Value
sublist-id	N	The list identifier stored at the specified position in the list.

Arguments	Type	Value or Action
list-id	N	Identifies the list to which the sublist item belongs.
index	N	Specifies the item's position in the list. *Index* defaults to 1, the first item in the list. If *index* is a positive number, the item is at position *index* from the beginning of the list. If *index* is a negative number, the item is at position abs(*index*) from the end of the list.

Description

The GETITEML function returns the list identifier stored as a sublist item in the SCL list identified by *list-id*. The item is specified by the number of its position in the list. To determine the type of an item in a list before using the GETITEML function, you can use the ITEMTYPE function.

Example

The following statements return the third and first sublist items from the list identified in the LISTID variable:

```
sublist=getiteml(listid,3);
sublist=getiteml(listid);
```

Notes

An error condition is produced if

- the indexed item is not a sublist
- the absolute value of *index* is zero or greater than the number of items in the list
- *list-id* is not a valid list identifier.

See Also

DELITEM, GETLATTR, GETITEMC, GETITEMN, GETNITEMC, GETNITEML, GETNITEMN, HASATTR, INSERTC, INSERTL, INSERTN, ITEMTYPE, LISTLEN, MAKELIST, MAKENLIST, POPC, POPL, POPN, SEARCHC, SEARCHL, SEARCHN, SETITEMC, SETITEML, SETITEMN, SETLATTR, SETNITEMC, SETNITEML, and SETNITEMN in this chapter for information on related SCL functions

GETITEMN

Returns the value a numeric item that is identified by its position in an SCL list

New SCL Function

List Function

Syntax

nval=GETITEMN(*list-id*⟨,*index*⟩);

Returns	Type	Value
nval	N	The numeric value stored at the specified position.

Arguments	Type	Value or Action
list-id	N	Identifies the list to which the numeric item belongs.
index	N	Specifies the item's position in the list. *Index* defaults to 1, the first item in the list. If *index* is a positive number, the item is at position *index* from the beginning of the list. If *index* is a negative number, the item is at position abs(*index*) from the end of the list.

Description

The GETITEMN function returns the value of a numeric item from the SCL list identified by *list-id*. The item is specified by the number of its position in the list. To determine whether a list item is numeric before using the GETITEMN function, you can use the ITEMTYPE function.

Example

The following statements return the third and first numeric items from the list identified in the LISTID variable:

```
nitem=getitemn(listid,3);
nitem=getitemn(listid);
```

Notes

An error condition is produced if

- the indexed item is not a number
- the absolute value of *index* is zero or greater than the number of item of in the list
- *list-id* is not a valid list identifier.

See Also

DELITEM, GETITEMC, GETITEML, GETNITEMC, GETNITEML, GETNITEMN, GETLATTR, HASATTR, INSERTC, INSERTL, INSERTN, ITEMTYPE, LISTLEN, MAKELIST, MAKENLIST, POPC, POPL, POPN, SEARCHC, SEARCHL, SEARCHN, SETITEMC, SETITEML, SETITEMN, SETLATTR, SETNITEMC, SETNITEML, and SETNITEMN in this chapter for information on related SCL functions

GETLATTR

Reports the attributes of an SCL list or an item in an SCL list

SCL Function

List Function

Syntax

attributes=GETLATTR(*list-id*⟨,*index*⟩);

Returns	Type	Value
attributes	C	The attributes assigned to the list or the list item.

Arguments	Type	Value or Action
list-id	N	Identifies the list whose attributes are to be reported or the list containing the item whose attributes are to be reported.
index	N	Specifies the item's position in the list. If this argument is specified, the GETLATTR function returns the attributes associated with the indexed item instead of the entire list. *Index* defaults to 1, the first item in the list. If *index* is a positive number, the item is at position *index* from the beginning of the list. If *index* is a negative number, the item is at position abs(*index*) from the end of the list.

Description

The GETLATTR function reports the attributes associated with the SCL list or an item in the SCL list identified by *list-id*. The attributes contained in *attributes* may be used to assign attributes to another list or item. The variable assigned as *attributes* contains a blank around each attribute so it is easy to determine if an attribute exists by searching the variable for an attribute name.

Example

The following statements obtain the attributes for the list identified in the LISTID variable, and for an item in that list:

```
listattrs=getlattr(listid);
itemattrs=getlattr(lisltid,i);
```

See Also

HASATTR, MAKELIST, MAKENLIST, and SETLATTR in this chapter for information on related SCL functions

GETNITEMC

Returns the value of a character item identified by its name in an SCL list

New SCL Function

List Function

Syntax

cval=GETNITEMC(*list-id*,*name*⟨,*occurrence*⟨,*index*⟨,*default*⟩⟩⟩);

Returns	Type	Value
cval	C	The value of the character item that is identified by its name.

Arguments	Type	Value or Action
list-id	N	Identifies the list to be searched.
name	C	Specifies the name of the item to fetch from the list. Item names are converted to uppercase and trailing blanks are ignored when searching the list for a matching name. Thus, the names 'abc' and 'Abc' are converted to 'ABC'.
occurrence	N	Specifies the number of the occurrence of the named item to be returned. The default is 1 for the first occurrence of the item.
index	N	Specifies the position to start searching the list for the item. *Index* defaults to 1, the first item in the list. If *index* is a positive number, the search starts at position *index* from the beginning of the list and continues to the end of the list. If *index* is a negative number, the search starts at position abs(*index*) from the end of the list and continues to the beginning of the list.
default	C	Specifies a default character value to return from GETNITEMC if the specified item is not found.

Description

The GETNITEMC function returns the value of the character item that is identified by its name in the SCL list specified by *list-id*. By default, the function starts searching at the beginning of the list and returns the first item found with the specified name. However, you can specify that the search start at a different place in the list by specifying an *index* other than 1. You can also specify a different occurrence of the item (for example, the second, tenth, or twentieth) by specifying an *occurrence* other than 1. If the search does not succeed and you have specified a default character value as the last parameter, that default value is returned instead of an error condition.

The GETNITEMC function combines the actions of the NAMEDITEM function and the GETITEMC function. For example, the statement

```
s=getnitemc(directors,'Software Sales',2,-1);
```

is equivalent to the following statements:

```
ssi=nameditem(directors,'Software Sales',2,-1);
s=getitemc(directors,ssi);
```

Note that the preceding statements halt the program if there are fewer than two items named 'Software Sales' in the list identified by DIRECTORS. Omitting the default value from the GETNITEMC statement designates that the character item must exist in the list. If your application is more general and the named item may not be in the list, you should supply a character value for DEFAULTC in the GETNITEMC statement.

```
ssi=nameditem(directors,'Software Sales',2,-1);
if ssi ne 0 then
   s=getitemc(directors,ssi);
else
   s=defaultc;
```

The preceding program statements can be written more efficiently as

```
s=getnitemc(directorid,'Software Sales',2,-1,defaultc);
```

Notes

An error condition results if

- the named item specified is not a character value
- the named item does not exist and no default value is specified in the GETNITEMC statement
- the absolute value for *index* is zero or greater than the number of items in the list
- *list-id* is not a valid list identifier.

See Also

DELNITEM, GETITEMC, GETITEML, GETITEMN, GETLATTR, GETNITEML, GETNITEMN, HASATTR, INSERTC, INSERTL, INSERTN, ITEMTYPE, MAKELIST, MAKENLIST, NAMEDITEM, NAMEITEM, POPC, POPL, POPN, SETITEMC, SETITEML, SETITEMN, SETLATTR, SETNITEMC, SETNITEML, and SETNITEMN in this chapter for information on related SCL functions

GETNITEML

Returns the identifier for the sublist item identified by its name in an SCL list

New SCL Function

List Function

Syntax

sublist-id=GETNITEML(*list-id*,*name*⟨,*occurrence*⟨,*index*⟨,*default-list-id*⟩⟩⟩);

Returns	Type	Value
sublist-id	N	The list identifier of the sublist item that is identified by its name.

Arguments	Type	Value or Action
list-id	N	Identifies the list to be searched.
name	C	Specifies the name of the item to fetch from the list. Item names are converted to uppercase and trailing blanks are ignored when searching the list for a matching name. Thus, the names 'abc' and 'Abc ' are converted to 'ABC'.
occurrence	N	The number of the occurrence of the named item to be returned. The default is 1 for the first occurrence of the item.
index	N	Specifies the position to searching the list for the item. *Index* defaults to 1, the first item in the list. If *index* is a positive number, the search starts at position *index* from the beginning of the list and continues to the end of the list. If *index* is a negative number, the search starts at position abs(*index*) from the end of the list and continues toward the beginning of the list.
default-list-id	N	Specifies a default list identifier to return if the specified sublist is not found.

Description

The GETNITEML function returns the list identifier of the sublist item that is identified by its name in the SCL list identified by *list-id*. By default, the function starts searching at the beginning of the list and returns the first item found with the specified name. However, you can specify that the search start at a different place in the list by specifying an *index* other than 1. You can also specify a different occurrence of the item (for example, the second, tenth, or twentieth) by specifying an *occurrence* other than 1. If the search does not succeed and you have specified a default list identifier as the last parameter, that default value is returned instead of an error condition.

The GETNITEML function combines the actions of the NAMEDITEM functions and the GETITEML function. For example, the following statement

```
listid=getniteml(emp_list,'Marketing',2,-10);
```

is equivalent to the statements

```
mpos=nameditem(emp_list,'Marketing',2,-10);
listid=getniteml(emp_list,mpos);
```

Note that the preceding statements halt the program if there are fewer than two items named 'Marketing' in the EMP_LIST list. Omitting the default value from the GETNITEML statement specifies that the sublist item must exist in the list. If your application is more general and the named item may not be in the list, you should supply a list identifier value for DEFAULT in the GETNITEML statement.

```
mpos=nameditem(emp_list,'Marketing',2,-1);
if ssitemnum ne 0 then
   sslistid=getiteml(emp_list,mpos);
else
   sslistid=defaultlistid;
```

The preceding program statements can be more efficiently written as:

```
sslistid=getniteml(emp_list,'Marketing',2,-1,defaultlistid);
```

Notes

An error results if

- the named item does not contain a sublist
- the absolute value for *index* is zero or greater than the number of items in the list
- the named item does not exist
- *list-id* is not a valid list identifier.

See Also

DELNITEM, GETITEMC, GETITEML, GETITEMN, GETLATTR, GETNITEMC, GETNITEMN, HASATTR, INSERTC, INSERTL, INSERTN, ITEMTYPE, MAKELIST, MAKENLIST, NAMEDITEM, NAMEITEM, POPC, POPL, POPN, SETITEMC, SETITEML, SETITEMN, SETLATTR, SETNITEMC, SETNITEML, and SETNITEMN in this chapter for information on related SCL functions

GETNITEMN

Returns the numeric value of a list item identified by its name in an SCL list

New SCL Function

List Function

Syntax

nval=GETNITEMN(*list-id,name*⟨*,occurrence*⟨*,index*⟨*,default*⟩⟩⟩);

Returns	Type	Value
nval	N	The value of a numeric item that is identified by its name. The numeric value of the item identified by *name* in the list identified by *list-id*.

Arguments	Type	Value or Action
list-id	N	Identifies the list to be searched.
name	C	Specifies the name of the item to fetch from the list. Item names are converted to uppercase and trailing blanks are ignored when searching the list for a matching name. Thus, the names 'abc' and 'Abc' are converted to 'ABC'.
n	N	Specifies the number of the occurrence of the named item to be returned. The default is 1 for the first occurrence of the item.
index	N	Specifies the position to start searching the list for the item. *Index* defaults to 1, the first item in the list. If *index* is a positive number, the search starts at position *index* from the beginning of the list and continues to the end of the list. If *index* is a negative number, the search starts at position abs(*index*) from the end of the list and continues to the beginning of the list.
default	N	Specifies a default numeric value to return if the specified item is not found.

Description

The GETNITEMN function returns the value of the numeric item that is identified by its name in the SCL list identified by *list-id*. By default, the function starts searching at the beginning of the list and returns the first item found with the specified name. However, you can specify that the search start at a different place in the list by specifying an *index* other than 1. You can also specify a different occurrence of the item (for example, the second, tenth, or twentieth) by specifying an *occurrence* other than 1. If the search does not succeed and you have specified a default numeric value as the last parameter, that default value is returned instead of an error condition.

The GETNITEMN function combines the actions of the NAMEDITEM function and the GETITEMN function. For example, the following statement

```
numval=getnitemn(revenue,'Eastern Region');
```

is equivalent to the statements

```
eastpos=nameditem(revenue,'Eastern Region');
numval=getniteml(revenue,eastpos);
```

Note that the preceding statements halt the program if there are fewer than two items named 'Eastern Region' in the list identified by DIRECTORID. Omitting the default value from the GETNITEMN statement specifies that the numeric item must exist in the list. If your application is more general and the named item may not be in the list, you should supply a numeric value for DEFAULTN in the GETNITEMN statement.

```
eastpos=nameditem(revenue,'Eastern Region');
if eastpos ne 0 then
   ssval=getnitenm(revenue,eastpos);
else
   ssval=defaultnum;
```

The preceding program statements can be more efficiently written as:

```
ssval=getnitemn(revenue,'Eastern Region',1,1,defaultnum);
```

Notes

An error condition results if

- the named item does not contain a numeric value
- the named item does not exist
- the absolute value for *index* is zero or greater than the number of items in the list
- *list-id* is not a valid list identifier.

See Also

DELNITEM, GETITEMC, GETITEML, GETITEMN, GETLATTR, GETNITEMC, GETNITEML, HASATTR, INSERTC, INSERTL, INSERTN, ITEMTYPE, MAKELIST, MAKENLIST, NAMEDITEM, NAMEITEM, POPC, POPL, POPN, SETITEMC, SETITEML, SETITEMN, SETLATTR, SETNITEMC, SETNITEML, and SETNITEMN in this chapter for information on related SCL functions

GRAY

Grays a single station or an entire choice group

New SCL Function

Choice Group Function

SAS/AF software only

Syntax

rc=GRAY(*choice-group*⟨,*station*⟨,*row*⟩⟩);

Returns	Type	Value	
rc	N	0	Specified choice group or station was successfully grayed
		≠0	Specified choice group or station could not be grayed

Arguments	Type	Value or Action
choice-group	C	Choice group name assigned in the ATTR window
station	N	Number of the field within the choice group. This value should be greater than 0 and no larger than the total number of stations defined for the choice group. Use the value 0 as a placeholder if the entire choice group at a specified row is to be grayed.
row	N	Valid row number when the choice group is in the scrollable section of an extended table.

Description

The GRAY function grays the specified station of a choice group or the entire choice group in a SAS/AF application. A grayed station or choice group cannot be selected by users.

Example

The following statements use the GRAY function to prohibit users from making a selection from the choice group WINE when the value of the AGE variable is less than 21.

```
if (age<21) then
   rc=gray('wine')
else
   rc=ungray('wine');
```

Notes

You can also use the ACTIVATE function to gray a station in a choice group by passing the negative value of the station number.

For linked action fields in choice groups, the ACTION-type pair is considered one station. For example, the following line in a DISPLAY window defines three linked action fields:

```
& &A_____      & &B_____      & &C_____
```

To gray the linked action pair for field B, you pass in 2 for the value of *station*, not 4.

See Also

ACTIVATE, CURWORD, and ISACTIVE
: in Chapter 8 in *SAS Screen Control Language: Reference* for information on related SCL functions

ISGRAY and UNGRAY
: in this chapter for information on related SCL functions

HASATTR

Reports whether an SCL list or list item has a specified attribute

New SCL Function

List Function

Syntax

rc=HASATTR(*list-id*,*attribute*⟨,*index*⟩);

Returns	Type	Value
rc	N	Indicator of the success of the operation. 1 The list or item has the specified attribute. 0 The list or item does not have the specified attribute.

Arguments	Type	Value or Action
list-id	N	Identifies the list to be queried. This value was returned by the function that created the list.
attribute	C	Specifies the name of an SCL list attribute, as described in the entry for the SETLATTR function. In addition, you can test for the following special attributes: G returns 1 if the list is a global list L returns 1 if the list is a local list
index	N	Specifies the position of the list item whose attribute is to be reported. *Index* defaults to 1, the first item in the list. If *index* is a positive number, the item is at position *index* from the beginning of the list. If *index* is a negative number, the item is at position abs(*index*) from the end of the list.

Description

The HASATTR function reports whether a list or list item has the specified SCL list attribute. If no value is specified for *index*, this function queries the attribute of the list. If a value that is not 0 is specified for *index*, it queries the attribute of an item in the list. For example, the following statement clears the list identified by MYLIST only if it has the UPDATE attribute.

```
if hasattr(mylist,'UPDATE') then rc=clearlist(mylist);
```

Example

The following statement shows how to determine if the third item in a list has the FIXEDTYPE attribute:

```
isfixed=hasattr(mylist,'FIXEDTYPE',3);
```

Notes

An error condition results if

- the absolute value for *index* is greater than the number of items in the list.
- *list-id* is not a valid list identifier.

See Also

GETLATTR, MAKELIST, MAKENLIST, and SETLATTR in this chapter for information on related SCL functions

ICON

Associates an icon number with the window

New SCL Function

Window Function

Syntax

rc=ICON(*icon-number*);

Returns	Type	Value	
rc	N	0	specified icon number was associated with the window
		$\neq 0$	An error or warning condition occurred during the operation

Arguments	Type	Value or Action
icon-number	N	Icon number. See the Appendix for a list of the available Institute-supplied icons.

Description

The ICON function associates an icon number with the window. When users reduce the window into an icon, display manager uses the specified icon to represent the window.

Note: Not all hosts support this feature.

Example

The following statement associates icon number 59 with the current window. Icon 59 is the icon for SAS/EIS software in the Institute-supplied set of icon definitions.

```
rc=icon(59);
```

See Also

Chapter 6, "Support for Icons," for more information on using icons in SAS/AF applications

IMPORT

Creates a SAS data set from an external file

Enhanced SCL Function

Utility Function

Syntax

name=IMPORT(*data-set-name,file*⟨,'DEFINE'⟩);

Note: The syntax for the IMPORT function is unchanged from Release 6.06. See Chapter 8 in *SAS Screen Control Language: Reference* for details.

Updated Functionality

The IMPORT function opens the IMPORT window for you to define the new data set. If you use the VERIFY option with the RUN command to allow interactive error correction while data are being read in, the function will open the VERIFY window in which you can modify invalid data values.

The CONTINUE, GO, and CANCEL commands were formerly valid in the VERIFY window. With Release 6.07, the valid commands for the VERIFY window are changed to

RUN
: the value was corrected and continuous error checking is desired.

GO
: the value may or may not have been corrected and no continuous error checking is desired. This also causes the statistics window not to be updated anymore.

CANCEL
: cancel the RUN command.

If you do not specify the VERIFY option with the RUN command, the statistics window is no longer updated after every 40 records.

The following additional commands are now valid in the IMPORT window:

SAVE *entry*
: saves the contents of the IMPORT window to a catalog entry. The value for *entry* must be a four-level name, and the fourth level must be SOURCE.

FILE *fileref* | "*filename*"
: saves the contents of the IMPORT window to an external file.

INSERTC

Inserts a character item into an SCL list

New SCL Function

List Function

Syntax

new-list-id=INSERTC(*list-id,cval*⟨,*index*⟨,*name*⟩⟩);

Returns	Type	Value
new-list-id	N	The list identifier of the modified list. The returned value is the same as the *list-id* argument.

Arguments	Type	Value or Action
list-id	N	Identifies the list to be inserted into.
cval	C	Specifies the character value to insert into the list.
index	N	Specifies the position at which the character item is to be inserted. *Index* defaults to 1, the first item in the list. If *index* is a positive number, the item is inserted at position *index* from the beginning of the list. If *index* is a negative number, the item is inserted at position abs(*index*) from the end of the list.
name	C	Specifies the optional item name for the inserted character item. *Name* is converted to uppercase and trailing blanks are removed. If omitted, the item is not given a name.

Description

The INSERTC function inserts a character item into the SCL list identified by *list-id*. The character item is inserted by increasing the length of the list by one and shifting all items between position *index* and the end of the list down by one and then assigning the item at position *index* to the new value. Thus, after you insert a character item at position *index*, you can retrieve it from position *index* with the GETITEMC function.

The INSERTC function does not make a copy of the list. The insertion is performed in place. You can append an item to an SCL list of length *n* by inserting at *index*=n+1 or at *index* −1.

Examples

The following examples assume that LISTID already exists and contains some values.

The following statement inserts `Australia` at the beginning of the list:

```
listid=insertc(listid,'Australia');
```

The following statement inserts `U.S.A.` at the end of the list:

```
listid=insertc(listid,'U.S.A.',-1);
```

The following statement inserts **CANADA** at the third position in the list:

```
listid=insertc(listid,'CANADA',3);
```

After this insertion, the following statement returns the value that was third in the list before inserting **CANADA** shifted it from the third to the fourth position.

```
cval=getitemc(listid,4);
```

Notes

An error condition results if:

- *list-id* is not a valid list identifier
- the value for *index* is greater than the number of items in the list.
- the list has any of the following attributes:
  - NOUPDATE
  - FIXEDLENGTH
  - NUMONLY
  - SASNAMES, and the variable for *name* is omitted or it is not a valid SAS name
  - NODUPNAMES, and the value for *name* duplicates the name of a list item.

To check the attributes of a list or list item, use the HASATTR function. To change these attributes, use the SETLATTR function.

See Also

DELITEM, DELNITEM, GETITEMC, GETITEML, GETITEMN, GETLATTR, GETNITEMC, GETNITEML, GETNITEMN, HASATTR, INSERTL, INSERTN, ITEMTYPE, LISTLEN, MAKELIST, MAKENLIST, NAMEDITEM, NAMEITEM, POPC, POPL, POPN, SEARCHC, SEARCHL, SEARCHN, SETITEMC, SETITEML, SETITEMN, SETLATTR, SETNITEMC, SETNITEML, and SETNITEMN in this chapter for information on related SCL functions

INSERTL

Inserts a sublist item into an SCL list

New SCL Function

List Function

Syntax

new-list-id=INSERTL(*list-id*,*sublist-id*⟨,*index*⟨,*name*⟩⟩);

Returns	Type	Value
new-list-id	N	The list identifier of the modified list. This value is the same as *list-id*.

Arguments	Type	Value or Action
list-id	N	Identifies the list to be inserted into.
sublist-id	N	Specifies the identifier for the sublist to insert into the list.
index	N	Specifies the position at which the identifier for the sublist item is to be inserted. *Index* defaults to 1, the first item in the list. If *index* is a positive number, the item is inserted at position *index* from the beginning of the list. If *index*is a negative number, the item is inserted at position abs(*index*) from the end of the list.
name	C	Specifies the optional item name for the inserted sublist item. *Name* is converted to uppercase and trailing blanks are removed. If omitted, the item is not given a name.

Description

The INSERTL function inserts a sublist item in the SCL list identified by *list-id*. The item is inserted by increasing the length of the list by one and shifting all items between position *index* and the end of the list down by one and then assigning the item at position *index* to the new value. Thus, after you insert a list item at position *index*, you can retrieve it with the GETITEML function.

The INSERTL function does not make a copy of the list. The insertion is performed in place. You can append an item to an SCL list of length *n* by inserting at *index*=n+1 or at *index*=−1.

Examples

The following examples assume that LISTID already exists and contains some values.

The following statement inserts a sublist at the beginning of the list.

```
listid=insertl(listid,newlist);
```

The following statement inserts a sublist at the end of the list.

```
listid=insertl(listid,newlist,-1);
```

The following statement inserts the sublist NEWLIST so it becomes the third item from the end of the list.

```
listid=insertl(listid,newlist,-3);
```

Notes

An error condition results if

- the list has any of the following attributes:
  - NOUPDATE
  - FIXEDLENGTH
  - NUMONLY
  - CHARONLY
  - SASNAMES, and the variable for *name* is omitted or it is not a valid SAS name
  - NODUPNAMES, and the value for *name* duplicates the name of a list item.
- you attempt to insert a local list into a global list
- the absolute value of *index* is zero or greater than the number of items in the list.
- *sublist-id* is not a valid list identifier
- *list-id* is not a valid list identifier

To check the attributes of a list or list item, use the HASATTR function. To change these attributes, use the SETLATTR function.

See Also

DELITEM, DELNITEM, GETITEMC, GETITEML, GETITEMN, GETLATTR, GETNITEMC, GETNITEML, GETNITEMN, HASATTR, INSERTC, INSERTN, ITEMTYPE, LISTLEN, MAKELIST, MAKENLIST, NAMEDITEM, NAMEITEM, POPC, POPL, POPN, SEARCHC, SEARCHL, SEARCHN, SETITEMC, SETITEML, SETITEMN, SETLATTR, SETNITEMC, SETNITEML, and SETNITEMN in this chapter for information on related SCL functions

INSERTN

Inserts a numeric item into an SCL list

New SCL Function

List Function

Syntax

new-list-id=INSERTN(*list-id*,*nval*⟨,*index*⟨,*name*⟩⟩);

Returns	Type	Value
new-list-id	N	The list identifier of the modified list. This variable is the same as the *list-id* argument.

Arguments	Type	Value or Action
list-id	N	Identifies the list to be inserted into.
nval	N	Specifies the numeric value to insert into the list.
index	N	Specifies the position at which the numeric item is to be inserted. *Index* defaults to 1, the first item in the list. If *index* is a positive number, the item is inserted at position *index* from the beginning of the list. If *index* is a negative number, the item is inserted at position abs(*index*) from the end of the list.
name	C	Specifies the optional item name for the inserted numeric item. *Name* is converted to uppercase and trailing blanks are removed. If omitted, the item is not given a name.

Description

The INSERTN function inserts a numeric item in the SCL list specified by *list-id*. The item is inserted by increasing the length of the list by one and shifting all items between position *index* and the end of the list down by one and then assigning the item at position *index* to the new value. Thus, after you insert a numeric item at position *index*, you can retrieve it with the GETITEMN function.

The INSERTN function does not make a copy of the list. The insertion is performed in place. You can append an item to an SCL list of length *n* by inserting at *index*=n+1 or at *index*=−1.

Example

Assume the list MYLIST contains four items, named A, B, C, and D, with the values 1, 4, 9, and 16, respectively. The following statements insert two new items: a string at the default position 1 (the beginning of the list), and a number at position -1 (the end of the list). The new number is given the name E.

```
call putlist(mylist,'Before: ',0);
mylist=insertc(mylist,'Squares');
mylist=insertn(mylist,25, -1,'E');
call putlist(mylist,'After: ',0);
```

The previous statements produce the following output:

```
Before: (A=1
         B=4
         C=9
         D=16
         )
After: ('Squares'
        A=1
        B=4
        C=9
        D=16
        E=25
        )
```

Notes

An error condition results if

- the list has any of the following attributes:
  - NOUPDATE
  - FIXEDLENGTH
  - CHARONLY
  - SASNAMES, and the variable for *name* is omitted or it is not a valid SAS name
  - NODUPNAMES, and the value for *name* duplicates the name of a list item.
- *list-id* is not a valid list identifier
- the absolute value for *index* is greater than zero or the number of items in the list.

To check the attributes of a list or list item, use the HASATTR function. To change these attributes, use the SETLATTR function.

See Also

DELITEM, DELNITEM, GETITEMC, GETITEML, GETITEMN, GETLATTR, GETNITEMC, GETNITEML, GETNITEMN, HASATTR, INSERTC, INSERTL, ITEMTYPE, LISTLEN, MAKELIST, MAKENLIST, NAMEDITEM, NAMEITEM, POPC, POPL, POPN, SEARCHC, SEARCHL, SEARCHN, SETITEMC, SETITEML, SETITEMN, SETLATTR, SETNITEMC, SETNITEML, and SETNITEMN in this chapter for information on related SCL functions

ISGRAY

Indicates whether a choice group or station is grayed

New SCL Function

Choice Group Function

SAS/AF Software Only

Syntax

rc=ISGRAY(*choice-group*⟨,*station*⟨,*row*⟩⟩);

Returns	Type	Value	
rc	N	1	Specified station is grayed.
		0	Specified station in not grayed. If the *station* argument is omitted, a return code of 0 indicates that no station in the specified choice group is grayed.
		−*n*	Entire choice group is grayed, where *n* is the total number of stations.
		m	Not entire choice group is grayed, but *m* stations are.

Arguments	Type	Value or Action
choice-group	C	Choice group name assigned in the ATTR window
station	N	Number of the field within the choice group. A valid station has to be greater than 0 and no larger than the total stations defined for the choice group.
row	N	Valid row number when the choice group is in the scrollable section of an extended table.

Description

The ISGRAY function returns whether a choice group or station is grayed out. Passing in the station number returns TRUE (1) if that station is grayed; otherwise, FALSE (0).

If a station number is not passed in, the ISGRAY function returns one of the three values:

−*n* All stations in the choice group are grayed out, where n is the total number of stations.

0 None of the stations in the choice group is grayed.

m Not all stations in the choice group are grayed out, but m of them are.

Examples

The following statements test whether the choice group WINE at the third row of an extended table is grayed.

```
if (isgray('wine',0,3)) then
   do;
      /* SCL program statements */
   end;
```

You could also find out how many stations are defined for a choice group using the following statements:

```
rc=gray('wine');
total=-isgray('wine');
```

See Also

ACTIVATE, CURWORD, ISACTIVE
: in Chapter 8 in *SAS Screen Control Language: Reference* for information on related SCL functions

GRAY and UNGRAY
: in this chapter for information on related SCL functions

ITEMTYPE

Reports the type of an item in an SCL list

New SCL Function

List Function

Syntax

type=ITEMTYPE(*list-id*⟨,*index*⟩);

Returns	Type	Value
type	C	The type of the item being queried. C The item is a character item. N The item is a numeric item. L The item is a sublist item.

Arguments	Type	Value or Action
list-id	N	Identifies the list containing the item being queried.
index	N	Specifies the item's position in the list. *Index* defaults to 1, the first item in the list. If *index* is a positive number, the item is at position *index* from the beginning of the list. If *index* is a negative number, the item is at position abs(*index*) from the end of the list.

Description

The ITEMTYPE function reports the type of an item in the SCL list identified by *list-id*. An item's type is determined by the function that creates the item.

The item type ...	Is created by the function ...
C (character)	SETITEMC, SETNITEMC, INSERTC
N (numeric)	SETITEMN, SETNITEMN, INSERTC
L (sublist)	SETITEML, SETNITEML, INSERTC

Notes

An error condition results if

- the absolute value of *index* is zero or greater than the number of items in the list
- *list-id* is not a valid list identifier.

See Also

GETITEMC, GETITEML, GETITEMN, GETNITEMC, GETNITEML, GETNITEMN, INSERTC, INSERTL, INSERTN, MAKELIST, MAKENLIST, POPC, POPL, POPN, SEARCHC, SEARCHL, SEARCHN, SETITEMC, SETITEML, SETITEMN, SETNITEMC, SETNITEML, and SETNITEMN in this chapter for information on related SCL functions

LASTCMD

Returns the text of the last command issued from the application window

New SCL Function

Command Function

Syntax

cval=LASTCMD();

Returns	Type	Value
cval	C	Text of the last command issued from application window

Description

The LASTCMD function returns the last command that users issued in the application's window.

Example

The following statements use the LASTCMD function to retrieve the last command issued in the window and execute a subroutine based on that command name.

```
MAIN:
   cmd=lastcmd();
   if cmd='GO' then
      link gopart;
   else
      link nogopart;
```

See Also

WORD in Chapter 8 in *SAS Screen Control Language: Reference* for information on a related SCL function

LASTKEY

Returns the number of the last function key issued from the window

New SCL Function

Key Function

Syntax

nval=LASTKEY();

Returns	Type	Value	
nval	N	≥0	Function key number issued from the application window. This number corresponds to the order in which the keys are displayed in the KEYS window.
		0	No function key was pressed.

Description

The LASTKEY function returns the number of the last function key issued by users in the application window. The value returned is the ordinal position of the key definition in the KEYS window.

Example

The following statements return the number of the last function key the user pressed:

```
keynum=lastkey();
if (keynum ne 0) then
   put 'Last function key is ' keynum;
else
   put 'Last function key is not defined';
```

Notes

To retrieve the name of the last function issued by a user, use the FKEYNAME function.

See Also

FKEYNAME in Chapter 8 in *SAS Screen Control Language: Reference* for information on a related SCL function

LIBLIST

Displays a selection list window containing libref names and returns user selections

Enhanced SCL Function

Selection List Function

Syntax

selections=LIBLIST(⟨*sel-excl*⟨,*engine*⟨,*message*⟨,*autoclose*⟨,*num-sel*⟩⟩⟩⟩⟩);

The following argument has been added for Release 6.07. Refer to *SAS Screen Control Language: Reference* for details of the other syntax elements.

Arguments	Type	Value or Action
num-sel	N	Maximum number of items users can select from the list. Use 0 for no selections, that is, a list displayed for reference only.

Updated Functionality

The LIBLIST function now permits more than one selection. It also now places values in the current environment list.

When the LIBLIST function is invoked, the current environment list is cleared. After invoking the LIBLIST function, the environment list has the following named elements:

Element	Type	Description
TAG	C	Identifies the list as one created by the LIBLIST function.
COUNT	N	Number of elements selected. If no selections are made, or if users issue a CANCEL command in the list window, COUNT is 0.
LIBREF	C	Name of each libref selected. There is one LIBREF element for each selection made.
LIBNAME	C	Physical name of the operating system file for each libref selected. There is one LIBNAME element for each selection made.

Example

The following statements display all librefs except MYLIB1 and MYLIB2. Users can make up to five selections. The selections are retrieved from the current environment list.

```
listid=makelist();
rc=curlist(listid);
select=liblist('^mylib1 mylib2',' ','Choose a libref','n',5);
n=getnitemn(listid,'COUNT');
do i=1 to n;
   libref=getitemc(listid,'LIBREF',i);
   physname=getitemc(listid,'LIBNAME',i);
   put libref= physname=;
end;
```

LISTC

Displays a selection list window containing character values and returns user selections

Enhanced SCL Function

Selection List Function

Syntax

cval=LISTC(*entry*⟨,*message*⟨,*autoclose*⟨,*num-sel*⟩⟩⟩);

The following argument has been added for Release 6.07. Refer to *SAS Screen Control Language: Reference* for details of the other syntax elements.

Arguments	Type	Value or Action
num-sel	N	Maximum number of items users can select from the list. Use 0 for no selections, that is, a list displayed for reference only.

Updated Functionality

The LISTC function now permits more than one selection. It also now places values in the current environment list.

When the LISTC function is invoked, the current environment list is cleared. After invoking the LISTC function, the current environment list contains one element for each item selected. The selections can be retrieved using the GETITEMC function.

Example

The following statements open the entry MYLIST.LIST in the current catalog and display it as a selection list. Users can make up to four selections. The selected values are retrieved from the current environment list:

```
listid=makelist();
rc=curlist(listid);
selection=listc('mylist.list',' ','n',4);
n=listlen(listid);
do i=1 to n;
   item=getitemc(listid,i);
   put item=;
end;
```

LISTN

Displays a selection list window containing numeric values and returns user selections

Enhanced SCL Function

Selection List Function

Syntax

cval=LISTN(*entry*⟨,*message*⟨,*autoclose*⟨,*num-sel*⟩⟩⟩);

The following argument has been added for Release 6.07. Refer to *SAS Screen Control Language: Reference* for details of the other syntax elements.

Arguments	Type	Value or Action
num-sel	N	Maximum number of items users can select from the list. Use 0 for no selections, that is, a list displayed for reference only.

Updated Functionality

The LISTN function now permits more than one selection. It also now places values in the current environment list.

When the LISTN function is invoked, the current environment list is cleared. After invoking the LISTN function, the environment list contains one element for each item selected. The selections can be retrieved using the GETITEMC function.

Example

The following statements open the entry MYLIST.LIST in the current catalog and display it as a selection list. Users can make up to four selections. The selected values are retrieved from the current environment list:

```
listid=makelist();
rc=curlist(listid);
selection=listn('mylist.list',' ','n',4);
n=listlen(listid);
do i=1 to n;
   item=getitemc(listid,i);
   put item=;
end;
```

LISTLEN

Reports the length of an SCL list

New SCL Function

List Function

Syntax

n=LISTLEN(*list-id*);

Returns	Type	Value
n	N	The length of the SCL list. ≥0 The length of a nonempty list. −1 The list identifier is invalid. 0 The list is empty.

Arguments	Type	Value or Action
list-id	N	Identifies the list to be queried.

Description

The LISTLEN function reports the length of the SCL list identified by *list-id*. Because the LISTLEN functions returns -1 if *list-id* is an invalid list identifier, you can use a LISTLEN statement to check that a list has not been deleted, as shown in the following statements.

```
listid=getniteml(envlist('G'),'MYLIST'));
invalid=(listlen(listid)=-1);
if invalid then
   do;
      put 'MYLIST in the global environment has been deleted.';
      stop;
   end;
```

Example

The following statements create the empty list A and then insert list A into a copy of itself, list B. The lengths of the two lists are then computed and stored in the variables LEN_A and LEN_B.

```
LISTA=makelist();
LISTB=copylist(LISTA);
LISTB=insertl(LISTB,LISTA);
len_a=listlen(LISTA);
len_b=listlen(LISTB);
_msg_='Length of A is '||len_a||' and length of B is '||len_b;
```

This example shows that the length of A is 0 while the length of B is 1.

See Also

MAKELIST and MAKENLIST in this chapter for information on related SCL functions

LOCK

Locks or unlocks a SAS file or SAS catalog entry

New SCL Function

Utility Function

SAS/SHARE software required

Syntax

sysrc=LOCK(*member*⟨,*action*⟩);

Returns	Type	Value	
sysrc	N	0	The specified action was successfully performed
		≠0	An error or warning condition occurred during the operation

Arguments	Type	Value or Action
member	C	Name of a SAS data library member or SAS catalog entry. The value you specify can be a one-, two-, three-, or four-level name. A one-level name is presumed to be a libref, while a two-level name defaults the SAS file type to DATA.
action	C	Action to be performed on the SAS file or SAS catalog entry.

Action	Description
CLEAR	Unlock the specified SAS file(s) or SAS catalog entry.
LOCK	Lock the specified SAS file(s) or SAS catalog entry.
QUERY	Query the lock status of a SAS file or a SAS catalog entry. Compare the value returned by the LOCK function against the following predefined SAS macros to determine the lock state: _SWNOLKH indicates object is not currently locked _SWLKUSR indicates object is locked by another user _SWLKYOU indicates object is locked by the caller.

Description

The LOCK function enables you to lock, unlock, or query the lock state of the specified SAS files or SAS catalog entry. If the *action* argument is not given, it defaults to LOCK. If the *member* argument is a one- or two-level name, the type of SAS file defaults to DATA.

The member identified in the *member* argument must be accessed using the SHARE engine. Otherwise, you get an error message when the statement executes.

LOCK

continued

Examples

The following statements illustrate the different actions you can perform with the LOCK function:

```
   rc=lock('a');                      /* locks data library a */
   rc=lock('lib.a.view','clear');     /* unlocks data view lib.a */
   rc=lock('lib.a.b.program');        /* locks b.program in catalog /go
lib.a */
   rc=lock('foo.one.data','query'); /* query the lock state of */
   if (rc=%sysrc(_SWLKUSR) or        /* data set foo.one        */
      rc=%sysrc(_SWLKYOU)) then
     _msg_='foo.one.data is currently locked.';
```

LVARLEVEL

Fills an SCL list with the unique formatted values of a variable from a SAS data set

New SCL Function

List Function

Syntax

rc=LVARLEVEL(*dsid*,*varname*,*nlevel*⟨,*list-id*⟩);

Returns	Type	Value
rc	N	Indicator of the success of the operation. 0 The list was successfully filled with the formatted values. ≠0 An error or warning occurred, and the list was not filled with the formatted values.

Arguments	Type	Value or Action
dsid	N	Identifies the data set (returned from the OPEN function).
varname	C	Specifies the data set variable whose unique formatted values are to be reported.
nlevel	N	Variable to contain the number of unique, formatted values of the variable. This argument must be specified as a variable name and not as a literal value.
list-id	N	Identifies the list to be filled. This value was returned by the function that created the list or the CURLIST function.

Description

The LVARLEVEL function fills an SCL list with all of the unique formatted values of a specified variable in the data set identified by *dsid*. The values are placed in the list identified by *list-id*, or in the current list if *list-id* is not specified. The values placed in the list are always character values.

The specification for *nlevel* must be the name of a variable because the LVARLEVEL function uses it to store the number of unique, formatted values found for the data set variable. The SCL program must precede the LVARLEVEL statement with a statement initializing this variable to 0.

Examples

The following examples illustrate placing values in the current list and placing them in a specified list.

LVARLEVEL

continued

Placing values in the current list

The following statements call the LVARLEVEL function to get the unique formatted values for the data set variable X. The values are placed in the current list, and retrieved by the GETITEMC function.

```
dsid=open('sample.data','i');
nlevels=0;
listid=makelist();
rc=curlist(listid);
rc=lvarlevel(dsid,'x',nlevels);
put nlevels=;
call putlist(listid,'levels',0);
```

Placing values in a specified list

The following statements use the LVARLEVEL function to get the unique formatted values for the data set variable X. The values are placed in the list specified, and retrieved by the GETITEMC function.

```
dsid=open('sample.data','i');
nlevels=0;
listid=makelist();
rc=lvarlevel(dsid 'x',nlevels,listid);
put nlevels=;
call putlist(listid,'levels',0);
```

See Also

VARLEVEL and VARSTAT in Chapter 8 in *SAS Screen Control Language: Reference* for information on related SCL functions

MAKELIST

Creates an SCL list

New SCL Function

List Function

Syntax

list-id=MAKELIST(⟨*n*⟨,*class*⟩⟩);

Returns	Type	Value
list-id	N	List identifier for the new list. >0 The list identifier. 0 The list could not be created.

Arguments	Type	Value or Action
n	N	Specifies the number of items to place in the list initially. By default, *n* is 0.
class	C	Designates whether the list is to be local or global. G The list is global to all applications executing in the same SAS session. L The list is local to the current SAS application. This is the default.

Description

The MAKELIST function creates an empty list or a list of *n* missing values, if *n* is specified. The list identifier returned is used with all other SCL list functions.

Values in a list that is local can be shared only by the SAS application in which the list is created, for example, the SAS/AF application. A local list is deleted when the application ends. Values in a list that is global can be shared by all SAS applications during a SAS session. A global list is deleted when the SAS session ends.

Example

The following statements use the MAKELIST function to create lists in the local and global environments:

```
n = 12;
   /*  Make an empty local list.  */
list1=makelist();
   /*  Make a list with 24 items.  */
list2=makelist(2*n);
   /*  Make an empty global list.  */
list3=makelist('G');
   /*  Get the global environment list.    */
genv=envlist(0, 'G');
   /*  Put list3 into the global environment.  */
genv=setniteml(genv,list3,'Acme Acct Info');
```

MAKELIST

continued

See Also

COPYLIST, CURLIST, DELITEM, DELLIST, DELNITEM, ENVLIST, FILLIST, GETITEMC, GETITEML, GETITEMN, GETLATTR, HASATTR, GETNITEMC, GETNITEML, GETNITEMN, INSERTC, INSERTL, INSERTN, ITEMTYPE, LISTLEN, MAKENLIST, NAMEDITEM, NAMEITEM, POPC, POPL, POPN, POPMENU, PUTLIST, REVLIST, ROTLIST, SAVELIST, SEARCHC, SEARCHL, SEARCHN, SETITEMC, SETITEML, SETITEMN, SETLATTR, SETNITEMC, SETNITEML, SETNITEMN, and SORTLIST in this chapter for information on related SCL functions

MAKENLIST

Creates a named list with named items

New SCL Function

List Function

Syntax

list-id=MAKENLIST(*class*,*name-1*⟨, . . .,*name-n*⟩);

Returns	Type	Value
list-id	N	Identifies the new list >0 List identifier of the new list. 0 The list could not be created.

Arguments	Type	Value or Action
class	C	Specifies the environment for the list. G The list is global to all applications executing in the same SAS session. L The list is local to the current SAS application. This is the default.
name-1, ..., *name-n*	C	Specifies the name of each element in the list. Item names are converted to uppercase and trailing blanks are removed. Each name can be any valid SCL string. The same name can be used more than once.

Description

The MAKENLIST function creates a list with a number of items equal to the number of names in the argument list. Each list item value is a missing value. The list identifier returned is used with all remaining functions that manipulate the list. When you create a list with named items, you can assign or access list values by their names instead of their positions.

The MAKENLIST function can be used to create structures, which group related information in one list. For example, an observation in a SAS data set could be placed in a named list, where each item name corresponds to the data set variable name.

Note that the environment argument ('L' or 'G') is required and is the first argument, unlike the MAKELIST function. Note also that this function does not use an *n* argument.

Using the MAKENLIST function is a shortcut for using MAKELIST and naming each item independently.

Example

The following statement

```
mylist=makenlist('L','A','B','C');
```

is equivalent to using these four statements:

```
mylist=makelist(3,'L');
mylist=nameitem(mylist,'A',1);
mylist=nameitem(mylist,'B',2);
mylist=nameitem(mylist,'C',3);
```

MAKENLIST

continued

See Also

DELNITEM, MAKELIST, NAMEDITEM, NAMEITEM, SETNITEMC, SETNITEML, and SETNITEMN in this chapter for information on related SCL functions

METHOD

Executes a method block defined in an SCL entry

New SCL Routine

Method Block Routine

Syntax

CALL METHOD(*entry*,*label*⟨,*parameters*⟩);

Returns	Type	Value
entry	C	Name of a catalog entry of type SCL If you specify a one- or two-level name (that is, *name* or *name.type*), the procedure assumes the entry is in the current catalog. Use a three- or four-level name to specify an entry in a different catalog. If the one- or three-level name is used, the type of SCL is assumed.
label	C	Name of the method block in a SCL entry. This name is a SAS label name.
parameters	C	Arguments given from the third argument are assumed to be parameters. The entry that receives these parameters must declare each of them within a METHOD statement.

Description

The METHOD routine executes a method block defined in another SCL entry. The name of this entry must be specified in the first argument of the CALL METHOD routine. The method block is identified by a preceding SCL label in the METHOD statement. The name of this label must be specified in the second argument of the CALL METHOD routine. These two arguments are required for the CALL METHOD routine. The remaining arguments are optional parameters passed to the method block.

The method block containing a sequence of SCL statements is an external called routine. The method block needs to declare parameters using the METHOD statement that begins the method block. The syntax of the METHOD statement is similar to the ENTRY statement. The number of arguments from the third arguments in a CALL METHOD routine should agree with the number of parameters in the corresponding METHOD statement. The relative positions of the arguments from the third argument in the CALL METHOD routine should match the parameters in the called METHOD statement. Also, both sets of variables must agree in data type. The argument names in the CALL METHOD routine do not have to match the parameter names in the METHOD statement.

When the executed method block is exited, control returns to the calling METHOD routine.

Parameters are passed one of the following ways:

Call by reference

This mechanism is used to pass variables and enables values to be returned to the CALL METHOD routine. This approach enables the called method block to modify values, then return them.

An example of a call by reference is:

```
call method('b.scl',var1,name,field2);
```

If you do not want to return the values, use the NOCHANGE() routine.

METHOD

continued

Call by value

This mechanism is used for all numeric constants, character constants, and expressions. It does not return values to the calling METHOD routine.

An example of a call by value is:

```
call method('b.scl',100,'hello',x+y);
```

Example

The following statement uses the METHOD routine to call the method block labeled ABC in the SCL entry CODE. The following three parameters are passed: the contents of the variable A, the literal value 3, and the contents of the variable C:

```
call method('code.scl','abc',a,3,c);
```

The method block can return modified values to the variables A and C.

See Also

DISPLAY and NOCHANGE

in Chapter 8 in *SAS Screen Control Language: Reference* for information on related SCL functions

METHOD statement and METHOD routine

in this chapter for information on related SCL functions

METHOD

Begins a statement block that can be called by the METHOD routine

New SCL Statement

Method Block Statement

Syntax

METHOD ⟨*argument-list-1*⟩ ⟨OPTIONAL=*argument-list-2*⟩;

Arguments	Type	Value or Action
argument-list-1	C	List of variables to receive parameter values passed from the METHOD routine

The parameter specifications have the same form as in the ENTRY statement:

variable-1 ⟨. . . *variable-n*⟩ ⟨$⟩ *length*

where

variable
: names the variable to receive the value from the parameter in the corresponding position of the argument list for the CALL METHOD statement

$
: is the symbol that designates the preceding variable or variables as character type.

length
: is a numeric constant that specifies the length of the preceding variable or variables. The length of character variables do not have to match the length of the corresponding passed parameters. SCL pads or truncates as necessary.

The arguments specified after the OPTIONAL= keyword are optional arguments. If the calling METHOD routine does not declare them in the parameter list, SCL assumes that they all have an initial value of _BLANK_.

Description

The METHOD statement begins a method block. A *method block* is a labeled statement block that begins with a METHOD statement, ends with an ENDMETHOD statement, and contains one or more SCL statements. A method block is a way to make a frequently used routine available to many different programs.

Executing method blocks
Execution of the method block starts at the METHOD statement and ends with the ENDMETHOD statement. After executing a method block, control returns to the calling routine or the command line.

Calling method blocks
Other SCL programs call the method block by specifying its label in a CALL METHOD statement. Only SCL entries can contain method blocks.

Testing method blocks
A method block can be tested individually by invoking a TESTAF command with the label=*label* option, for example:

```
testaf label=nsort
```

METHOD

continued

Scope of method block variables
All the variables defined in a method block are global to that entry. There is no variable scoping implied within a method block. You cannot use a GOTO or a LINK statement to jump into the method block in the current entry. The label for the method block is the only entry point to a METHOD block.

Passing parameters to method blocks
The parameter-receiving mechanism for the METHOD statement is very similar to that mechanism for the ENTRY statement. The METHOD statement receives parameters from the third argument of the calling METHOD routine. The calling METHOD routine must agree with the corresponding METHOD statement in the following ways or SCL halts the execution of the calling METHOD routine:

- The number of arguments passed must be the same as the number of parameters received.
- The relative positions of the arguments passed must match the parameters in the corresponding METHOD statement.
- The data types of both sets of variables must agree.

The argument names in the calling METHOD routine do not have to match the parameter names in the METHOD statement.

Returning values to the calling routine
A called method block can modify any argument it receives. However, it cannot return new values to METHOD routine arguments that are numeric literals, character literals, or expressions. By default, values for variables are returned to the calling METHOD routine. If you want a called method block to receive values but not return values to its calling METHOD routine, use the NOCHANGE routine. The value of each argument is completely determined by the status of the program stack because all the variables defined in a method block are global to the current entry. If a method block is invoked by a LINK statement or by a TESTAF command, no parameters can be passed.

Example

The following program contains two method blocks:

- NSORT, which sorts numeric arrays
- CSORT, which sorts character arrays.

```
array narr(100) _temporary_;
array carr(100) $ 200 _temporary_;
length msg $ 200;
length ntemp 8 ctemp $ 200;

   /* This method sorts a numeric array. */
NSORT:
   method size 8 msg $ optional=narr 8;
      msg=' ';   /* set return value */
      if (size<=0) then
         do;
            _msg_='Array size is too small';
            return;
```

```
         end;
      if (size>100) then
         do;
            _msg_='Array size is over 100';
            return;
         end;
         /*  Do a bubble sort.  */
      do i=1 to size-1;
         do j=i+1 to size;
            if narr(i)>narr(j) then
               do;
                     /* Swap */
                  ntemp=narr(i);
                  narr(i)=narr(j);
                  narr(j)=ntemp;
               end;
         end;
      end;
   endmethod;

   /* This method sorts a character string array. */
CSORT:
   method size 8 msg $ optional=carr $;
      _msg_=' ';   /* set return value */
      if (size<0) then
         do;
            _msg_='Array size is too small';
            return;
         end;
      if (size>100) then
         do;
            _msg_='Array size is over 100';
            return;
         end;
          /*  Do a bubble sort. */
       do i=1 to size-1;
          do j=i+1 to size;
             if carr(i)>carr(j) then
                do;
                      /* Perform a swap. */
                   ctemp=carr(i);
                   carr(i)=carr(j);
                   carr(j)=ctemp;
                end;
          end;
       end;
   endmethod;
```

Example of calling a method
Assume that the method block CSORT is defined in SCL entry ABC. To call CSORT, you can use the following statement in any SCL entry or FSEDIT SCREEN entry to call the method block CSORT, which is equivalent to an external called routine.

```
call method('abc.scl','csort',arrdim,msg,arr);
```

METHOD

continued

If the preceding method blocks are defined in an SCL entry, the block NSORT is equivalent to an internal called routine when it is invoked by the following LINK statement.

```
MAIN:
   link nsort;
   other SCL statements
return;
```

Example of testing a method block

During the development stage, the NSORT block can be tested individually by using the following TESTAF command line:

```
testaf label=nsort
```

NAMEDITEM

Searches an SCL list for the item with the specified name

New SCL Function

List Function

Syntax

position=NAMEDITEM(*list-id*,*name*⟨,*occurrence*⟨,*index*⟩⟩);

Returns	Type	Value
position	N	The item's position in the list. >0 The position number of the named item. 0 The item being searched for was not found.

Arguments	Type	Value or Action
list-id	N	Identifies the list to be searched.
name	C	Specifies the name of the item to search for. If *name* is blank, the first unnamed item is returned. Its name is converted to uppercase and trailing blanks are removed before searching.
occurrence	N	Specifies the number of the occurrence of the named item to search for. The default is 1 for the first occurrence of the item.
index	N	Specifies the position to start searching the list for the item. *Index* defaults to 1, the first item in the list. If *index* is a positive number, the search starts at position *index* from the beginning of the list and continues to the end of the list. If *index* is a negative number, the search starts at position abs(*index*) from the end of the list and continues to the beginning of the list.

Description

The NAMEDITEM function searches a list for the item with the specified name and returns the number of its position in the list. This function only searches the top level of the list specified by *list-id*; that is, it does not search sublists. Several functions that access items in a list by position have counterparts that access items by their names. Since it is more efficient to retrieve an item by the number of its position rather than by its name, you can use the NAMEDITEM function to find the position and then use the functions that access items by position number rather than by name.

For forward searches, the search continues only to the end of the list and does not wrap back to the front of the list. For backward searches, the search continues only to the beginning of the list and does not wrap back to the end of the list.

NAMEDITEM

continued

Examples

The following statements swap the numeric values associated with the first and last occurrence of the item named X.

```
   /*  Return first occurence of X.  */
first=getnitemn(listid,'X');
   /*  Return last occurence of X.   */
last=getnitemn(listid,'X',1,-1);
list=setnitemn(listid,last,'X');
list=setnitemn(listid,first,'X',1 -1);
```

The following statements show a slightly more efficient way to perform the swap operation. This method does not require a second search for the item, and it can also detect when item X does not exist in the list.

```
   /*  Return the position number of the first item X. */
ifirst=nameditem(listid,'X');
if (ifirst>0) then
   do;
      first=getitemn(listid,ifirst);
         / * Return the position of the last item X.  */
      ilast=nameditem(listid,'X',1,-1);
      list=setitemn(listid,getitemn(list,ilast),ifirst);
      list=setitemn(listid,first,ilast);
   end;
```

Notes

An error condition occurs if

- the absolute value of *index* is zero or greater than the number of items in the list
- *list-id* is not a valid list identifier.

See Also

DELNITEM, GETITEMC, GETITEML, GETITEMN, GETNITEMC, GETNITEML, GETNITEMN, INSERTC, INSERTL, INSERTN, ITEMTYPE, MAKELIST, MAKENLIST, NAMEITEM, SEARCHC, SEARCHL, SEARCHN, SETITEMC, SETITEML, SETITEMN, SETNITEMC, SETNITEML, and SETNITEMN in this chapter for information on related SCL functions

NAMEITEM

Returns and optionally replaces the name of an item in an SCL list

New SCL Function

List Function

Syntax

item-name=NAMEITEM(*list-id*⟨,*index*⟨,*new-name*⟩⟩);

Returns	Type	Value
item-name	C	The name of the list item. Returns blank if the item does not have a name.

Arguments	Type	Value or Action
list-id	N	Identifies the SCL list containing the item whose name is being reported or changed.
index	N	Specifies the number of the position in the list containing the item whose name is to be reported or changed. *Index* defaults to 1, the first item in the list. If *index* is a positive number, the item is at position *index* from the beginning of the list. If *index* is a negative number, the item is at position abs(*index*) from the end of the list.
new-name	C	Specifies the new name to assign to the list item.

Description

The NAMEITEM function returns the name of the item at the list position specified by the value for *index*. If a value for *name* is also provided, the function assigns that name to the item, replacing the old name.

Notes

An error condition results if

- the value for *name* is provided and the list has the:
  - NOUPDATE attribute
  - SASNAMES attribute and the variable for *name* is not a valid SAS name
  - NODUPNAMES attribute and the value for *name* duplicates the name of another item in the list.
- the absolute value of *index* is zero or is larger than the number of items in the list
- *list-id* is not a valid list identifier number.

To check the attributes of a list or list item, use the HASATTR function. To change these attributes, use the SETLATTR function.

NAMEITEM

continued

See Also

DELNITEM, GETLATTR, GETNITEMC, GETNITEML, GETNITEMN, HASATTR, INSERTC, INSERTL, INSERTN, MAKELIST, MAKENLIST, NAMEDITEM, SETLATTR, SETNITEMC, SETNITEML, and SETNITEMN in this chapter for information on related SCL functions

OBSINFO

Returns information on the current observation in an FSEDIT application

New SCL Function

Data Set Function

FSEDIT applications only

Syntax

rc=OBSINFO(*info-item*);

Returns	Type	Value
rc	N	Depends on the information requested. See the descriptions of the individual *info-type* argument values for details.

Arguments	Type	Value or Action
info-item	C	One of the following information items:

CUROBS
: Returns the observation number of the currently displayed observation. For this argument, the function returns one of the following values:
  - *n* the observation number of the currently displayed observation
  - −1 the SAS data set is accessed using an engine that does not support observation numbers

DELETED
: Tests whether the currently displayed observation is marked for deletion. For this argument, the function returns one of the following values:
  - 1 the currently displayed observation is marked for deletion
  - 0 the currently displayed observation is not marked for deletion

LOCKED
: Tests whether the currently displayed observation is locked by another user. For this argument, the function returns one of the following values:
  - 1 another user has locked the currently displayed observation
  - 0 the currently displayed observation is not locked

NEW
: Tests whether the currently displayed observation is newly added and not yet saved. For this argument, the function returns the following values:
  - 1 the currently displayed observation is a new observation
  - 0 the currently displayed observation already exists in the data set

OBSINFO

continued

MODIFIED — Tests whether users have modified any variable in the currently displayed observation. For this argument, the function returns the following values:

1 — users have modified data set variables in the currently displayed observation

0 — users have not yet modified any data set variables in the currently displayed observation

Description

The OBSINFO function can be used to obtain information about the observation that is currently displayed in the FSEDIT window.

Example

The following statements use the OBSINFO function to obtain information about the observation currently displayed in the FSEDIT window.

```
rc=obsinfo('curobs');
rc=obsinfo('deleted');
rc=obsinfo('locked');
rc=obsinfo('new');
rc=obsinfo('modified');
```

See Also

CUROBS in Chapter 8 in *SAS Screen Control Language: Reference* for information on a related SCL function

OPEN

Opens a SAS data set

Enhanced SCL Function

Data Set Function

Syntax

data-set-id=OPEN(⟨*data-set-name*⟨,*mode*⟩⟩);

The following argument has changed for Release 6.07. Refer to *SAS Screen Control Language: Reference* for details of the other syntax elements.

Arguments	Type	Value or Action
mode	C	Mode in which the data set is opened. In addition to I, N, U, and V, new valid values are: IS Open data set in INPUT mode and data set will be read in sequential instead of the default random order. IN Open data set in INPUT mode and data set will be read multiple times. US Open data set in UPDATE mode and data set will be read in sequential order. UN Open data set in UPDATE mode and data set will be read multiple times.

Updated Functionality

The OPEN function now supports additional open modes that allow you to specify whether the data set is opened for sequential or random access.

Notes

The OPEN function formerly defaulted to random access when opening files in INPUT or UPDATE modes. With Release 6.07, the OPEN function defaults to the strongest access mode available in the engine. That is, if the engine supports random access, the OPEN function still defaults to random access when files are opened in INPUT or UPDATE mode. Otherwise, files are opened with sequential access and a system level warning (_SWSEQ) is set. For example, accessing DB2 view descriptors from the ACCESS window will trigger this warning. You should use the SYSRC function to check for this warning.

PATHNAME

Returns the physical name of a SAS data library or an external file

New SCL Function

Utility Function

Syntax

filename=PATHNAME(*fileref*);

Returns	Type	Value
filename	C	Physical name of an external file or library

Arguments	Type	Value or Action
fileref	C	Fileref associated with an external file or a library

Description

The PATHNAME function returns the actual name of an external file or library in the form required by the host operating system.

Example

The following statement verifies that the fileref MYFILE is associated with an external file, then uses the PATHNAME function to retrieve the actual name of the external file.

```
if (fileref('myfile')) then
   fname=pathname('myfile');
```

See Also

FILENAME, FILEREF, FEXIST, and FILEEXIST in Chapter 8 in *SAS Screen Control Language: Reference* for information on related SCL functions

POPC

Removes a character item from a list and returns the value stored there

New SCL Function

List Function

Syntax

cval=POPC(*list-id*⟨,*index*⟩);

Returns	Type	Value
cval	C	The value of character the item removed from the list.

Arguments	Type	Value or Action
list-id	N	Identifies the list from which to remove the item.
index	N	Specifies the number of the item's position in the list. *Index* defaults to 1, the first item in the list. If *index* is a positive number, the item is at position *index* from the beginning of the list. If *index* is a negative number, the item is at position abs(*index*) from the end of the list.

Description

The POPC function returns the value of a character item in the SCL list identified by *list-id* and removes the item from the list. The POPC function is useful for implementing stacks and queues.

Examples

The following statement:

```
cval=popc(listid);
```

is equivalent to the following statements:

```
cval=getitemc(listid);
listid=delitem(listid);
```

The following statement returns the character value of the last item in the list and then deletes it from the list:

```
cval=popc(listid,-1);
```

Notes

An error condition results if

- the item has the NODELETE attribute
- the list has the FIXEDLENGTH or NOUPDATE attribute
- the list is empty
- the specified item is not a character item
- the absolute value of *index* is zero or greater than the number of items in the list
- *list-id* is not a valid list identifier.

POPC

continued

To check the attributes of a list or list item, use the HASATTR function. To change these attributes, use the SETLATTR function.

See Also

DELITEM, DELNITEM, GETITEMC, GETITEML, GETITEMN, GETLATTR, HASATTR, INSERTC, INSERTL, INSERTN, ITEMTYPE, LISTLEN, MAKELIST, MAKENLIST, POPL, POPN, SETITEMC, SETITEML, SETITEMN, SETLATTR, SETNITEMC, SETNITEML, and SETNITEMN in this chapter for information on related SCL functions

POPL

Removes a sublist item from a list and returns the identifier for the sublist stored there

New SCL Function

List Function

Syntax

sublist-id=POPL(*list-id*⟨,*index*⟩);

Returns	Type	Value
sublist-id	N	Identifier of the sublist item removed from the list.

Arguments	Type	Value or Action
list-id	N	Identifies the list from which to remove the item.
index	N	Specifies the number of the item's position in the list. *Index* defaults to 1, the first item in the list. If *index* is a positive number, the item is at position *index* from the beginning of the list. If *index* is a negative number, the item is at position abs(*index*) from the end of the list.

Description

The POPL function returns the list identifier of a sublist item in the SCL list identified by *list-id* and removes the item from the list. The POPL function is useful for implementing stacks and queues.

Examples

The following statement:

```
list=popl(listid);
```

is equivalent to the following statements:

```
list=getitemc(listid);
listid=delitem(listid);
```

The following statement returns the sublist identifier of the last item in the list and then deletes it from the list:

```
list=popl(listid,-1);
```

Notes

An error condition results if

- the item has the NODELETE attribute
- the list has the FIXEDLENGTH or NOUPDATE attribute
- the list is empty
- the specified item is not a sublist item
- the absolute value of *index* is zero or greater than the number of items in the list
- *list-id* is not a valid list identifier.

POPL

continued

To check the attributes of a list or list item, use the HASATTR function. To change these attributes, use the SETLATTR function.

See Also

DELITEM, DELNITEM, GETITEMC, GETITEML, GETITEMN, GETLATTR, HASATTR, INSERTC, INSERTL, INSERTN, ITEMTYPE, LISTLEN, MAKELIST, MAKENLIST, POPC, POPN, SETITEMC, SETITEML, SETITEMN, SETLATTR, SETNITEMC, SETNITEML, and SETNITEMN in this chapter for information on related SCL functions

POPMENU

Displays a popup menu containing character elements of an SCL list

New SCL Function

List Function

Syntax

selection=POPMENU(*list-id*);

Returns	Type	Value
selection	N	The position number of the item selected from the menu. ≥0 The list position of the item selected from the popup menu. 0 The user cancelled the menu, the list is empty, or the list contains blank characters or numeric or sublist items.

Arguments	Type	Value or Action
list-id	N	Identifies the list whose items are to be displayed in the popup menu.

Description

The POPMENU function displays a menu containing the character items in the list identified by *list-id* and returns the list position of the item users select. An item in the list that has the INACTIVE attribute cannot be selected and is greyed on devices that support graying, but it is still displayed in the menu. You can use the SETLATTR function to assign an item the INACTIVE attribute or restore the item to an ACTIVE state.

The maximum number of items that POPMENU can display depends on your display device. If your list is longer than that supported by the device, the extra items are not displayed, and users cannot select them. Thus, you should not try to pop up a menu of more than 20 items in applications supported on all display devices.

Notes

An error condition results if *list-id* is not a valid list identifier.

See Also

FILLIST, GETITEMC, GETITEML, GETITEMN, GETLATTR, HASATTR, LISTLEN, MAKELIST, MAKENLIST, and SETLATTR in this chapter for information on related SCL functions

POPN

Removes a numeric item from a list and returns the value stored there

New SCL Function

List Function

Syntax

nval=POPN(*list-id*⟨,*index*⟩);

Returns	Type	Value
nval	N	The value of the numeric item removed from the list.

Arguments	Type	Value or Action
list-id	N	Identifies the list from which to remove the item.
index	N	Specifies the number of the item's position in the list. *Index* defaults to 1, the first item in the list. If *index* is a positive number, the item is at position *index* from the beginning of the list. If *index* is a negative number, the item is at position abs(*index*) from the end of the list.

Description

The POPN function returns the value of a numeric item in the SCL list identified by *list-id* and removes the item from the list. The POPN function is useful for implementing stacks and queues.

Examples

The following statement:

```
nval=popn(listid);
```

is equivalent to the following statements:

```
nval=getitemn(listid);
listid=delitem(listid);
```

The following statement returns the numeric value of the last item in the list and then deletes it from the list:

```
nval=popn(listid,-1);
```

Notes

An error condition results if

- the first item in the list has the NODELETE attribute
- the list has the FIXEDLENGTH or NOUPDATE attribute
- the list is empty
- the specified item is not a numeric item
- the absolute value of *index* is zero or greater than the number of items in the list
- *list-id* is not a valid list identifier.

To check the attributes of a list or list item, use the HASATTR function. To change these attributes, use the SETLATTR function.

See Also

DELITEM, DELNITEM, GETITEMC, GETITEML, GETITEMN, GETLATTR, HASATTR, INSERTC, INSERTL, INSERTN, ITEMTYPE, LISTLEN, MAKELIST, MAKENLIST, POPC, POPL, SETITEMC, SETITEML, SETITEMN, SETLATTR, SETNITEMC, SETNITEML, and SETNITEMN in this chapter for information on related SCL functions

PREVIEW

Manipulates submitted statements in the PREVIEW buffer

Enhanced SCL Function

Submit Block Function

SAS/AF software only

Syntax

rc=PREVIEW(*action*⟨,*argument-1*⟨,*argument-2*⟨,*argument-3*⟩⟩⟩);

The following argument has changed for Release 6.07. Refer to *SAS Screen Control Language: Reference* for details of the other syntax elements.

Arguments	Type	Value or Action
action	C	In addition to the actions described in Chapter 8 in *SAS Screen Control Language: Reference*, the following actions have been added or changed for Release 6.07:

FILE
: You can now specify 'APPEND' for *argument-3* to append the contents of the preview buffer to the previous contents of the external file.

HISTORY
: Saves or appends the statements submitted from SCL programs to a catalog member.

With the HISTORY action, you must specify the name of an entry as *argument-1*. Use one of the following forms:

entry

Saves the submitted statements in the catalog entry SASUSER.PROFILE.*entry*.SOURCE.

entry.type

Saves the submitted statements in the catalog entry SASUSER.PROFILE.*entry.type*. The only valid value for the *type* argument is `SOURCE`.

libref.catalog.entry

Saves the submitted statements in the catalog entry *libref.catalog.entry*.SOURCE.

libref.catalog.entry.type

Saves the submitted statements in the catalog entry *libref.catalog.entry.type*. The only valid value for the *type* argument is `SOURCE`.

	Once a history destination is set, it stays through the application until a reset is performed. To clear the destination, simply invoke the PREVIEW function again by passing the HISTORY action but without any succeeding argument. The application would then stop appending the submitted statements to the previously specified SOURCE entry. You can also optionally specify a description for the entry as *argument-2*. Only the first 40 characters of the description are saved.
PRINT	You can optionally specify a form name, fileref, and append mode. *Argument-1* specifies the name of a FORM entry to use for printing. Use *name.FORM* or simply *name* to specify a form entry in the current catalog. To specify a form in a different catalog, use *libref.catalog.name.FORM* or *libref.catalog.name*. *Argument-2* specifies a valid fileref for a print file. If blank or not specified, the printout is sent to the default system printer. *Argument-3* specifies the append mode. An 'A' is used to append the output to the print file. If blank or not specified, each new set of print output replaces the contents of the print file.

Updated Functionality

The PREVIEW function now allows you to

- append the contents of the preview buffer to an external file
- save all submitted statements in a catalog entry
- print the contents of the preview buffer.

Example

The following statements use the HISTORY action to save all submitted statements in a catalog entry:

```
   /* Open the history entry. */
rc=preview('history','sasuser.history.submit.source');
   /* Submitted statements will be saved in the catalog entry. */
submit continue;
   data one;
      x=1;
   run;
endsubmit;
   More SCL statements
```

PREVIEW

continued

```
submit;
   data two;
      y=2;
   run;
endsubmit;
   More SCL statements
   /* Close the history entry. */
rc=preview('history');
   /* Submitted statements not saved because the */
   /* history entry is now closed.               */
submit;
   data three;
      z=3;
   run;
endsubmit;
```

Notes

The PREVIEW function can now be used in FSEDIT and FSVIEW applications to manipulate the preview buffer.

See Also

ENDSUBMIT, SUBMIT, and WREGION in Chapter 8 in *SAS Screen Control Language: Reference* for information on related SCL functions

PUTLIST

Displays the contents of a list in the MESSAGE window

New SCL Routine

List Routine

Syntax

CALL PUTLIST(*list-id*⟨,*label*⟨,*indent*⟩⟩);

Arguments	Type	Value or Action
list-id	N	Identifies the list to be displayed. This value was returned by the function that created the list.
label	C	Specifies the label for the printed output.
indent	N	Specifies the number of characters to indent list items in the printed list.

Description

The PUTLIST routine displays the contents of a list in the MESSAGE window. After printing the optional label, the PUTLIST routine prints a left parenthesis '(' to mark the beginning of the list, followed by the list of items separated by blanks. Each named item is preceded by its name and an equal sign (=), but nothing is printed before items that do not have names. The PUTLIST routine ends the list with a right parenthesis ')', followed by the list's identifier number within square brackets.

If a value for *indent* is greater than or equal to 0, the list is printed in a vertical format where each list item is printed on its own line. Sublists are indented the number of spaces to the right that is specified by *indent*.

The PUTLIST routine identifies an invalid list identifier with the text `<invalid list id>[`*`listid`*`]` if the list contains sublists that have been deleted.

Examples

The following examples are based on an SCL list whose list identifier is stored in the variable A. This list contains the numbers 17 and 328 and the character value "Any Characters." These examples display the list

- in its simplest form
- with values indented
- after a numeric item is replaced with a sublist item
- after the list is added to itself as a sublist.

List in simplest form
The statement

```
call putlist(a);
```

displays the following:

```
(17 328 'Any characters' )[7]
```

PUTLIST

continued

List with values indented
The following statement

```
call putlist(lista,'A=',2);
```

displays:

```
A=(  17
     328
     'Any string'
   )[7]
```

This example shows the result of specifying an indent with the PUTLIST routine.

List with sublist item replacing numeric item
The following statements replace the second item in the list A with the list identifier for sublist B, which contains the values -4.75 and 12.875.

```
   /*  Assign the second item to list B.  */
a=setiteml(listb,b,2);
name=nameitem(listb,1,'MIN');
name=nameitem(listb,2,'B');
call putlist(listb,'A=',2);
```

The previous statements display the following output in the MESSAGE window. Note that the list B has a list identifier of 5.

```
A=(  MIN=17
     B=(  -4.75
          12.875
     )[5]
     'Any string'
   )[7]
```

List added to itself as a sublist
If a sublist appears more than once in the list being printed, the PUTLIST routine prints only

(...) [*listid*]

for the second and subsequent occurrences of the list. You should scan the output of the PUTLIST routine for another occurrence of

[*listid*]

to view the full contents of the list. This prevents infinite loops if a list contains itself.

The following statements create and display a recursive list.

```
r1=makenlist('L','R1','SELF');
r1=setnitemn(r1,1,'X');
r1=setniteml(r1,r1,'R1');
call putlist(r1,'R1=',2);
```

These statements display the following information in the MESSAGE window. Note that the full contents of the list with the identifier 7 is printed only once. The other occurrence is represented with (...)[7].

```
R1=(  X=1
      SELF=(...)[7]
    )[7]
```

See Also

MAKELIST, MAKENLIST, and NAMEITEM in this chapter for information on related SCL functions

REFRESH

Updates field values and redisplays the window

New SCL Statement

Window Statement

Syntax

REFRESH;

Description

The REFRESH statement updates all fields with the corresponding window variable values and then redisplays the application's window.

Example

The following statements clear the window's message line if any message is currently displayed:

```
if (_msg_ ne _blank_) then
   do;
      _msg_=_blank_;
      refresh;
   end;
```

RENAME

Renames a SAS data set, view, catalog, or catalog entry

Enhanced SCL Function

Utility Function

Syntax

sysrc=RENAME(*old-name,new-name*⟨,*type*⟨,*description*⟩⟩);

The following argument has been added for Release 6.07. Refer to *SAS Screen Control Language: Reference* for details of the other syntax elements.

Returns	Type	Value
description	C	Description for the catalog entry. Only valid when the value of the *type* argument is **CATALOG**.

Updated Functionality

The RENAME function now supports an extra parameter to describe the catalog entry to be renamed.

To rename an entry in a catalog, specify the four-level name for the *old-name* argument and a one-level name for the *new-name* argument. Specify CATALOG for the *type* argument when rename an entry in a catalog, along with a description for the *description* argument if the renamed entry should have a different description.

To change the description of a catalog entry without renaming the entry, the *new-name* argument should be the same member name that occurs in the *old-name* argument.

Examples

The following statement renames a SAS data set from DATA1 to DATA2:

```
rc1=rename('sasuser.data1','data2');
```

The following statement renames a catalog entry from A.PROGRAM to B.PROGRAM and changes the catalog entry description to B.PROGRAM SOURCE.

```
rc2=rename('sasuser.profile.a.program','b','catalog',
           'B.PROGRAM source');
```

The following statement changes the description of A.PROGRAM to `A.PROGRAM source`.

```
rc1=rename('sasuser.profile.a.program','a','catalog',
           'A.PROGRAM source');
```

REVLIST

Reverses the order of the items in an SCL list

New SCL Function

List Function

Syntax

new-list-id=REVLIST(*list-id*);

Returns	Type	Value
new-list-id	N	The list identifier of the modified list. This value is equal to the argument *list-id*.

Arguments	Type	Value or Action
list-id	N	Identifies the list to be reversed. This value was returned by the function that created the list.

Description

The REVLIST function reverses the order of the items in the list specified by *list-id*. Any attributes that are assigned to list items remain with the items when they are reversed.

The REVLIST function does not make a copy of the list before reversing the order of the list items. The list is modified in place. To store a copy of both lists, use the COPYLIST function before the REVLIST function.

Example

The following statement makes a non-recursive copy of the list identified by MYLISTID, reverses the items in the copy, and assigns the new list identifier to the variable REVLISTID.

```
revlistid = revlist(copylist(mylistid));
```

Notes

An error condition results if

- □ the list has the NOUPDATE attribute
- □ *list-id* is not a valid list identifier.

To check the attributes of a list or list item, use the HASATTR function. To change these attributes, use the SETLATTR function.

See Also

COPYLIST, MAKELIST, MAKENLIST, ROTLIST, and SORTLIST in this chapter for information on related SCL functions

RLINK

Determines whether a link exists between the current SAS session and a remote SAS session

Modified SCL Function

SAS/CONNECT Software Interface Function

SAS/CONNECT software required

Syntax

rc=RLINK(*remote-session-id*);

The following argument has been changed for Release 6.07. Refer to *SAS Screen Control Language: Reference* for details of the other syntax elements.

Argument	Type	Value or Action
remote-session-id	C	Name of the remote session (REMOTE= value) that is being tested.

Description

The RLINK function verifies whether a link exists between the local SAS session and a remote SAS session.

Example

The following statements test whether a link exists between the local SAS session and the remote SAS session with the identifier REMSESS.

```
rc=rlink('REMSESS');
if (rc=0) then
   _msg_='No link exists.';
else
   _msg_='A link exists.';
```

Notes

Release 6.06 or a later release of the SAS System must be running on both the local and remote host systems in order to use this function.

See Also

SAS/CONNECT Software: Usage and Reference, Version 6, First Edition
for details on accessing remote hosts from the SAS System

RSESSION and RSTITLE in this chapter
for information on related SCL functions

ROTLIST

Rotates the order of the items in an SCL list

New SCL Function

List Function

Syntax

new-list-id=ROTLIST(*list-id*⟨,*n*⟩);

Returns	Type	Value
new-list-id	N	The list identifier of the modified list. This value is equal to *list-id*.

Arguments	Type	Value or Action
list-id	N	Identifies the list whose items are to be rotated.
n	N	Specifies the number of times to rotate the list. The default is 1.

Description

The ROTLIST function rotates the items in the list specified by *list-id*. The items are rotated the number of times specified by *n*. If the value for *n* is positive, the items are rotated from right to left. This means that each rotation moves the item at the front of the list to the end of the list (that is, from position 1 to position -1). If the value for *n* is negative, the items are rotated from left to right. This moves the item at the end of the list to the front of the list (that is, from position -1 to position 1).

When a list is rotated, item names and attributes are moved with the elements.

Fetching a named item from a list that has more than one item with that same name may return a different item from the list after rotating than was returned before rotating.

The ROTLIST function does not make a copy of the list before rotating the order of items in the list. The list is modified in place.

Examples

This example manipulates the list identified by LISTID, which contains the five character values A, B, C, D, and E.

The following statements display the list, rotate it left to right one time and display that list, and then rotate it right to left. twice and display that list.

```
call putlist(listid,'Input list=');
listid = rotlist(listid); /* Rotate 1 time */
call putlist(listid,'Rotated  1=');
listid = rotlist(listid,-2);
call putlist(listid,'Rotated -2=');
```

The preceding statements produce the following changes. The net result is that the list is rotated backwards one time.

```
Input list=('A' 'B' 'C' 'D' 'E')[3]
Rotate   1=('B' 'C' 'D' 'E' 'A')[3]
Rotate  -2=('E' 'A' 'B' 'C' 'D')[3]
```

Notes

An error condition results if

□ the list has the NOUPDATE attribute

□ *list-id* is not a valid list identifier.

To check a list's attributes, use the HASATTR function. To change these attributes, use the SETLATTR function.

See Also

MAKELIST, MAKENLIST, REVLIST, and SORTLIST in this chapter for information on related SCL functions

RSESSION

Returns the name, description, and SAS System version of a remote session

New SCL Function

SAS/CONNECT Software Interface Function

SAS/CONNECT software required

Syntax

cval=RSESSION(*n*);

Returns	Type	Value
cval	C	Character string containing the following information: Characters 1 through 8 the session identifier (REMOTE= value) Characters 9 through 40 the description Characters 41 through 44 the SAS release of remote session

Arguments	Type	Value or Action
n	N	Number of the remote session for which to get session information

Description

The RSESSION function returns the session identifier and corresponding description for a remote session established with SAS/CONNECT software. You must have previously defined the description using the RSTITLE function.

If no remote link exists, the returned value is blank. If a link exists but no description has been specified, characters 9 through 40 in the returned value are blanks.

Example

The following statements check which release of SAS System software is running in remote session 1:

```
value=rsession(1);
if substr(value,41,4)='6073' then
   _msg_='Remote session is Release 6.07.03 of the SAS System';
else if substr(value,41,4)='6060' then
   _msg_='Remote session is Release 6.06 of the SAS System';
else if substr(value,41,4)='5180' then
   _msg_='Remote session is Release 5.18 of the SAS System';
else
   _msg_='Error in remote session';
```

Notes

Release 6.07 of the SAS System must be running on both the local and remote host systems in order to use this function.

See Also

SAS/CONNECT Software: Usage and Reference, Version 6, First Edition
for more information about establishing a link between local and remote hosts

RLINK and RSTITLE in this chapter
for information on related SCL functions

RSTITLE

Defines a description for an existing connection to a remote session

New SCL Function

SAS/CONNECT Software Interface Function

SAS/CONNECT software required

Syntax

sysrc=RSTITLE(*session-id,description*);

Returns	Type	Value	
sysrc	N	0	Description was saved
		≠0	The operation failed

Arguments	Type	Value or Action
session-id	C	Name of the remost session (REMOTE= value). The string can be up to eight characters long
description	C	Description to associate with the remote session. The string can be up to 40 characters long.

Description

The RSTITLE function saves the session identifier and description for an existing connection to a remote session. This information can be retrieved using the RSESSION function to build a list of connections. The list can then be used to select a connection when submitting statements to a remote host.

Example

The following statements define the description `MVS Payroll Data` for the remote session with the identifier A:

```
session='A';
descrip='MVS Payroll Data';
rc=rstitle(session,descrip);
```

Notes

Release 6.07 of the SAS System must be running on both the local and remote host systems in order to use this function.

See Also

SAS/CONNECT Software: Usage and Reference, Version 6, First Edition
for more information about establishing a link between local and remote hosts

RLINK and RSESSION in this chapter
for information on related SCL functions

SAVELIST

Stores SCL list items in a SAS file or an external file

New SCL Function

List Function

Syntax

rc=SAVELIST(*type*,*source*,*list-id*⟨,*attr-list-id*⟨,*description*⟩⟩);

Returns	Type	Value
rc	N	Indicator of the success of the operation. 0 The list was successfully stored. ≠0 The list was not stored.

Arguments	Type	Value or Action
type	C	Specifies the type of file in which the list items are stored. CATALOG Save text in a catalog entry. FILE Save text in an external file named in SOURCE. FILEREF Save text in an external file identified by a fileref in SOURCE.
source	C	Specifies the name of the catalog entry, external file, or fileref into which the list items are stored. For catalog entries, this must be a four-level name (*libref.catalog.name.etype*).
list-id	N	Identifies the list to be stored in the SAS file or external file. For text catalog entries, the first character in each item in the list contains the Fortran carriage control: 1 means a new page starts with this line. All other control codes can be safely ignored for now.
attr-list-id	N	Identifies the list to fill with text attribute information when the value for *type* is CATALOG.
description	C	The catalog entry description text. This argument is ignored if the value for *type* is FILE or FILEREF. (The description is displayed in the catalog directory.)

SAVELIST

continued

Description

The SAVELIST function stores the items from an SCL list into a SAS file or an external file, or stores the list itself in a SLIST catalog entry.

When storing a list into a text file (when the value for *type* is CATALOG, FILE or FILEREF), each item in the list identified by *list-id* must be a character string. When the type is CATALOG, and a value is specified for *attr-list-id*, the list items must also contain text. Each string is stored as a separate line of text. See the description of FILLIST for a description of the attribute specifications. The length of the list determines the number of lines of text in the file. If the value for *attr-list-id* is omitted or is 0, then no attributes are stored with the text files. Any value specified for *attr-list-id* is ignored when a list is stored in an external file or an SLIST catalog entry.

When the value for *type* is CATALOG and the entry type is SLIST, the list can be re-created, including names and list and item attributes, with the FILLIST function, although the list identifier will be different. The lists you save with the SAVELIST function can persist across SAS sessions if you save them in a permanent catalog.

When the SAVELIST function writes a list, each item that has the NOWRITE attribute is not written to the file. This is useful for placing temporary run time values on a list that should not be written to the file because of their transient nature. For example, if you place data set identifiers in lists to be saved with the SAVELIST function and restored with the FILLIST function in another task or another SAS session, the data set identifiers will become invalid. Thus, you should use the SETLATTR function to set the NOWRITE attribute on that list item.

Example

The following statements perform operations similar to copying a list recursively with COPYLIST(mylistid,'Y'):

```
   /* Assume the catalog WORK.TEMP exists: */
rc=savelist('catalog','work.temp.mylist.slist',mylistid);
newlistid=makelist();
rc=fillist('catalog','work.temp.mylist.slist',newlistid);
rc=delete('work.temp.mylist','catalog');
```

Notes

An error condition results if

- *list-id* is not a valid list identifier
- *attr-list* is not a valid list identifier.

(Do not confuse text attributes, like color and highlight, with list attributes as specified with the SETLATTR function.)

See Also

GETITEMC, GETLATTR, HASATTR, LISTLEN, MAKELIST, POPC, SAVELIST, SETITEMC, and SETLATTR in this chapter for information on related SCL functions

SEARCH

Creates or manipulates the current catalog search path

New SCL Function

Utility Function

Syntax

rc=SEARCH(*cat-name*);

Returns	Type	Value	
rc	N	0	The operation was successful
		−1	A problem occurred

Arguments	Type	Value or Action
cat-name	C	Name of the catalog to push to the front of the current search list Alternatively, you can specify one of the following values in place of a specific catalog name: -DISABLE Disable the current search list. -ENABLE Enable the current search list. If there is no disabled list, the current search list remains empty. -POP Remove the first name in the current search list. -POPALL Clear the current search list. **Note:** You must include the hyphen (-) as the first character in each of these argument values. Otherwise, the value will be treated as a catalog name in the WORK library.

Description

The SEARCH function enables you to manipulate the search path used by certain functions to locate catalog entries. It is not necessary to know the exact location of a catalog member, only that it is in one of the catalogs in the current search path.

When a function that uses the current search path is called, the catalogs in the search path are opened from first to last until the specified entry is found, or until the end of the search path is reached.

If there is no current search path, or if the current search path has been disabled or overridden, the search is limited to the current catalog.

Example

The following statements set up a search list with MYLIB1.CAT1, MYLIB1.CAT2 and MYLIB1.CAT3. Each time SEARCH is called, the new value of the argument is pushed to the front of the list, so MYLIB1.CAT3 is

SEARCH

continued

searched first. If MYPROG.PROGRAM only exists in MYLIB1.CAT1, it still executes correctly, since MYLIB1.CAT1 also is in the search path.

```
rc=search('mylib1.cat1');
rc=search('mylib1.cat2');
rc=search('mylib1.cat3');
call display('myprog.program');
```

See Also

CEXIST, DISPLAY, FSEDIT, FSLIST, FSVIEW, LETTER, LISTC, LISTN, and PREVIEW
: in Chapter 8 in *SAS Screen Control Language: Reference* for information on related SCL functions

BUILD and CALC
: in this chapter for information on related SCL functions

SEARCHC

Searches for the value of a character item in an SCL list and returns its position number

New SCL Function

List Function

Syntax

position=SEARCHC(*list-id*,*cval*⟨,*occurrence*⟨,*index*⟨,*ignore-case*⟨,*prefix*⟩⟩⟩⟩);

Returns	Type	Value
position	N	The number of the item's position in the SCL list. >0 The list position of the character value. 0 The value was not found.

Arguments	Type	Value or Action
list-id	N	Identifies the list to be searched.
cval	C	Specifies the character value to search for.
occurrence	N	Specifies the number of the occurrence of the value to search for. The default is 1, for the first occurrence of the item.
index	N	Specifies the position to start searching the list for the item. *Index* defaults to 1, the first item in the list. If *index* is a positive number, the search starts at position *index* from the beginning of the list and continues toward the end of the list. If *index* is a negative number, the search starts at position abs(*index*) from the end of the list and continues toward the beginning of the list.
ignore-case	C	Specifies how to compare string values: Y Ignore the case of the character strings. N Do not ignore case when comparing character strings. This is the default.
prefix	C	Specifies that the value is a prefix. Y Do a prefix comparison. This means search for any items which have *cval* as a prefix. The SEARCHC compares only the first *m* characters, where *m* is the length of search string *cval*. N Do not do a prefix search but compare all characters to *cval*. This is the default.

Description

The SEARCHC function searches an SCL list for a character value and returns the number of the position where the value is found or 0 if the value is not in the list. This function does not search any sublists of the list identified by *list-id* for the character value. The value for *cval* is compared only to the character values in the list identified by *list-id*.

SEARCHC

continued

Examples

The following statement searchs for the third occurrence of the string 'ABC' in the list identified by MYLISTID:

```
third=searchc(mylistid,'ABC',3);
```

The following statement finds the position of the second-to-last occurrence of a string that begins with 'SAS', ignoring case:

```
last2=searchc(mylistid,'sas',2,-1,'Y','Y');
```

Notes

The NAMEDITEM function searches for items by their name rather than their value.

An error condition results if

- the absolute value of *index* is zero or greater than the number of items in the list
- *list-id* does not contain a valid list identifier.

See Also

ITEMTYPE, MAKELIST, MAKENLIST, NAMEDITEM, SEARCHC, and SEARCHN in this chapter for information on related SCL functions

SEARCHL

Searches for the list identifier of a sublist item in an SCL list and returns its position number

SCL Function

List Function

Syntax

position=SEARCHL(*list-id,sublist-id*⟨,*n*⟨,*index*⟩⟩);

Returns	Type	Value
position	N	The number of the item's position in the SCL list. >0 The list position of the found value. 0 The value was not found.

Arguments	Type	Value or Action
list-id	N	Identifies the list to be searched.
sublist-id	N	Specifies the sublist identifier to search for.
occurrence	N	Specifies the number of the occurrence of the list identifier to search for. The default is 1, for the first occurrence of the item.
index	N	Specifies the position to start searching the list for the item. *Index* defaults to 1, the first item in the list. If *index* is a positive number, the search starts at position *index* from the beginning of the list and continues toward the end of the list. If *index* is a negative number, the search starts at position abs(*index*) from the end of the list and continues toward the beginning of the list.

Description

The SEARCHL function searches an SCL list for a sublist identifier and returns the number of the position where the identifier is found or 0 if the identifier is not in the list. This function does not search any sublists of the list identified by *list-id* for the sublist identifier. The value for *sublist-id* is compared only with the list values in the list identified by *list-id*.

Example

The following statement searches the list identified by MYLISTID for the third occurrence of the identifier for the sublist item identified by the value of NAMELISTID:

```
third=searchl(mylistid,namelistid,3);
```

Notes

The NAMEDITEM function searches for items by their name rather than their value.

An error condition results if

- the absolute value of *index* is zero or greater than the number of items in the list
- *list-id* is not a valid list identifier.

SEARCHL

continued

See Also

ITEMTYPE, MAKELIST, MAKENLIST, NAMEDITEM, SEARCHC, and SEARCHN in this chapter for information on related SCL functions

SEARCHN

Searches for the value of a numeric item in an SCL list and returns its position number

New SCL Function

List Function

Syntax

position= SEARCHN(*list-id*,*nval*⟨,*occurrence*⟨,*index*⟩⟩);

Returns	Type	Value
position	N	The number of the item's position in the SCL list. >0 The list position of the found value. 0 The value was not found.

Arguments	Type	Value or Action
list-id	N	Identifies the list to be searched.
nval	N	Specifies the numeric value to search for.
occurrence	N	Specifies the number of the occurrence of the value to search for. The default is 1, for the first occurrence of the item.
index	N	Specifies the position to start searching the list for the item. *Index* defaults to 1, the first item in the list. If *index* is a positive number, the search starts at position *index* from the beginning of the list and continues toward the end of the list. If *index* is a negative number, the search starts at position abs(*index*) from the end of the list and continues toward the beginning of the list.

Description

The SEARCHN function searches an SCL list for a numeric value and returns the number of the position where the value is found or 0 if the value is not in the list. This function does not search any sublists of the list identified by *list-id* for the numeric value. The value for *nval* is compared only to the numeric values in the list identified by *list-id*.

Example

The following statement searches for the third occurrence of the number 46 in the list identified by MYLISTID:

```
third = searchc(mylistid,46,3);
```

Notes

The NAMEDITEM function searches for items by their name rather than their value.

An error condition results if

- the absolute value of *index* is zero or greater than the number of items in the list
- *list-id* is not a valid list identifier.

SEARCHN

continued

See Also

ITEMTYPE, MAKELIST, MAKENLIST, NAMEDITEM, SEARCHC, and SEARCHL in this chapter for information on related SCL functions

SETITEMC

Assigns a new value to a character item in an SCL list or a value to a new character item

New SCL Function

List Function

Syntax

new-list-id=SETITEMC(*list-id*,*cval*⟨,*index*⟨,*autogrow*⟩⟩);

Returns	Type	Value
new-list-id	N	The list identifier of the modified list. This value is the same as *list-id*.

Arguments	Type	Value or Action
list-id	N	Identifies the list to be modified.
cval	C	Specifies the character value to store in the list.
index	N	Specifies the number of the item's position in the list. *Index* defaults to 1, the first item in the list. If *index* is a positive number, the item is at position *index* from the beginning of the list. If *index* is a negative number, the item is at position abs(*index*) from the end of the list.
autogrow	C	Specifies whether the list can expand to accommodate a new item. Y — The list's size can increase to accommodate a new item that is being added to the list. N — The list's size cannot change. This is the default.

Description

Using the SETITEMC function is analogous to assigning a value to an indexed item in an array. The SETITEMC function assigns a specified character value to an item in the list identified by *list-id*.

The value for *index* specifies the list position of the item whose value is assigned. If the value of *autogrow* is 'Y', the value of *index* can be greater than the length of the list. The SETITEMC function then expands the list to a total of *index*items, sets all new items to missing values, and places the new value into the list.

The SETITEMC function will replace an existing item in a list and even change its type, unless the item or the list has the FIXEDTYPE attribute.

The SETITEMC function does not make a copy of the list before assigning the new character item. The list is modified in place.

Notes

An error condition results if

- the list or item has the NOUPDATE attribute.
- the absolute value of *index* is greater than the length of the list and the list has the FIXEDLENGTH attribute (even if *autogrow* is Y)
- the list has the NUMONLY attribute

SETITEMC

continued

- the list or item has the FIXEDTYPE attribute and the function attempts to set the item to a different type. For example, if item 4 is numeric and has the FIXEDTYPE attribute, the following statement fails.

```
list=setitemc(list,'abc',4);
```

- the absolute value of *index* is greater than the length of the list and *autogrow* is 'N'
- *list-id* is not a valid list identifier.

See Also

DELITEM, GETITEMC, GETITEML, GETITEMN, GETLATTR, GETNITEMC, GETNITEML, GETNITEMN, HASATTR, INSERTC, INSERTL, INSERTN, ITEMTYPE, LISTLEN, MAKELIST, MAKENLIST, NAMEDITEM, SETITEML, SETITEMN, SETLATTR, SETNITEMC, SETNITEML, and SETNITEMN in this chapter for information on related SCL functions

SETITEML

Assigns a new identifier value to a sublist item or an identifier value to a new list item

New SCL Function

List Function

Syntax

new-list-id=SETITEML(*list-id*,*sublist-id*⟨,*index*⟨,*autogrow*⟩⟩);

Returns	Type	Value
new-list-id	N	The list identifier of the modified list. This value is the same as *list-id*.

Arguments	Type	Value or Action
list-id	N	Identifies the list to be modified.
sublist-id	N	The list identifier to store in the list.
index	N	Specifies the number of the item's position in the list. *Index* defaults to 1, the first item in the list. If *index* is a positive number, the item is at position *index* from the beginning of the list. If *index* is a negative number, the item is at position abs(*index*) from the end of the list.
autogrow	C	Specifies whether the list can expand to accommodate a new item. Y specifies that the list's size can increase to accommodate a new item that is being added to the list. N specifies that the list's size cannot change. This is the default.

Description

Using the SETITEML function is analogous to assigning a value to an indexed item in an array. The SETITEML function assigns a sublist to an item in the list identified by *list-id* .

The value for *index* specifies the list position to which the sublist item is assigned. If the value of *autogrow* is 'Y', the value of *index* can be greater than the length of the list. The SETITEML function then expands the list to a total of *index* items, sets all new items to missing values, and places the new sublist into the list.

The SETITEML function replaces an existing item in a list and even change its type, unless the item or the list has the FIXEDTYPE attribute.

The SETITEML function does not make a copy of the list before assigning the new character item. The list is modified in place.

Notes

An error condition results if

- *sublist-id* identifies a local list and *list-id* identifies a global list (you cannot place local lists into global lists)
- the absolute value of *index* is greater than the length of the list and *autogrow* is 'N'

SETITEML

continued

- the list or item has the NOUPDATE attribute.
- the absolute value of *index* is greater than the length of the list and the list has the FIXEDLENGTH attribute (even if *autogrow* is Y)
- the list has the CHARONLY or NUMONLY attribute
- the list or item has the FIXEDTYPE attribute and the function attempts to set the item to a different type. For example, if item 4 is numeric and has the FIXEDTYPE attribute, the following statement fails.

```
list=setiteml(listid,mylist-id,4);
```

- *sublist-id* is not a valid list identifier
- *list-id* is not a valid list identifier.

See Also

DELITEM, GETITEMC, GETITEML, GETITEMN, GETLATTR, GETNITEMC, GETNITEML, GETNITEMN, HASATTR, INSERTC, INSERTL, INSERTN, ITEMTYPE, LISTLEN, MAKELIST, MAKENLIST, NAMEDITEM, SETLATTR, SETITEMC, SETITEMN, SETNITEMC, SETNITEML, and SETNITEMN in this chapter for information on related SCL functions

SETITEMN

Assigns a new value to a numeric item in an SCL list or a value to a new numeric item

New SCL Function

List Function

Syntax

new-list-id=SETITEMN(*list-id,nval*⟨,*index*⟨,*autogrow*⟩⟩);

Returns	Type	Value
new-list-id	N	The list identifier of the modified list. This value is the same as *list-id*.

Arguments	Type	Value or Action
list-id	N	Identifies the list to be modified.
nval	N	The numeric value to store in the list.
index	N	Specifies the number of the item's position in the list. *Index* defaults to 1, the first item in the list. If *index* is a positive number, the item is at position *index* from the beginning of the list. If *index* is a negative number, the item is at position abs(*index*) from the end of the list.
autogrow	C	Specifies whether the list can expand to accommodate a new item. Y specifies that the list's size can increase to accommodate a new item that is being added to the list. N specifies that the list's size cannot change. This is the default.

Description

Using the SETITEMN function is analogous to assigning a value to an indexed item in an array. The SETITEMN function assigns a numeric value to an item in the list identified by *list-id*.

The value for *index* specifies the list position to which the sublist item is assigned. If the value of *autogrow* is 'Y', the value of *index* can be greater than the length of the list. The SETITEMN function then expands the list to a total of *index* items, sets all new items to missing values, and places the numeric value into the list.

The SETITEMN function replaces an existing item in a list and even changes its type, unless the item or the list has the FIXEDTYPE attribute.

The SETITEMN function does not make a copy of the list before assigning the new character item. The list is modified in place.

Notes

An error condition results if

- the absolute value of *index* is greater than the length of the list and *autogrow* is 'N'
- the list or item has the NOUPDATE attribute
- the list has the CHARONLY attribute

SETITEMN

continued

- the absolute value of *index* is greater than the length of the list and the list has the FIXEDLENGTH attribute (even if *autogrow* is Y)
- *list-id* is not a valid list identifier
- the list or item has the FIXEDTYPE attribute and the function attempts to set the item to a different type. For example, if item 4 is character and has the FIXEDTYPE attribute, the following statement fails.

```
list=SETITEMN(list,5000,4);
```

See Also

DELITEM, GETITEMC, GETITEML, GETITEMN, GETLATTR, GETNITEMC, GETNITEML, GETNITEMN, HASATTR,INSERTC, INSERTL, INSERTN, ITEMTYPE, LISTLEN, MAKELIST, MAKENLIST, NAMEDITEM, SETLATTR, SETNITEMC, SETNITEML, and SETNITEMN in this chapter for information on related SCL functions

SETKEY

Defines an index key for retrieving observations from a SAS data set

New SCL Function

Data Set Function

Syntax

nval=SETKEY(*data-set-id*⟨,*key-name*⟨, *condition*⟩⟩);

Returns	Type	Value	
nval	N	0	An active key was successfully set or cleared
		≠0	An error or warning condition occurred during the operation

Arguments	Type	Value or Action
data-set-id	N	Data set identifier returned by the OPEN function
key-name	C	Name of a defined index key to be used for retrieval
condition	C	Comparison criteria for the key value. Specify one of the following: EQ Equal to the key value. This is the default. GT Greater than the key value. GE Greater or equal to the key value.

Description

The SETKEY function enables you to set an active key in an open data set to a simple or composite key. It establishes a set of criteria for reading SAS data set observations by evaluating the value of the variables from the SDV against the key value in the observations.

If the active key is a composite key and the *condition* parameter was set to GT or GE, the data set will be subset into observations whose primary key variable values meet the specified criteria. Consequently, you still have to check the values of other key parts against the data vector to narrow down the subset of observations.

Example

The following program applies a key retrieval to the data set MYDATA which subsets the data set into only those observations where the variable AGE has a value greater than or equal to 20.

```
   /* assuming a simple key SEX has been defined */
age='20';
dsid=open('MYDATA','I');
call set(dsid);
rc=setkey(dsid,'age','ge');
do while(fetch(dsid) ne -1);
   name=getvarc(dsid,1);
   put name=;
end;
```

The following program searches the data set CHILDREN all boys who are 5 years old or older. The composite key ATTR is used for retrieval. The FETCH function within the DO-loop returns all observations with variable

SETKEY

continued

AGE>=5. Because some of the observations might not have a matched concatenated key part, an additional check on the value of variable SEX is needed to skip unmatched observations.

```
dsid =open ( 'children', 'v');

   /* create a composite key ATTR with AGE as primary key variable */
rc=icreate(dsid,'attr','age sex');
call set(dsid);
age=5;
sex='M';
rc=setkey(dsid,'attr','ge');
do while(rc=0);
      /* FETCH function applies the retrieval criteria and */
      /* retrieves all observations for which AGE>=5       */
   rc=fetch(dsid);
   if (rc) then leave;
      /* filter out observations for which SEX is not 'M' */
   sex_val=getvarc(dsid,5);
   if (sex_val ne sex) then
      continue;
   child = getvarc(dsid,3);
   put child=;
end;
```

Notes

The SETKEY function work only after the SET function has been called in the SCL program. Once an active key was set through the SETKEY function, it remains active until

- □ the data set is closed.
- □ another key is set.
- □ the current setting is cleared by passing the data set identifier alone to the SETKEY function.

The data set is automatically positioned at the first observation that meets the specified criteria.

See Also

ICREATE, IREVIEW, and WHERE in Chapter 8 in *SAS Screen Control Language: Reference* for information on related SCL functions

SETLATTR

Changes the attributes of a list or a list item

New SCL Function

List Function

Syntax

rc=SETLATTR(*list-id*,*attributes*⟨,*index*⟩);

Returns	Type	Value
rc	N	Indicator of the success of the change operation. 0 The attributes were set without error. ≠0 An error occurred trying to set an attribute.

Arguments	Type	Value or Action
list-id	N	List identifier
attributes	C	A character string containing one or more attributes to assign to the list or the list item. The following attributes are recognized for both lists and list items: DEFAULT A combination of all default attributes. DELETE Allow deletions of the list or item. This is a default attribute. NODELETE Do not allow deletion. When this attribute is assigned to an item, the item may not be deleted. When this attribute is assigned to a list, the list may not be deleted (but individual items that do not have the NODELETE attribute may be deleted). You may delete a list that contains items with the NODELETE attribute. UPDATE When this attribute is assigned to a list item, updates to the value are allowed. When this attribute is assigned to a list, updates are allowed to each item that does not have the NOUPDATE attribute. This is a default attribute. NOUPDATE When this attribute is assigned to a list item, updates to the value are not allowed. When this attribute is assigned to a list, updates are not allowed to any item, even if it has an UPDATE attribute. This enables you to make a list read-only in one step, without having to make each individual item read-only.

SETLATTR

continued

NOFIXEDTYPE
: When this attribute is assigned to a list item, the type of an item may change. When this attribute is assigned to a list, the type of each item may change as long as the list does not have the CHARONLY or NUMONLY attribute and the item does not have a FIXEDTYPE attribute. This is a default attribute.

FIXEDTYPE
: When this attribute is assigned to a list item, the type of the item may not change. See also the NUMONLY and CHARONLY list attributes. When this attribute is assigned to a list, the type of individual items may not change.

The following attributes are valid for lists only. If you try to assign these attributes to list items, they are ignored. Thus, you can create a single attribute string which you can apply to lists or list items.

ANYNAMES
: Item names can be any character string, although names are always converted to uppercase and trailing blanks are removed. This is a default attribute.

SASNAMES
: All items in the list must be named, and all names must be valid SAS names, with no leading or trailing blanks.

DUPNAMES
: Duplicate names are allowed. This is a default attribute.

NODUPNAMES
: All item names must be unique.

NOCHARONLY
: All items need not have character values. This is a default attribute.

CHARONLY
: Items must all have character values.

NOFIXEDLENGTH
: The list length may change. This is a default attribute.

FIXEDLENGTH
: The list length cannot change.

NONUMONLY
: All items need not have numeric values. This is a default attribute.

NUMONLY
: All items must have numeric values.

The following attributes are valid for list items only. They are ignored if you try to assign them to a list.

ACTIVE	The item will be active when presented in the POPMENU function. This is a default attribute.
INACTIVE	The item will not be active when presented in the POPMENU function (users cannot select it).
WRITE	The item will be written when the list is stored via SAVELIST. This is a default attribute.
NOWRITE	The item will not be written by SAVELIST.

index N The number of the item's position in the list. If *index* is not 0, the named attributes are assigned to the specified item instead of the entire list. If *index* is a negative number, the item is at position abs(*index*) from the end of the list.

Description

The SETLATTR function assigns attributes to a list or an item in a list. If the number for *index* is omitted or zero, the attributes are assigned to the list. Otherwise the attributes are assigned to the item at the position specified by *index*. Item attributes are attached to the items in the list, not the position in the list, so that an item keeps its attributes after rotating or reversing the list or after inserting and deleting other items. That is, if you assign a NODELETE attribute to the fourth item in the list and then delete the item at position 2, the item still has the NODELETE attribute even though it is now at position 3.

Distinction between NODELETE list and NODELETE item attributes
The NODELETE list attribute means the list itself cannot be deleted with the DELLIST function. The NODELETE item attribute indicates an item cannot be deleted from the list, regardless of the item's type.

The following statements show this distinction.

```
a=makelist(3);
b=makelist();
a=setiteml(a,b,3);   /*  Set 3rd item in A to B.  */
   /* Give the list B the NODELETE attribute.      */
   /* DELLIST(b) will be an error.                 */
rc=setlattr(b,'NODELETE');
   /* give the 3rd item in A the NODELETE attribute */
   /* DELITEM(a, 3) will be an error               */
rc=setlattr(a,'NODELETE',3);
   /* Move B to second item in list and set        */
   /* third item with 0.                           */
a=setiteml(a,b,2);
a=setitemn(a,0,3);
   /* Remove B from the list A, but B still exists  */
a=delitem(a,2);
   /* DELITEM(a,2) will be an error now            */
```

SETLATTR

continued

Protecting list attributes from modification
You can assign a password to list attributes, which enables you to protect them. The password is stored with the list and must be supplied in subsequent SETLATTR function statements in order to modify either list or item attributes. The password is specified as

PASSWORD=*pwd*

in the attribute string. The password may not contain any blanks, but case is significant (the passwords frobble and FROBBLE are different).

The following statements illustrate assigning a password.

```
pwd='password=grombaq';
myattr='nodelete noupdate';
setlattr(mylistid,myattr||pwd );
```

If an SCL program attempts to modify the value of one of the items in MYLIST, the program will halt because the list has the NOUPDATE attribute. If you want to permit updates of the list again, you can execute:

```
rc=setlattr(mylist,'update'||pwd);
```

You can remove the password from a list with the NOPASSWORD= attribute, allowing any SCL program to change attributes or to set the password. Either of the following statements remove the previously set password from the list identified by MYLIST.

```
rc=setlattr(mylist,'no'||pwd);
rc=setlattr(mylist,nopassword=grombaq');
```

Note that you must supply the correct password in order to remove it.

Attributes
The attributes for lists and list items come in mutually exclusive pairs. For example, the NOUPDATE attribute designates that the UPDATE attribute is off. Setting one attribute of a mutually exclusive pair automatically turns off the other. The attribute pairs are shown in the following table. The first column indicates which attributes are default attributes, the second column shows its complement, and the third column designates whether attributes apply to lists (L), items (I), or both (B).

ACTIVE	INACTIVE	I
ANYNAMES	SASNAMES	L
DELETE	NODELETE	B
DUPNAMES	NODUPNAMES	L
NOCHARONLY	CHARONLY	L
NOFIXEDLENGTH	FIXEDLENGTH	L
NOFIXEDTYPE	FIXEDTYPE	B
NONUMONLY	NUMONLY	L
UPDATE	NOUPDATE	B

Notes

The attributes of a list (such as CHARONLY, NUMONLY, FIXEDTYPE, and NOUPDATE) do not apply to sublists contained within them. You must set these attributes on the sublists if you wish them to have these attributes.

Both list and item attributes are copied by COPYLIST, but not the password.

Most of the list functions that alter lists or their contents are affected in some way by list and item attributes. See the documentation for the individual functions to see how they are affected.

An error condition results if

- *index* is an invalid list index other than 0
- *list-id* is not a valid list identifier.

See Also

COPYLIST, DELITEM, DELLIST, DELNITEM, ENVLIST, FILLIST, GETITEMC, GETITEML, GETITEMN, GETLATTR, GETNITEMC, GETNITEML, GETNITEMN, HASATTR, INSERTC, INSERTL, INSERTN, ITEMTYPE, LISTLEN, MAKELIST, MAKENLIST, NAMEDITEM, NAMEITEM, POPC, POPL, POPN, POPMENU, PUTLIST, REVLIST, ROTLIST, SAVELIST, SEARCHC, SEARCHL, SEARCHN, SETITEMC, SETITEML, SETITEMN, SETNITEMC, SETNITEML, and SETNITEMN in this chapter for information on related SCL functions

SETNITEMC

Assigns a character value to a named item in an SCL list

New SCL Function

List Function

Syntax

new-list-id=SETNITEMC(*list-id,cval,name*⟨*,occurrence*⟨*,index*⟨*,pos*⟩⟩⟩);

Returns	Type	Value
new-list-id	N	The list identifier of the modified list. This value is the same number as *list-id*.

Arguments	Type	Value or Action
list-id	N	Identifies the list to be modified. This value was returned by the function that created the list.
cval	C	Specifies the character value to assign to the named item.
name	C	Specifies the name of the character item. If this item is not in the list, it is inserted into the list. Item names are converted to uppercase and trailing blanks are ignored when searching the list for a matching name. Thus, the names 'abc' and 'Abc ' are converted to 'ABC'.
occurrence	N	The number of the occurrence of the named item to assign the specified value. The default is 1 for the first occurrence of the item.
index	N	Specifies the position to start searching the list for the item. *Index* defaults to 1, the first item in the list. If *index* is a positive number, the search starts at position *index* from the beginning of the list and continues toward the end of the list. If *index* is a negative number, the search starts at position abs(*index*) from the end of the list and continues toward the beginning of the list.
pos	N	Specifies a variable to contain the position of the modified or inserted item.

Description

The SETNITEMC function assigns a character value to a named item in the SCL list specified by *list-id*. If the named item is not found in the list (and the list does not have the FIXEDLENGTH attribute), the item is inserted into the list. If the value for *index* is a positive number, the new item is inserted at the end of the list, so as to not shift previous items that match the name. If the value for *index* is a negative number, the new item is inserted at the beginning of the list.

The result of using the SETNITEMC function is similar to combining the NAMEDITEM and the SETITEMC functions. For example, the statement:

```
mylist=setnitemc(mylist,'Jones','NAMES',1,1,i);
```

performs the same operations as the following statements:

```
i=nameditem(mylist,'NAMES');
   /* If NAMES isn't found, insert it at the end of the list. */
if i=0 then mylist=insertc(mylist,'Jones',-1,'NAMES');
else mylist=setitemc(mylist,'Jones',i);
```

If a value is specified for *pos*, the SETNITEMC function returns the position of the modified or inserted item. You can reference this position to update the same item with the SETITEMC function and other SCL list functions, as long as the items do not change positions (for example, as a result of an insert or delete operation). If the position of items in a list is stable, using the *pos* argument and subsequent index-based functions rather than name-based functions improves performance because the list does not have to be searched to find a name match.

The SETNITEMC function does not make a copy of the list before the item is modified or inserted. The list is modified in place.

Note that the SETNITEMC function automatically inserts the item into the list if the named item does not already exist. To control whether the item is inserted if it is not in the list, use the NAMEDITEM and INSERTC functions.

Notes

An error condition results if

- either the item or the list has the NOUPDATE or NUMONLY attribute
- either the item or the list has the FIXEDTYPE attribute and the new value is being assigned to a numeric or sublist item
- the absolute value of *index* is zero or greater than the number of items in the list
- *list-id* is not a valid list identifier.

To check the attributes of a list or list item, use the HASATTR function. To change these attributes, use the SETLATTR function.

See Also

DELNITEM, GETITEMC, GETITEML, GETITEMN, GETLATTR, GETNITEMC, GETNITEML, GETNITEMN, HASATTR, INSERTC, INSERTL, INSERTN, MAKELIST, MAKENLIST, NAMEDITEM, NAMEITEM, SETITEMC, SETITEML, SETITEMN, SETNITEML, SETNITEMN, and SETLATTR in this chapter for information on related SCL functions

SETNITEML

Assigns a sublist identifier to a named item in an SCL list

New SCL Function

List Function

Syntax

new-list-id=SETNITEML(*list-id,sublist-id,name*⟨*,occurrence*⟨*,index*⟨*,pos*⟩⟩⟩);

Returns	Type	Value
new-list-id	N	The list identifier of the modified list. This value is the same as *list-id*.

Arguments	Type	Value or Action
list-id	N	Identifies the list to be modified.
sublist-id	N	Specifies the sublist identifier to assign to the named item.
name	C	Specifies the name of the sublist item. If this item is not in the list, it is inserted into the list. Item names are converted to uppercase and trailing blanks are ignored when searching the list for a matching name. Thus, the names 'abc' and 'Abc ' are converted to 'ABC'.
occurrence	N	The number of the occurrence of the named item to assign the specified value. The default is 1 for the first occurrence of the item.
index	N	Specifies the position to start searching the list for the item. *Index* defaults to 1, the first item in the list. If *index* is a positive number, the search starts at position *index* from the beginning of the list and continues to the end of the list. If *index* is a negative number, the search starts at position abs(*index*) from the end of the list and continues to the beginning of the list.
pos	N	Specifies the number of the position of the modified or inserted item.

Description

The SETNITEML function assigns a sublist value to a named item in the SCL list specified by *list-id*. If the named item is not found in the list (and the list does not have the FIXEDLENGTH attribute), the item is inserted into the list. If the value for *index* is a positive number, the new item is inserted at the end of the list, so as to not shift previous items that match the name. If the value for *index* is a negative number, the new item is inserted at the beginning of the list.

If a value is specified for *pos*, the SETNITEML function returns the position of the modified or inserted item. You can reference this position to update the same item with the SETITEML function and other SCL list functions, as long as the items do not change positions (for example, as a result of an insert or delete operation). If the position of items in a list is stable, using the *pos* argument and subsequent index-based functions rather than name-based functions improves performance because the list does not have to be searched to find a name match.

The result of using the SETNITEML function is similar to combining the NAMEDITEM and the SETITEML functions. For example, the statement:

```
mylist=setniteml(mylist,employeelistid,'NAMES',1,1,i);
```

performs the same operations as the following statements:

```
i=nameditem(mylist,'NAMES');
   /* If NAMES isn't found, insert it at the end of the list. */
if i=0 then mylist=insertl(mylist,employeelistid,-1,'NAMES');
else mylist=setiteml(mylist,employeelistid,i);
```

The SETNITEML function cannot assign the new sublist value if either the item or the list has the

- NOUPDATE, NUMONLY, or CHARONLY attribute
- FIXEDTYPE attribute, and the new value being is being assigned to a character or numeric item.

(To check the attributes of a list or list item, use the HASATTR function. To change these attributes, use the SETLATTR function.)

The SETNITEML function does not make a copy of the list before the item is modified or inserted. The list is modified in place.

Note that the SETNITEML function automatically inserts the item into the list if the named item does not already exist. To control whether the item is inserted if it is not in the list, use the NAMEDITEM and INSERTL functions.

Notes

An error condition results if

- *sublist-id* identifies a local list and *list-id* identifies a global list, because you cannot place local lists into global lists
- the absolute value of *index* is zero or greater than the number of items in the list
- *sublist-id* is not a valid identifier
- *list-id* is not a valid identifier.

See Also

DELNITEM, GETITEMC, GETITEML, GETITEMN, GETLATTR, GETNITEMC, GETNITEML, GETNITEMN, HASATTR, INSERTC, INSERTL, INSERTN, MAKELIST, MAKENLIST, NAMEDITEM, NAMEITEM, SETITEMC, SETITEML, SETITEMN, SETNITEMC, SETNITEMN, and SETLATTR in this chapter for information on related SCL functions

SETNITEMN

Assigns a numeric value to a named item in an SCL list

New SCL Function

List Function

Syntax

new-list-id=SETNITEMN(*list-id,nval,name*⟨,*occurrence*⟨,*index*⟨,*pos*⟩⟩⟩);

Returns	Type	Value
new-list-id	N	The list identifier of the modified list. This value is the same as *list-id*.

Arguments	Type	Value or Action
list-id	N	Identifies the list to be modified. This value was returned by the function that created the list.
nval	N	Specifies the numeric value to assign to the named item.
name	C	Specifies the name of the numeric item. If this item is not in the list, it is inserted into the list. Item names are converted to uppercase and trailing blanks are ignored when searching the list for a matching name. Thus, the names 'abc' and 'Abc ' are converted to 'ABC'.
occurrence	N	The number of the occurrence of the named item to assign the specified value. The default is 1 for the first occurrence of the item.
index	N	Specifies the position to start searching the list for the item. *Index* defaults to 1, the first item in the list. If *index* is a positive number, the search starts at position *index* from the beginning of the list and continues to the end of the list. If *index* is a negative number, the search starts at position abs(*index*) from the end of the list and continues to the beginning of the list.
pos	N	Specifies the number of the position of the modified or inserted item.

Description

The SETNITEMN function assigns a numeric value to a named item in the SCL list specified by *list-id*. If the named item is not found in the list (and the list does not have the FIXEDLENGTH attribute), the item is inserted into the list. If the value for *index* is a positive number, the new item is inserted at the end of the list, so as to not shift previous items that match the name. If the value for *index* is a negative number, the new item is inserted at the beginning of the list.

If a value is specified for *pos*, the SETNITEMN function returns the position of the modified or inserted item. You can reference this position to update the same item with the SETITEMN function and other SCL list functions, as long as the items do not change positions (for example, as a result of an insert or delete operation). If the position of items in a list is stable, using the *pos* argument and subsequent index-based functions rather than name-based functions improves performance because the list does not have to be searched to find a name match.

The result of using the SETNITEMN function is similar to combining the NAMEDITEM and the SETITEMN functions. For example, the statement:

```
mylist=setnitemn(mylist,5000,'AMOUNTS',1,1,i);
```

performs the same operations as the following statements:

```
i=nameditem(mylist,'AMOUNTS');
   /* If AMOUNTS isn't found, insert it at the end of the list. */
if i=0 then mylist=insertn(mylist,5000,-1,'AMOUNTS');
else mylist=setitemn(mylist,5000,i);
```

Note that the SETNITEMN function automatically inserts the item into the list. To control whether the item is inserted if it is not in the list, use the NAMEDITEM and INSERTN functions.

Notes

An error condition results if

- either the item or the list has the NOUPDATE or CHARONLY attribute
- either the item or the list has the FIXEDTYPE attribute, and the new value is being assigned to a character or sublist item
- the absolute value of *index* is zero or greater than the number of items in the list
- *list-id* is not a valid list identifier.

To check the attributes of a list or list item, use the HASATTR function. To change these attributes, use the SETLATTR function.

See Also

DELNITEM, GETITEMC, GETITEML, GETITEMN, GETLATTR, GETNITEMC, GETNITEML, GETNITEMN, HASATTR, INSERTC, INSERTL, INSERTN, MAKELIST, MAKENLIST, NAMEDITEM, NAMEITEM, SETITEMC, SETITEML, SETITEMN, SETNITEMC, SETNITEML, and SETLATTR in this chapter for information on related SCL functions

SORTLIST

Sorts the items in an SCL list

New SCL Function

List Function

Syntax

new-list-id=SORTLIST(*list-id*
⟨,*options*⟨,*start-index*⟨,*n-items*⟩⟩⟩);

Returns	Type	Value
new-list-id	N	The list identifier of the sorted list. This value is the same as *list-id*.

Arguments	Type	Value or Action
list-id	N	Identifies the list to be sorted.
options	C	Specify how the sort operation is performed. Multiple options can be specified, separated by blanks. Each option can be abbreviated to a unique substring, which is the first character for all options except NAME and NODUP which may be abbreviated to two characters, NA or NO.

Option	Description
ASCENDING	Sort the list in ascending order. This is default sort order.
DESCENDING	Sort the list in descending order.
VALUE	Sort the list by item value. This is the default. In an ascending sort, missing values appear first in the sorted list, followed by string values, followed by numeric values, followed by list id's.
NAME	Sort the list by item name. Unnamed items appear before named items in an ascending sort.
IGNORECASE	Ignore case when comparing string values. Case is always ignored when sorting by NAME because names are always converted to uppercase.
OBEYCASE	Obey case when comparing string values. This is the default when sorting by VALUE.
NODUP	Delete duplicate items when sorting. If your are sorting by value (name), then all but the first item in the sort range which have the same value (name) are deleted. The default is not to delete duplicates.

start-index	N	Specifies the position to start the sort operation. *Start-index* defaults to 1, the first item in the list. If *start-index* is a positive number, *index* is the first item in the sublist. If *start-index* is a negative number, abs(*start-index*) marks the last item in the sublist, counted from the end of the list.
n-items	N	Specifies the number of items in the list to sort. The default is all items. To explicitly specify all items, specify -1.

Description

The SORTLIST function sorts items in a list, and returns the sorted list. The SORTLIST function does not make a copy of the list before it is sorted. The list is modified in place.

Examples

The following statement sorts the first 10 items in a list in descending order:

```
list=sortlist(list,'D',1,10);
```

The following statement sorts the last 16 items in a list in ascending order.

```
list=sortlist(list,'',-1,16);
```

The following statement sorts the second ten items in a list in ascending name order, deleting duplicate.

```
list=sortlist(list,'NODUP ASCENDING NAME',11 10);
```

Notes

Sublists contained in the sorted list are not sorted recursively.

When you specify the NODUP and IGNORECASE options, the list then items or names that are spelled the same but differ only in case are considered duplicates and all but the first occurrence are removed from the sorted list.

An error condition results if *list-id* is not a valid list identifier.

See Also

COPYLIST, CURLIST, DELLIST, FILLIST, GETLATTR, LISTLEN, MAKELIST, PUTLIST, REVLIST, ROTLIST, and SETLATTR in this chapter for information on related SCL functions

STRATTR

Defines a color and highlighting attribute string

New SCL Function

Field Function

Syntax

cval=STRATTR(*color,attribute,start,length*);

Returns	Type	Value
cval	C	String containing information about given color and highlighting attribute

Arguments	Type	Value or Action
color	C	Color name to store in the attribute string. The following values are valid for the *color* argument: BLACK CYAN MAGENTA RED BLUE GRAY ORANGE WHITE BROWN GREEN PINK YELLOW
attribute	C	Highlighting attribute name to store in the attribute string. The following values are valid for the *attribute* argument: ALLOFF HIREV BLINKING REVERSE HIGHLIGHT UNDERLINE
start	N	Starting character position to store in the attribute string.
length	N	Number of character positions to store in the attribute string.

Description

The STRATTR function defines a string that you can use with the FLDATTR function to change the color and highlighting attribute of fields or portions of fields in the application's window.

Example

The following statement uses the STRATTR function to define an attribute string named ABC that sets the third through seventh character positions of a field to red and high intensity:

```
abc=strattr('red','highlight',3,5);
```

Notes

If the contents of remaining character string position is not between the start position and start+length-1, the position does not change.

The function FLDCOLOR is equivalent to the combination of function STRATTR and function FLDATTR.

See Also

FLDATTR and FLDCOLOR in this chapter for information on related SCL functions

UNGRAY

Ungrays a single station or an entire choice group

New SCL Function

Choice Group Function

SAS/AF Software Only

Syntax

rc=UNGRAY(*choice-group*⟨,*station*⟨,*row*⟩⟩);

rc	N	0	Specified choice group or station was successfully ungrayed
		≠0	Specified choice group or station could not be ungrayed

Arguments	Type	Value or Action
choice-group	C	Choice group name assigned in the ATTR window
station	N	Number of the field within the choice group
row	N	Valid row number when the choice group is in the scrollable section of an extended table

Description

The UNGRAY function ungrays the specified station of a choice group or the entire choice group in a SAS/AF application.

The UNGRAY function, when used with the GRAY function, enables an AF application to control the availability of a choice group or a station based on the program flow.

Example

The following statements use the UNGRAY function to make a station available only when the value of variable DEPT is `ADMIN`.

```
if (dept='ADMIN') then
   rc=ungray('personal',3);
else
   rc=gray('personal',3);
```

Notes

You can also use the ACTIVATE function to ungray a grayed station of a choice group by passing a negative value of station number.

See Also

ACTIVATE, CURWORD, and ISACTIVE
: in Chapter 8 in *SAS Screen Control Language: Reference* for information on related SCL functions

GRAY and ISGRAY
: in this chapter for information on related SCL functions

VARLIST

Displays a selection list window that lists the variables in an open SAS data set and returns user selections

Enhanced SCL Function

Selection List Function

Syntax

cval=VARLIST(*data-set-id*,*var-type*,*num-sel*⟨,*message*⟨,*autoclose*⟨,*sel-order*
⟨,*exclude*⟨,*select*⟩⟩⟩⟩⟩);

Note: The syntax for the VARLIST function is unchanged from Release 6.06. See Chapter 8 in *SAS Screen Control Language: Reference* for details.

Updated Functionality

The VARLIST function now places values in the current environment list. When the VARLIST function is invoked, the current environment list is cleared. After invoking the VARLIST function, the environment list contains one element for each variable name selected. The selections can be retrieved using the GETITEMC function.

Example

The following statements display a selection list window containing the character variables from an open SAS data set, excluding the variables NAME and ADDRESS. User can make two selections. The selected variable names are retrieved from the current environment list. The LISTLEN function is used to return the number of selections because there is only one element in the list for each selection made.

```
listid=makelist();
rc=curlist(listid);
select=varlist(dsid,'c',2,'Choose a variable',' ','y',
               'name address');
n=listlen(listid);
do i=1 to n;
   varname=getitemc(listid,i);
   put varname=;
end;
```

WINFO

Returns information about the current window

Enhanced SCL Function

Window Function

Syntax

rc=WINFO(*info-item*);

The following argument has changed for Release 6.07. Refer to *SAS Screen Control Language: Reference* for details of the other syntax elements.

Arguments	Type	Value or Action	
info-item	C	Information item to be returned. In addition to the information items listed for the WINFO function in Chapter 8 in *SAS Screen Control Language: Reference*, the following new options are available:	
		GRAPHICS	Returns a 1 if the user's output device supports graphics.
		ICON	Returns the number of Institute-supplied icons available under the user's host operating system. Refer to host documentation for information on whether the SAS System supports icons under your host operating system.
		UICON	Returns the number of user-defined icons available under the user's host operating system.
		NSCREEN	Returned value varies according to the type of application: SAS/AF returns a 2 if you used ^^^ or ¬¬¬ to divide the entry's window into two or more frames. Otherwise, this argument value returns a 1. FSEDIT returns the number of screens defined for the current FSEDIT window. FSVIEW returns 4 to indicate the four parts of the FSVIEW window: the column title area, the row number or ID column area, the data area, and the area above the column titles.
		CURSCREEN	The number of the screen or frame where the cursor is situated.
		BATCH	Returns a 1 if the application is running in batch mode.

Updated Functionality

The WINFO function now returns additional information about the features available in the current window.

Example

The following statements use the new WINFO function options to obtain information about the current window:

```
sr=winfo('graphics');
si=winfo('icon');
ui=winfo('uicon');
ns=winfo('nscreen');
cs=winfo('curscreen');
bm=winfo('batch');
```

See Also

Chapter 6, "Support for Icons," for more information on using icons in SAS/AF applications

WOUTPUT

Manipulates the display manager OUTPUT window

Enhanced SCL Function

Window Function

Syntax

sysrc=WOUTPUT(*action*,⟨,*argument-1*⟨,. . .,*argument-3*⟩⟩);

The following argument has changed for Release 6.07. Refer to *SAS Screen Control Language: Reference* for details of the other syntax elements.

Arguments	Type	Value or Action
action	C	Action to perform on the OUTPUT window. In addition to the actions listed for the WOUTPUT function in Chapter 8 in *SAS Screen Control Language: Reference*, the following new options are available: POPOFF — turns off the AUTOPOP option of the OUTPUT window. POPON — turns on the AUTOPOP option of the OUTPUT window. NOTE — marks to get the next created output. The NOTE action has a direct effect on the FILE, PRINT and SAVE actions. When the output is written via the WOUTPUT function, the pointer is reset to the end of the current output. DROPNOTE — clears the note and causes it to use its default behavior to write only the last output.

Updated Functionality

The WOUTPUT function now provides additional features for controlling the behavior of the display manager output window.

Example

The following statements print the output generated by the two SUBMIT statements in the OUTPUT window and append it to the file designated by the fileref in the SCL variable EXTERN. If you omit the WOUTPUT statement with the NOTE option, only the output from the second SUBMIT statement is printed.

```
rc=woutput('note');
submit continue;
   data one;
      x=1;
      proc print;
   run;
      more SCL statements
endsubmit;
```

```
submit continue;
   data two;
      y=2;
      proc print;
   run;
endsubmit;
rc=woutput('print',' ',extern,'a');
rc=woutput('dropnote');
```

Notes

Once a note is set, it stays through the SAS session until it is explicitly reset.

CHAPTER 21 Dictionary of Enhanced SCL Debugger Commands

BREAK

Suspends program execution at an executable statement

Enhanced SCL Debugger Command

Manipulating Debugging Requests

Syntax

BREAK ⟨*location* ⟨AFTER *count*⟩⟨WHEN *clause* | DO *list*⟩⟩
B ⟨*location* ⟨AFTER *count*⟩⟨WHEN *clause* | DO *list*⟩⟩

Arguments	Description	
location	Specifies where to set a breakpoint.	
	label	Sets a breakpoint at the first executable statement of a specific labeled section in the program. Labeled sections can be user defined as well as system defined.

Updated Functionality

The BREAK command specified with one of the program's label names sets a breakpoint at the first executable statement in the specified labeled section. The label can be any program label, user-defined as well as system defined.

Examples

The following examples illustrate the use of the BREAK command with user-defined program labels.

□ Set a breakpoint at the label AAA.

```
DEBUG> B AAA
```

□ Set a breakpoint at the label AAA in the SAS/AF entry TEST1.PROGRAM.

```
DEBUG> B test1\AAA
```

GO

Starts or resumes execution of the active program

SCL Debugger Command

Controlling Program Execution

Syntax

GO ⟨*entry-name*\ | *line-num* | *label-name* | RETURN⟩
G ⟨*entry-name*\ | *line-num* | *label-name* | RETURN⟩

Arguments	Description
label-name	Specifies that execution is to be suspended at the first executable statement of the specified label section in the program. User-defined labels are now supported as well as system-defined labels.

Updated Functionality

The GO command specified with a program label starts or resumes program execution and suspends execution at the first executable statement in the specified section. Both user-defined and system-defined labels can be specified with the GO command.

Example

Suppose you want to resume program execution and then suspend execution at the first statement in the section you have labeled AAA. The temporary breakpoint in AAA will be cleared after the program is suspended at AAA.

```
DEBUG> GO AAA
```

PUTLIST

Displays the contents of an SCL list

New SCL Debugger Command

Syntax

PUTLIST </il arg-list/rg | *n*>+

Arguments	Description
arg-list	One or more SCL list identifiers returned by the MAKELIST or COPYLIST function. It can be specified in the form <*entry-name*\> *variable*, where *entry-name* — names a program entry where a succeeding variable is defined *variable* — identifies a standard SCL variable
n	one or more numeric literals that represent the list to be printed

Description

The PUTLIST command displays the contents of an SCL list in the DEBUGGER MESSAGE window. The list starts with left parenthesis '(' to mark the beginning of the list, followed by the list of items separated by blanks. Each named item is preceded by its name and an equal sign (=), but nothing is printed before items that do not have names. The PUTLIST function ends the list with a right parenthesis ')', followed by the list's identifier number within square brackets.

Examples

The following is the result of issuing the SCL debug command PUTLIST A where list A contains the numbers 17 and 328 and the character string 'Any string.'

```
DEBUG > putlist a

( 17
  328
  'Any string'
)  7
```

The following example prints the lists identified by numbers 7 and 5.

```
DEBUG> putlist 7 5

( STYLE=8
  SQFEET=8
  BEDROOMS=8
  BATHS=8
  STREET=16
  PRICE=8
)  7
( NAME=8
  SEX=1
  AGE=8
  HEIGHT=8
  WEIGHT=8
)  5
```

PUTLIST

continued

Notes

If a list appears more than once in the list being printed, the PUTLIST command displays just (. . .) *listid* for the second and subsequent occurrences of the list. You should scan the output of the PUTLIST command for another occurrence of *listid* to view the full contents of the list. This prevents infinite loops if a list contains itself as a sublist.

See Also

SCL routine PUTLIST

STEP

Executes statements one at a time in the active program

SCL Debugger Command

Controlling Program Execution

Syntax

STEP ⟨OVER | O⟩
ST ⟨OVER | O⟩

Updated Functionality

The STEP command when used to execute a SELECT statement jumps directly to the appropriate WHEN or OTHERWISE clause without stepping through any intervening WHEN statements.

Example

Suppose you are using the STEP command to execute your program, which is stopped at line 15. If VAL has a value of 99, the STEP command jumps to line 116 immediately.

```
line #
 15   select (val);
 16      when (1)
 17            call display('a1');
 18      when (2)
 19            call display('a2');
      ...............
113      when (98)
114            call display('a98');
115      when (99)
116            call display('a99');
117      when (100)
118            call display('a100');
119      otherwise
120            call display('other');
121   end;
```

Appendix Icons

1
KEYS

2
HELP

3
LOG

4
OUTPUT

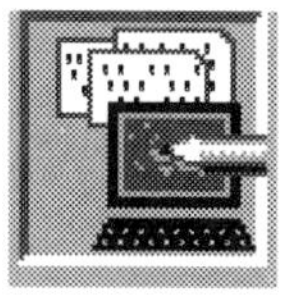

5
PROGRAM EDITOR

6
LIBNAME

7
DIR

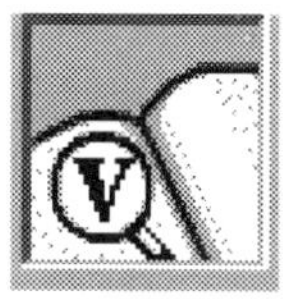

8
VAR

9
FILENAME

10
NOTEPAD

11
TITLES

12
FOOTNOTES

13
OPTIONS

14
SETINIT

16
GRAPH MANAGER

17
AF

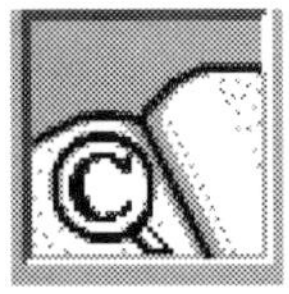

18
CATALOG

23
FSEDIT

24
FSBROWSE

25
FSVIEW

26
FSLIST

27
FSLETTER

28
APPOINTMENT

29
SYMBOL

30
PATTERN

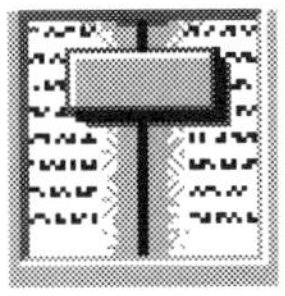

31
ASSIST

32
ACCESS

33
CALCULATOR

34
SQL

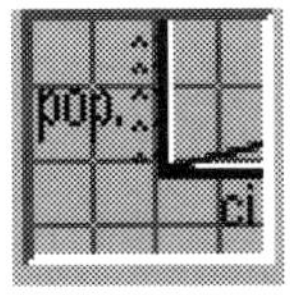

35
AXIS

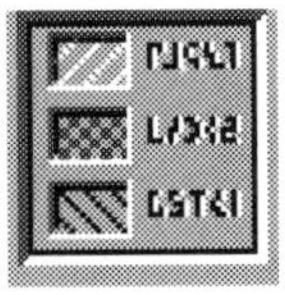

36
LEGEND

37
QUERY

39
SITEINFO

40
FSFORM

46
GRAPH 1

47
GRAPH 2

48
GRAPH 3

49
GRAPH 4

50
LAB

52
TRADER RECEIVE

54
INSIGHT

55
DESIGN OF E

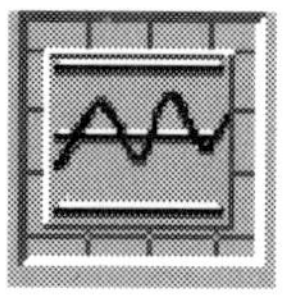

56
STATISTICAL QUALITY CNTL

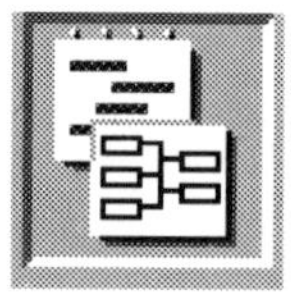

57
PROJECT MGMT

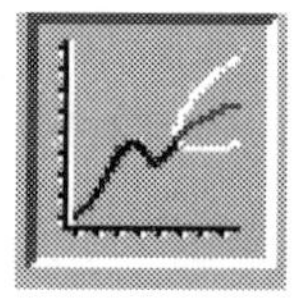

58
FORECASTIN

63
BUILD

64
CALC

102
TUTORIAL

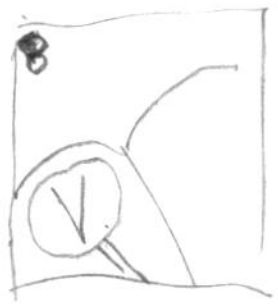

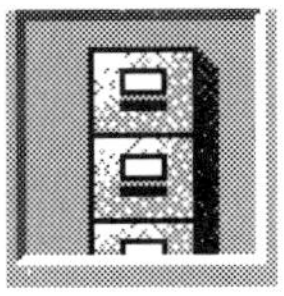

103
DATA MGMT

104
REPORT WRITING

105
DATA ANALYSIS

106
PLANNING TOOLS

107
EIS

108
RESULTS

109
SETUP

110
INDEX

111
EXIT

112
OVERVIEW

113
PRINCIPLES

114
DIRECTIONS

115
CUSTOMIZE

116
GOBACK

117
ACTIVE

118
EDIT

119
CREATE/IMPORT

120
DBMS ACCESS

121
COMBINE

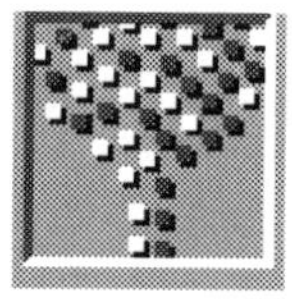

122
SORT

123
UTILITIES

124
LISTING

125
TABLES

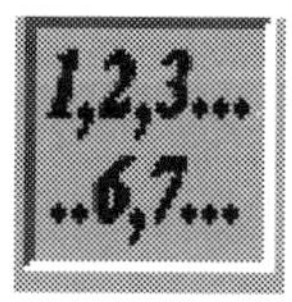

126
COUNTS

127
DESIGN REPORT

128
BAR CHARTS

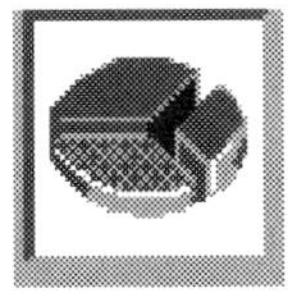

129
PIE CHARTS

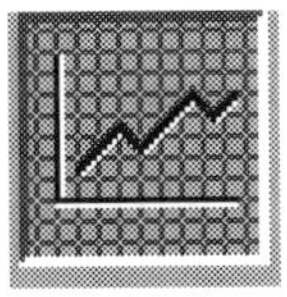

130
PLOTS

131
MAPS

132
ELEMENTARY

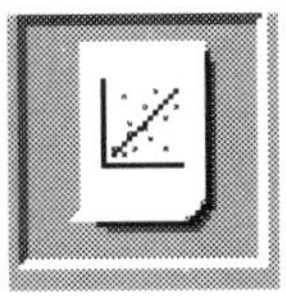

133
REGRESSION

134
ANOVA

135
MULTIVARIATE

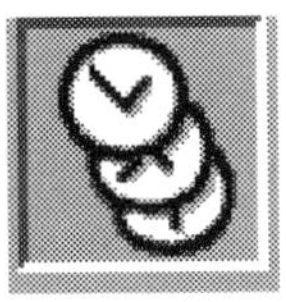

136
TIME SERIES

137
LOAN ANALYSIS

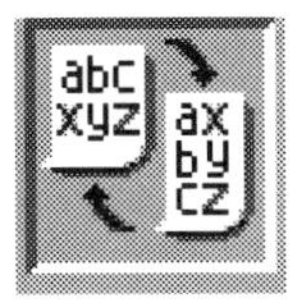

138
TRANSPOSE

139
DESIGN FORMAT

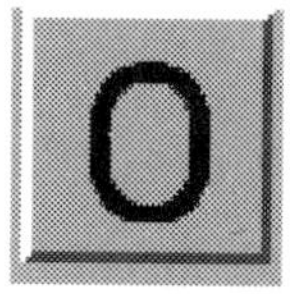

140
ZERO

141
ONE

142
TWO

143
THREE

144
FOUR

145
FIVE

146
SIX

147
SEVEN

148
EIGHT

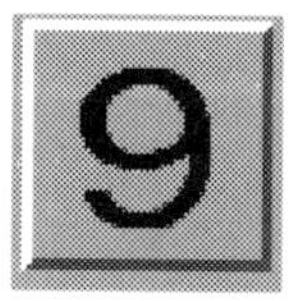

149
NINE

162
SUBSET/COPY

164
RIGHT ARROW

165
LEFT ARROW

166
UP ARROW

167
DOWN ARROW

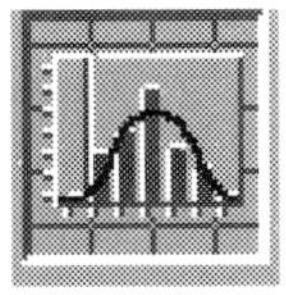

168
CAPABILITY

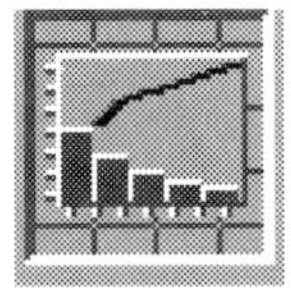

169
PARETO

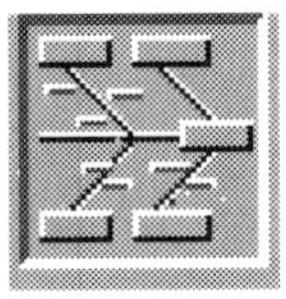

170
ISHIKAWA

171
SAMPLE DATA

172
SCHEDULE

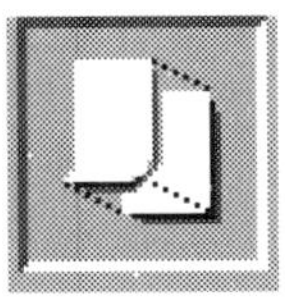

173
COPY

174
DELETE

175
IMPORT

176
DATA ENTRY

201
OK

202
CANCEL

301
DESKTOP

302
SAMPLE SYSTEMS

303
DEVELOPMENT

304
CREATE LABELS

305
APPLICATIONS

306
BUILD EIS

307
ADD NEW OBJECT

308
METABASE

309
PUBLIC APPLICATIONS

210
SG SUMMARY

203
SG WINDOW MENU

999
SPELL

Index

A

B

C

G

H

I

T

U

V

W

Special Characters

Your Turn

If you have comments or suggestions about SAS/AF software, SAS/FSP software, or SAS Screen Control Language or about SAS Technical Report P-216, *SAS/AF Software, SAS/FSP Software, and SAS Screen Control Language: Changes and Enhancements, Release 6.07*, please send them to us on a photocopy of this page.

Please return the photocopy to the Publications Division (for comments about this book) or the Technical Support Division (for suggestions about the software) at SAS Institute Inc., SAS Campus Drive, Cary, NC 27513.